Student Debt

Books in the **Contemporary World Issues** series address vital issues in today's society such as genetic engineering, pollution, and biodiversity. Written by professional writers, scholars, and nonacademic experts, these books are authoritative, clearly written, up-to-date, and objective. They provide a good starting point for research by high school and college students, scholars, and general readers as well as by legislators, businesspeople, activists, and others.

Each book, carefully organized and easy to use, contains an overview of the subject, a detailed chronology, biographical sketches, facts and data and/or documents and other primary source material, a forum of authoritative perspective essays, annotated lists of print and nonprint resources, and an index.

Readers of books in the Contemporary World Issues series will find the information they need in order to have a better understanding of the social, political, environmental, and economic issues facing the world today.

Student Debt

A REFERENCE HANDBOOK

William Elliott III and Melinda K. Lewis

An Imprint of ABC-CLIO, LLC
Santa Barbara, California • Denver, Colorado

Library of Congress Cataloging-in-Publication Data

Student Debt: A Reference Handbook
Library of Congress Cataloging in Publication Control
  Number: 2016042007

ISBN: 978-1-4408-4487-4
EISBN: 978-1-4408-4488-1

21 20 19 18 17   1 2 3 4 5

This book is also available as an eBook.

ABC-CLIO
An Imprint of ABC-CLIO, LLC

ABC-CLIO, LLC
130 Cremona Drive, P.O. Box 1911
Santa Barbara, California 93116–1911
www.abc-clio.com

This book is printed on acid-free paper ∞

Manufactured in the United States of America

5   DATA AND DOCUMENTS, 197

Preface

Readers may have picked up this book for a variety of reasons. Some may be impending high school graduates, contemplating financing options and wanting to carefully consider the implications of an offered "financial aid package" before agreeing to thousands of dollars in student borrowing. Others may be parents, alarmed at how little of their son's or daughter's higher education they are able to pay for and concerned with how this accounting may affect their child's chances. Some may be financial aid professionals or educators, looking both for answers to questions about how we got here and what it will mean and for resources to pass on to those they are expected to advise. Some may be observers of today's landscape of indebted young adults and their darkened horizon of future possibilities, individuals without a direct stake in the student loan debate but, nonetheless, a vested interest in the path we choose because of its significance for our collective fate.

It is our hope that this handbook offers something of real value to all its audiences. It contains data that illuminate some of the key trends in student debt today, including the growing polarization in student borrowing by race and class and the unprecedented increases since the 1980s in the incidence of borrowing and length of repayment. It traces the history of student loans and their growing prominence within the financial aid system, as a reminder that this debt dependence was constructed and, thus, can also be reversed. It analyzes some of the current debates on student debt, which often seem to surround us but, still, omit critical questions and crucial points. It features essays from students, financial aid administers, and researchers who offer advice to those contending with accrued student debt, those seeking to navigate a way through college without accumulating too much of it, and those looking for some reassurance that they are not alone in their sense that things were not supposed to work out this way, once they studied hard and made it to and through higher education.

This is a book, then, about student loans. It peels back the curtain on what many Americans have come to take for granted, that pursuit of higher education comes at a steep price, one that they will pay for years. It has statistics about average debt loads, research about the long-term financial implications of student borrowing, and recitations of key points when U.S. financial aid policy turned toward student debt. It asks readers to consider the consequences of relying on loans to pay for college and the ways in which that debt reverberates through our economic and educational landscapes. This is not, however, *just* a book about student loans. We care about student loans not for their own sake but because of the way in which dependence on debt as the mechanism—for many, the *only* mechanism—through which American students can access higher education may be derailing pursuit of those educational credentials and, in turn, distorting the path to prosperity. Our work lives at the intersection between wealth, education, and opportunity in this country. It is through this lens that we view student debt. It is by this benchmark that we judge our financial aid policies. Nor is student debt merely a scholarly interest of ours. Instead, it is also profoundly personal, as our own educational and career journeys have provided a vivid reminder of how wealth and its absence matter in determining educational outcomes and, then, why change is imperative. We share slices of our own stories not because we presume that they are broadly representative of others' journeys but because our own histories continue to motivate, inform, and frame our inquiry into the effects of debt-dependent education financing on individuals' ascent up the ladder of economic mobility and, in the aggregate, on the vitality of the American Dream.

Willie Elliott's Story

Today, I'm 45 years old, and although I can now see the proverbial light at the end of the tunnel, I have not yet achieved true financial well-being for me and my family. Despite having "succeeded," by many measures, as a college professor and noted scholar, I still stay up at night thinking about how I can pay down my student loans and not hinder my own children's opportunities. Student debt can never be just macroeconomic, to me. It is also real, on a daily basis. It influences how I see my life to this point and the future that stretches out in front of me. When we hear that student loan debt in America totals $1.3 trillion, we know it's a lot. It sounds insurmountable. What's even harder to grasp than the figure is what it really means. That student debt is an accumulation of millions of stories like mine, and of stories that took even more tragic turns, as some students borrowed for college degrees they never finished or to finance educations that have yet to translate into good jobs, or as some would-be students eschewed their one route to escape from poverty—a college education—because of the specter of student debt. I study and talk about education financing (and include my own story in the narrative) because my own history illustrates not only the promise we want to believe about the American Dream—that hard work can pay off, regardless of initial circumstances—but also the darker underside, that where one starts matters a lot for determining how well you do.

As a result of growing up in poverty, not only did I enter college behind academically, meaning that I had to work harder to overcome that disadvantage, but also my family had few financial resources to help pay for my schooling. My entrance into college was an even greater source of financial stress for my family than for many others, since it meant the interruption of the income I provided for their sustenance. Consequently, I relied heavily on student loans, the only way I could see to continue my education. I ended up graduating with a bachelor's degree and $40,000 in student debt. After paying off these student loans in U.S. military service, I went to graduate school to pursue my intellectual passions and a more positive career trajectory. I mapped out an ambitious path and earned a PhD from a prestigious institution. I have a productive and promising academic career. I also have $100,000 in student debt. My story represents the debt-dependent path to the American dream. Many Americans have stories—and balance sheets—like mine. But it does not have to be like that.

Melinda Lewis's Story

My life has mostly conformed to the ideal of education as a path to upward mobility and financial security. Raised in a family and community populated with college-educated adults, I grew up seeing college as an eventuality and paying for it as an afterthought. My family wasn't extraordinarily wealthy, but my parents' advanced education, purchased in part with support from their own parents, provided a human capital base. Ours was an upwardly-mobile lineage, with ascent fueled at strategic points by my maternal grandparents' infusions of assets, put to productive use in one generation and invested to ease the way for the next. The few thousand dollars they provided at critical moments in my childhood was a source of financial security for my parents, help I now realize is elusive for most young families. This laid a foundation for my parents' college saving and, then, became a platform of economic mobility. When I worked hard in school and earned scholarships to pay for college, this educational asset base was converted into a foundation for my future; we used those accumulated savings to pay off my husband's student loan (kept relatively small by his own parents' financial support for his education) and help with a down payment on our first house. After finishing graduate school, my husband and I started building home equity before we turned 25 and began to save for retirement. In other words, the assets I brought with me made a difference in how my effort paid off. It looked like my success, but it was in no way mine alone. As a result of this 'head start', we were well-positioned for college savings, opening the first account shortly after our oldest child was born and subsequently depositing the last of my grandparents' financial transfers. Even in today's superheated tuition increase environment, we are on track to have our four kids' education paid for before they finish high school. In a repeat of my own early beginnings, my children know that we are investing in their college educations. They can even see the statements to watch the balances grow. Insulated from the severe financial anxieties that characterize many families' college conversations, my children confidently plan for their future degrees. Their future achievements can only be accurately viewed within this context. Mine is an asset-empowered path to the American dream. It is one that conveys often hidden advantage, but that we must bring into clear focus. It is also one that policy can provide whereas families cannot. It still requires personal initiative and leveraged ability. It does not remove all of the obstacles that can thwart educational attainment or financial well-being. But it makes good on the promise we want to believe about the way this country works: that education is the route to prosperity, that hard work today will result in better times tomorrow, and that parents' hope of seeing their children surpass them is truly within reach.

This book offers some lifelines to those adrift in the country's sea of student debt. At its core, though, it is a cautionary tale, seeking to outline the ways in which reliance on student loans as the primary instrument for financing college has undermined education's equalizing force. This is the story we lived and that is underscored by the divergence in our respective outcomes. Moving beyond cataloguing the ills of student borrowing, the book highlights where public policy debates are overlooking the possibility of asset empowerment and suggests innovations that could bring wealth opportunities to more American children. And it introduces readers to some of the key players and critical resources active in this pivotal moment, not just in financial aid policy but in the future of the American dream itself. Our stories, like yours, continue to be written. Together, we can write a new ending to our collective narrative, one where equipping children with equitable opportunities for transformative asset ownership is just their beginning.

Student Debt

Introduction

As Adamson (2009) stated, "Of all the transformations that have taken place in the American university, . . . perhaps the most radical is the shift toward financing higher education through borrowed money" (p. 97). In 2000, student loans made up 38 percent of net tuition, fees, room, and board; by 2013 they made up 50 percent (Greenstone, Looney, Patashnik, & Yu, 2013). Current student debt levels exceed $1 trillion, and total student debt is higher now than credit card debt in the United States (Hartman, 2013). The average student leaves college with about $29,400 of student loan debt (Miller, 2014). While median debt is less (Edmiston, Brooks, & Shepelwich, 2012), borrowing has clearly become a common part of the American postsecondary educational experience. And the fact of borrowing may be more determinant than the amount for influencing outcomes; even debt levels as low as $5,000 can lead to financial hardships (Brown, Haughwout, Lee, Scally, & van der Klaauw, 2015).

Not surprisingly, people do not rely equally on student loans to pay for college. For instance, among different racial and ethnic groups, black students are the most likely to borrow when compared to white, Hispanic, and Asian students (Jackson & Reynolds, 2013). Ratcliffe and McKernan (2013) find that black adults are nearly twice as likely to have outstanding

Students wait outside Everest College hoping to get their transcripts, information on loan forgiveness, and transferring credits to other schools in Industry, California, on April, 28, 2015. Students at closed for-profit institutions may experience financial hardship and interruption of their academic careers. (AP Photo/Christine Armario) student debt. Furthermore, though they borrow about as much as white students, their life circumstances—including postgraduate employment and income, as well as family economic security—make these amounts harder to bear (Goldrick-Rab, Kelchen, & Houle, 2014). Lack of family income, particularly family assets, can account for many of these disparities in who borrows, whether they are loan averse in ways that may distort educational plans, how much they borrow, and the effect of that borrowing on their long-term financial health (e.g., Elliott & Lewis, 2015; Goldrick-Rab et al., 2014). Student debt is not only a young person's problem, however. According to the Federal Reserve Bank of New York, about 2.2 million Americans 60 years of age or older were liable for repayment of $43 billion in federal and private student loans in 2012, up $15 billion from 2007 (Greene, 2012).

This chapter will provide a brief history of federal student loan policy in the United States. Part of what will be suggested in this chapter is that the history of student loans in the United States is not a history based on the best empirical evidence or even a well-conceived plan for financing higher education, instead, a history based largely on political agendas. Moreover, it is contended that the U.S. financial aid model has been in a period of "normal science" for far too long, with facts used to make the case for maintenance and core assumptions unchecked. Since 1980, the debates over student aid, though at times heated, have involved only tweaks around the margins rather than proposals for fundamental reconsiderations (Archibald, 2002). Since the infrastructure of the student loan program as we know it today was laid in the 1980s, this chapter will primarily focus on the history of student loans up to the early 1990s.

1958: National Defense Student Loan Program

The first federal student loans were created as part of the National Defense Education Act (NDEA) of 1958: the National Defense Student Loan (NDSL). NDEA was signed into law by President Dwight D. Eisenhower. NDSL, later named the National Direct Loan System, eventually became what we know today as the Federal Perkins Loan (Fuller, 2014). NDSL provided higher education institutions with 90 percent of capital funds for low-interest direct loans for college students. The loans ranged from $1,000 to $5,000 and had to be paid back within 10 years after graduation with a 3 percent fixed interest rate. A goal of NDSL was to provide greater access to college among low-income students in response to the Soviet launch of Sputnik and the fear that the United States was falling behind in educating mathematicians and scientists (Morse, 1977).

Until the passage of NDEA, there had been strong resistance in the United States against providing federal financial aid for education. In the three years prior to the passage of NDEA, the Senate passed legislation to fund education largely through grants, but each year it died in the House of Representatives. However, the launch of Sputnik into space provided the opportunity for liberal legislators to frame the issue of federal funding of education as a defense issue, something more conservative members of the House understood as a vital government responsibility. This was reflected in the name of the bill, the National Defense Education Act.

Knowing that NDEA would still face resistance in the House, Stewart E. McClure, chief clerk of the Senate Committee on Labor, Education, and Public Welfare, devised a strategy with Alabama Democrat representative Carl Elliott to frame the debate around whether federal funds should be given to students as scholarships or as loans, not about whether federal funds should be spent on education in the first place (McClure, 1983). This framing was particularly shrewd because some conservative members of the House viewed scholarships as a form of socialism. Thus, Senator McClure and Representative Elliott concluded conservatives were much more likely to approve a bill if they were made to believe they won a victory by denouncing federal spending on what they thought were socialist scholarships in favor of spending on loans, a financing mechanism that more closely aligned with individual responsibility for paying for college (Morse, 1977). This deception facilitated the passage of NDEA, which established the precedent that it was legitimate to use federal funds to help students pay for higher education. This was a turning point in how higher education was funded in the United States.

A fact that seems to be lost on the current debate about student loans is that, like almost all education policy in the United States, student loan legislation represented a compromise between two disagreeing parties. As John F. Morse (1977), former director of Governmental Relations for the American Council on Education, explained, "I have long believed that the basic federal loan program was written by members of Congress who did not really believe in loans, enacted by a Congress the majority of whose member did not believe in federal aid to education" (p. 3). Morse played a significant role in the development of student loan policy and its administration and was acting director of NDSL for a short time. What should be clear from his statement is that it was not as though either faction saw student loans as the best policy for creating access to college or that borrowing gained legitimacy because of a strong body of empirical evidence that compelled legislators to create student loans. Instead, student loans were swallowed by conservative legislators because of the need to respond to the Soviet Union's entrance into space and accepted by liberals as a way to ease into their desired end of the federal government financing higher education.

Somewhere in the mind of liberal legislators had to be the idea that once the precedent was set, higher education could be paid for with federal dollars, and they would later be able to get their grand plan established, of a higher education system largely funded through federal grants, not loans. They put little thought into whether how they brought this about mattered; student loans just appeared as something they could sell to conservatives as a compromise. One reason there was little concern for student loans becoming the predominant way that education was financed is that neither liberals nor conservatives believed that many universities or students would actually use student loans. Of course, even though Congress did approve grant programs in the following decades, liberal legislators were never able to bring their vision of federal financing to fruition. Instead, the federal government would go on to spend amounts of money unimagined at the time on the student loan program. One reason they were not able to realize their dream was that they underestimated the appeal that paying for college with student loans would have.

It is important to point out that student loans were not a complete win for conservatives either. Conservatives believed that the federal government had little or no role to play in financing higher education. They too were willing to accept loans as a compromise because they also believed that few would use student loans as a way to pay for college and that, therefore, student loans would not lead to large spending by the federal government on higher education. To this day, then, loans remain a compromise. Loans are seen as a "better-than-nothing" policy that few believe actually can be the linchpin to creating a more equitable higher education system. Indeed, there is little evidence to suggest that student loans are better than grants for creating equity (Heller, 2008). But where one party sees no role for the federal government in financing college and the other sees the federal government paying all of the cost for education, legislators, educators, and others live in fear that any change will result in either more federal spending or no spending on higher education. The seeds of today's seemingly intractable stalemate were sown, then, in the origins of the student loan system.

The current impasse did not come entirely without warning, however. Even then, there were early warnings of the potential danger of viewing student loans as a way to set the precedent of federal spending on higher education:

> But I expressed deep concern that we had not even the remotest idea of what reasonable debt limits might be, and that having discovered loans, we might be tempted to

rely more and more on them as a substitute for, rather than a supplement to, societal and parental support. I feared we might place the heaviest burden of debt on our poorest citizens. And I expressed concern that if we did, collection and default would grow, to the disillusionment of all who created the problem. (Morse, 1977)

Morse's prophecy has largely come to pass. Today, we *still* do not know what a reasonable debt limit is (Akers, 2014; Brown et al., 2015). Student loans *have* grown to be the main way we finance education (Greenstone et al., 2013; Heller, 2011). The heaviest burden of debt *has* fallen on minority and our poorest children (Huelsman et al., 2015). Also, collection and default problems have become pervasive, monumental, and, in some cases, catastrophic (Greene, 2012; Herr & Burt, 2005).

1965: The Higher Education Act—Loan Guarantees

Even with the institution of financing options designed to increase participation in higher education, postsecondary studies remained the purview of the relatively elite. About NDEA, Francis Keppel (1987) said that it was meant to "educate gifted pupils and the upper portion of the college population" (p. 57). The Higher Education Act (HEA) of 1965 was signed into law by President Lyndon B. Johnson as part of his plan to create a Great Society where poverty and racial injustice did not exist. Increasing educational opportunities for all Americans was a key component of President Johnson's plan, and HEA was his main legislative instrument for making college accessible to all (Cervantes et al., 2005). He said, "The important role of the federal government is somehow to do something for the people who are down and out, and that's where its major energy in education ought to go" (Cervantes et al., 2005, p. 20).

HEA increased federal money given to universities, created scholarships, gave low-interest loans to students, and established a National Teachers Corps. In part, HEA represented a shift toward the liberal idea that education, particularly higher education, was a tool for building economic growth and that the federal government, therefore, had an important role to play in helping finance higher education. Further indication of this shift toward a more liberal understanding of the role of the federal government in paying for education was the inclusion of a national need-based scholarship as part of HEA, what was known as Basic Educational Opportunity Grants. In 1972 the Educational Opportunity Grant became what we know now as the Pell Grant, named after Democratic senator Claiborne Pell of Rhode Island. The Pell Grant was meant to serve as the "floor" of an undergraduate student's financial aid package.

The Guaranteed Student Loan (GSL) program, which in 1992 was renamed the Federal Family Education Loan (FFEL) program, was created as part of HEA under Title IV, part B. During the transition from NDEA to HEA, how the federal loan program was financed was changed. Instead of giving funding to institutes of higher education to distribute to students with financial need, bankers made the loans under HEA. But, to get private lenders to be willing to offer loans to students who, for the most part, had no credit history, the banks had to be given an assurance that they could recover their losses if a student defaulted. So it was established that if students defaulted, the government would guarantee that it would pay back the loan and take it over so bankers would not incur the risk. If a student failed to make timely payments and the federal government had to pay back the loan, the government owned the loan and the right to collect payments on the loan from the borrower. Further, HEA established loan insurance for students who did not have reasonable access to state or private nonprofit guaranty agencies. Therefore, the concessions in 1965 took student loans down a path that has resulted in a fairly unique debt instrument.

As in 1958, expansion of student loans through the creation of the GSL program came about through compromise. At the time, there was a debate over the "relative merits of institutional and student aid—the approach taken in HEA of 1965—as opposed to tax credits for educational expenses" (Archibald, 2002, pp. 34–35). Liberal legislators favored institutional and student aid over tax credits because tax credits offered little or no help to low-income families who did not have the money to pay for college upfront and later deduct a portion of what they paid from their taxes. And so, in order to get the grants they wanted, liberal legislators had to give conservatives an expanded student loan program meant to help middle-income students pay for college (Archibald, 2002; Lumina Foundation & Institute for Higher Education Policy, 2014). However, further development of the student loan program put more of the scaffolding in place that required individuals to shoulder most of the burden of paying for college while society was asked to shoulder less and less. In the 1970s, with the reauthorization of HEA, Congress continued to lay the scaffolding needed to produce the current financial aid system that honors privatization and individual responsibility over collective responsibility as the primary means for financing a college education.

1972: Education Amendments

In 1972, HEA was reauthorized under President Richard Nixon. By then, achieving equity in education through federal funding had become a guiding principle even for some conservatives at the time, a seemingly short-lived victory for liberals. President Richard Nixon (1972) said, "In March of 1970, I asked that aid to students enrolled in postsecondary institutions be expanded and redirected to assure every qualified student that he would be eligible for a combination of Federal grants and subsidized loans sufficient to make up the difference between his college costs and what his family is able to contribute."

The 1972 reauthorization of HEA set the basic framework of our current financial aid system "with students as the intermediaries of funds between the federal government and institutions" (Fuller, 2014, p. 54).

Ascendance of Student Loans within the Financial Aid System

According to Mendoza (2012), changes in 1972 to the HEA of 1965 opened the door for the privatization as well as the marketization of higher education. Never understood as a basic right for all persons but instead as a benefit to which there was also a significant social utility, higher education was less and less thought of as an integral part of the American welfare system (i.e., a way out of poverty for low-income students) and increasingly seen as a commodity to be sold by colleges and universities and purchased by students. This came about, at least in part, because the 1972 amendments help to establish giving aid directly to students instead of institutions. While seemingly more responsive to the unique financial circumstances of individual students, this shift of resources toward the individual as the unit of intervention set the stage for cost shifts. As a result of this subtle policy shift, over time, individuals and families have been increasingly expected to take on the bulk of the burden of paying for college, and, as a result, colleges have been thrust into competition with one another for students' tuition and financial aid dollars (Burd, 2013).

Both of these policy changes, privatization and individual aid, favored the wealthy, who were in a better position to take on increased responsibility for paying for college and then were more attractive to universities, particularly the more costly, selective ones (Elliott & Lewis, 2015). These market forces and their influence on the higher education system are critical parts of student loan history in the United States. Through this lens, it is not that wealthy students and their families acted to create laws that favored them, but that, because of their wealth advantage, they were able to benefit more from the changes that occurred and then to angle for perpetuation of a system they found to their satisfaction. At the same time, low-income families and minorities were disadvantaged in this emerging system for financing higher education. Without the resources to compete successfully with wealthy students, they could not

similarly work the rules established in the shift toward privatization to their advantage. Instead of financial aid redressing the
disparities these students confront in higher education, it has
come to multiply them (Elliott & Lewis, 2015).

Sallie Mae

Another unintended consequence of student loan policy is that
it created incentives for banks to act to protect the student loan
program from any potential threats to its survival. As Mettler
(2014) explains, "Then in turn, the profitability of the enterprise led the banks to engage in rent-seeking behavior, mobilizing to protect the student loan system and to make its terms all
the more favorable to them" (p. 54).

The Education Amendments of 1972 created the Student
Loan Marketing Association (SLMA). SLMA—pronounced
"Sallie Mae" (U.S. Department of Treasury, 2006)—started
out as a government-sponsored enterprise meant to increase
liquidity and capital in the GSL program by originating loans.
Though it was government sponsored, it is important to note
that Sallie Mae was a for-profit corporation; in 1983 it became
a publicly owned company listed and traded on the New York
Stock Exchange (U.S. Department of Treasury, 2006). Congress gave Sallie Mae benefits not afforded to other companies
such as "low funding costs in the 'agency' debt market, exemp-
tion from most state and local taxes, and low required capital
as compared to banks" (U.S. Department of Treasury, 2006,
p. 7). These advantages helped it become the largest private
student loan lender and one of the industry's largest profiteers.
By 1990 Sallie Mae held almost half of the guaranteed student
loan market (U.S. Department of Treasury, 2006). From 1995
to 2006 Sallie Mae's stock rose by almost 200 percent (Schorn,
2006). In 1996 lawmakers passed the Student Loan Marketing
Association Reorganization Act, making Sallie Mae a private
company. In 2010 Sallie Mae stopped originating federal loans
after the federal government legislated that all loans be made

directly from the government to students. But Sallie Mae continues to be important in the student loan industry, reported to have made $939 million dollars in net profit in 2012 (Hartman, 2013). Sallie Mae's history is a story of conflict between Congress' mandate for it to serve a public function of increasing access to college and its desire to maximize profits and please its shareholders as a private organization (U.S. Department of Treasury, 2006). We will revisit this topic later in this chapter.

1978: Middle-Income Student Assistance Act

Throughout the 1970s and 1980s, legislators and their constituents were increasingly demanding that federal resources be used to finance the education of middle- and upper-income students (Zumeta, 2001). The Middle-Income Student Assistance Act (MISAA) of 1978 did just that by expanding the availability of student loans and grants to more middle-class families (U.S. Congress, 1978). As a result, the number of guaranteed students expanded from 1 million in 1978 to 3.1 million in 1982 (Mumper, 1996). MISSAA of 1978 was being considered at the same time as a tax credit bill (designed to help middle-income families), and the competition between the two proposals yielded generous benefits to the middle class. MISSAA removed the income requirement for guaranteed student loans, making all students eligible.

Because more students were now eligible to receive a GSL loan, program administration costs increased (Dynarski & Scott-Clayton, 2013). To counter the escalating costs associated with the student loan program, in 1981 the student loan origination fee was created, allowing lenders to charge up to 5 percent of the loan in addition to the borrowed amount. MISAA was repealed in 1981 through the Omnibus Budget Reconciliation Act, but the origination fee remained (Lumina Foundation & Institute for Higher Education Policy, 2014). However, the shift toward making higher education more accessible for the middle class continued to intensify in 1992 when student loans were opened up to all income groups and federal financial needs calculations started to exclude home equity from the equation (Schenet, 1993).

1980s: Student Loans Become the Dominant Paradigm in Financial Aid

In the mid-1980s student loans became the largest source of student financial aid in the United States (Geiger & Heller, 2012). It also became normal to presume that colleges and universities are overcharging (Zumeta, 2001), mistrust fueled by the perception that increasing federal support for higher education incentivized higher education institutions to raise the cost of tuition, despite a lack of evidence of this practice (Hoxby, 2004). These perceptions flourished during the 1980s as part of the Reagan political agenda (Fuller, 2014).

As a result of this shift toward a more conservative, smaller government approach to federal aid, in the 1980s there was a noted shift from need-based to merit-based aid. Woo and Choy (2011) found that the proportion of undergraduates receiving merit aid rose from 6 percent in the academic year 1995–1996 to 14 percent in the academic year 2007–2008. Between 1982 and 2000, spending on need-based scholarships for undergraduates by the states increased 7.4 percent annually, while spending on merit programs increased 13.6 percent annually. The proportion of state grants awarded based on merit rose from 9 percent to 22 percent during this period (Heller, 2002; National Association of State Student Grant and Aid Programs, 2001). As of 2001, the 13 states with broad-based merit scholarship programs planned to distribute a combined $709 million in merit awards annually, more than twice the $325 million provided in need-based aid by those states in 1998–1999 (Selingo, 2001).

This shift resulted in a financial aid system that largely subsidized middle- to upper-income, white students attending college (Baum & Schwartz, 1988; Woo & Choy, 2011). In the case of merit-based aid, of which scholarships are the most common form, a student with little financial need is just as entitled to aid as students with high levels of financial need. Indeed, because research reveals strong correlations between economic advantage and academic performance, merit-based aid can serve to further intensify inequity in higher education (Kiley, 2013). Test scores are often the key factor for determining eligibility for merit aid, and privileged students enjoy advantages (e.g., better-performing schools, greater access to supportive services, less exposure to adverse inputs) that may translate into higher scores. This shift toward merit aid allowed many schools to leverage their financial aid budgets to bring in not only the brightest students but also those who could afford to attend without help, in order to maximize the institutions' revenue (Burd, 2013). For example, Burd (2013) finds that

> The competition for the wealthy is so strong that 10 percent of college admissions directors at four-year colleges (and nearly 20 percent of those at private liberal arts colleges) reported that they give affluent students a significant leg up in the admissions process—meaning that they are admitting full-pay students with lower grades and test scores than other applicants. (p. 4)

At the same time, some colleges and universities were deliberately offering low-income students financial aid packages that were underfunded in order to establish expectations that will discourage them from enrolling (Burd, 2013).

In line with the shift toward individual responsibility, in 1980, the Parent Loans for Undergraduate Students (PLUS) program was signed into law (Mumper, 1996). Parents as well as students became eligible for government-subsidized loans for education. Starting that same year, graduate and undergraduate students not financially dependent on their parents could get government-subsidized loans from the Supplemental Loans for Students program. Initially, the PLUS program limited borrowing to $3,000 per year with a total limit of $15,000 (Education Amendments of 1980). By 1986 loan limits had risen to $4,000 per year and a total limit of $20,000. The borrowing limit was increased again in 1992 to the amount of a student's unmet financial need, and the lifetime limit was removed altogether (Education Amendments of 1980). The PLUS program offered interest rates lower than private loans but considerably higher than subsidized and unsubsidized loans (Goldrick-Rab et al., 2014). PLUS loans have been characterized as a type of "last resort" financial aid because they are intended for use after students have already accepted their federal subsidized and unsubsidized Stafford loans but only if they meet credit requirements (Goldrick-Rab et al., 2014, p. 6). As a result of the credit check requirement for PLUS loans, many of the neediest children and their families do not qualify despite having high unmet need after they receive their financial aid package (Goldrick-Rab et al., 2014).

In 1988, Congress renamed the Federal Guaranteed Loan program the Robert T. Stafford Student Loan program, in honor of U.S. senator Robert Stafford, a Republican from Vermont. According to Wei and Skomsvold (2010), a persistent and concerning pattern of borrowing arose with the adoption of the Stafford Student Loan program. In a given year, about 60 percent of students taking out Stafford loans took out the maximum allowable amount. A reason for the increasing reliance on student loans is the diminishing purchasing power of the Pell Grant. In fact, Goldrick-Rab et al. (2014) suggest that the purchasing power of the Pell Grant has diminished to the degree it serves as a "gateway to student loans for most families" (p. 7).

In 1992 the student loan program fell under the Federal Family Education Loan (FFEL) program. FFEL had four components: Subsidized Stafford Loans, Unsubsidized Stafford Loans, PLUS Loans, and Federal Consolidation Loans. About this time, however, there was a movement to have direct lending replace guaranteed loans in the Omnibus Reconciliation Act of 1993. But this initial attempt to switch to direct lending was derailed by lobbyists for the student loan industry who, according to a *U.S. News & World Report* article "used money and favors, along with their friends in Congress and the Department of Education, to get what they wanted" (McCann, 2015, paragraph 10) and block wide adoption of direct lending. But, in 2010, under President Obama's administration, the federal government mandated that all loans be made directly from the government to students. The Congressional Budget Office estimated that eliminating subsidies paid to private lenders would save $68.7 billion over the next 10 years after 2010 (McCann, 2015).

Changing Perceptions of Student Loans

Shortly after the NDSL program was enacted, the media and the public were largely enthusiastic about the program. Morse (1977) tells the story of being approached by two *U.S. News & World Report*'s reporters after a talk he gave on the program while in the position as director of the program:

> The next morning I received a telephone call saying they had been so excited by the "revolutionary" ideas they had heard that they wanted to do an exhaustive interview as a cover story. The story appeared in February 1960, and judging from the mail I received later, had tremendous impact. (p. 6)

Not only did the media respond positively toward the federal entrance into the student loan business, but contrary to the predictions when student loans were first introduced, there was widespread use of them. By the 1975–1976 school year, or 16 years after NDSL was enacted, $12.2 billion dollars had been borrowed in NDSL and the GSL program (Johnstone, 1977). During that school year, spending on the federal student loan program made up 43 percent of the total $2.2 billion federal aid budget.

Prior to the Great Recession, the national policy conversation on student loans was largely about how to provide people with more access to loans to pay for college. Further, the media largely portrayed student loans as a net positive, and parents saw taking out student loans as a "badge of good parenthood" (Goldrick-Rab et al., 2014, p. 7). Not only was taking out loans for college seen as a badge of good parenthood, but banks saw home-equity loans for college as a safe source of collateral. For instance, Lovenheim (2011) finds that for each $10,000 in home equity a lower-income family has, the probability of enrolling in college increased by about 5.7 percentage points. However, after the Great Recession hit and the value of homes began to plummet precipitously, providing home-equity loans to help pay for college became more risky (Tedeschi, 2009). In 2010, housing prices had dropped 35 percent from their peak in 2006 (Urahn, Currier, Wechsler, Wilson, & Colbert, 2012). The recession hit low- and middle-income households the hardest, as many homeowners ended up with negative equity (mortgage debt higher than the value of the property). For homeowners with income of less than $70,000, home equity is estimated to have declined by 54 percent between 2006 and 2010 (Urahn et al., 2012). Alongside these devastating financial losses and in the face of the economic insecurity they portend, the narrative around parents helping their children pay for college shifted. Now, parents are advised to have their children take on more of the burden of paying for college and save for their own retirement first (Carrns, 2014).

This shift in how people and the media talk and think about student loans as a way to pay for college is not only because of changes in families' economic status since the Great Recession; it also is the shrinking power of education to change their child's financial outlook. Especially since the beginning of the 20th century, few institutions have been more important in sustaining the American dream than public schools, colleges, and universities (see, e.g., Hochschild & Scovronick, 2003). As early as the 19th century, Horace Mann called education "the great equalizer of the conditions of men" (1848, p. 59). Since then, a widespread belief has persisted that economic disparity can be narrowed through effort in school and the pursuit of higher education. However, whereas before the Great Recession there was little questioning in the general public and media about whether college was "worth it," afterward the national conversation increasingly raises questions about the ability of a college degree to deliver on the American dream.

Between 2000 and 2010 unemployment among college graduates rose from 2 percent to 5.7 percent (Mishel, Bivens, Gould, & Shierholz, 2013). The unemployment rate among college graduates is higher among racial minorities, compounding the disadvantages of the racial wealth gap. Between 2000 and 2010 the unemployment rate increased for white workers with a college degree from 1.8 percent to 4.9 percent, but for black college graduates it increased from 2.8 percent to 9.8 percent (Mishel et al., 2013). In addition to rising unemployment rates among college graduates, there is a growing productivity-wage gap (Gomme & Rupert, 2004; Mishel et al., 2013; Rodriguez & Jayadev, 2010), making college a risker investment than it was in previous years. Although during the recent recession workers with a college degree fared slightly better than workers with only a high school diploma, they have also experienced declining wage growth over the past several years. For example, between 2000 and 2011 their wages grew a modest 0.2 percent; between 2002 and 2011, they declined by –2.2 percent, and between 2003 and 2011 by –1.9 percent, on average (Mishel et al., 2013). It is simply not the case that a college degree is a universal ticket to prosperity—or even a guaranteed hedge against deprivation—and Americans' contemplation of financial aid increasingly recognizes this reality.

The shift in how people and the media talk and think about student loans as a way to pay for college has also been influenced by a renewed focus on equity. The Great Recession drew the United States' attention to the issue of equity in a way that it maybe had not been since the Great Depression. Average household wealth declined 15 percent between 2007 and 2010 and has only recovered 45 percent of its value

(Boshara & Emmons, 2013). This was a catastrophic financial disaster that will leave its mark on the nation—and on individual and household balance sheets—for generations. For millions of American households, the Great Recession produced an economic devastation almost unimaginable; because wealth is so unevenly distributed, median declines were even more dramatic, with a median household wealth drop of 39 percent (Emmons, 2012). Three-fifths or more of families across all income groups reported a decline in wealth between 2007 and 2009 (Bricker, Kennickell, Moore, & Sabelhaus, 2012), and the typical household lost nearly one-fifth of its wealth. With so many seeing their own futures as increasingly bleak, questions of distribution, the differential effects of policy on particular groups, and the inadequacy of government protection against hardship took on new relevance and, indeed, urgency.

The national focus on inequality during and after the Great Recession heightened the spotlight on higher education's ability to deliver as the "Great Equalizer." A recent study finds that college graduates who grow up in families that are below 185 percent of the federal poverty level earn 91 percent more over the course of their careers than high school graduates who grow up in families that are 185 percent of the federal poverty level (Hershbein, 2016). Graduating from college clearly has benefit for the poor when compared with poor children who do not graduate. The same analysis also finds, however, that a college degree benefits the nonpoor more. Hershbein (2016) finds that college graduates who grow up in families with incomes above 185 percent of the poverty level earned 162 percent more over their careers than high school graduates who grow up in families that are above 185 percent of the poverty level. This suggests that while education improves the outcomes of poor children in adulthood, it may not be acting as an equalizer. These findings may also suggest that policies that build families' economic background (i.e., particularly income and wealth) and education together may be more powerful tools for reducing inequality than those that address each separately.

Kuhn (1962) suggests that during periods of normal science researchers identify questions to investigate based on existing knowledge. The insights gained from these analyses are constrained, then, by the limits of the prevailing paradigm; one can seldom discover what one is not seeking. Up until the Great Recession, this has largely been the case with regard to studying the relationship between student loans and the equalizing power of higher education. Under the prevailing financial aid paradigm that emphasized borrowing as a way to pay for college, the question asked is, "Is a student who graduates from college and takes out student loans better off than if he or she had not graduated from college?" However, some researchers are beginning to challenge the existing paradigm and ask, "Is a student who graduates from college and has to take out loans to pay for it better off than a student who graduates from college and does not have to take out loans?" The prior question is focused on whether students are better off by not going to college, whereas the latter question is about whether student loans empower education to act as an equalizer or not.

Similar to Hershbein's (2016) findings calling into question equitable return on degree, research on student debt also finds that a degree is worth less for students with debt than students without debt. According to the Government Accounting Office (2003), assuming a standard 10-year payback at 7 percent annual interest, average cumulative undergraduate educational debt exceeded $18,000 in 2000, which corresponds to a $6,000 premium borrowers' pay for a college education. Prior to the Great Recession, this line of inquiry garnered relatively little attention and made little impact in the trajectory of attitudes about financial aid. After the Great Recession, however, a clear body of research examined student loans through the new lens of equity. Elliott and Lewis (2015) provide a more extensive chronicling of this research, but, in short, researchers using the new lens find that having outstanding student debt drives graduates away from low-paying and public-sector jobs (Rothstein & Rouse, 2011), delays marriage (Gicheva, 2011), reduces satisfaction when they marry (Dew, 2008), delays child-bearing and family formation (American Student Assistance, 2013; also see Baum & O'Malley, 2003), reduces net worth (Elliott & Nam, 2013; Hiltonsmith, 2013) and retirement savings (Egoian, 2013; Hiltonsmith, 2013), reduces credit scores (Brown & Caldwell, 2013), delays purchasing a home (Cooper & Wang, 2014), and reduces home equity if they buy (Hiltonsmith, 2013). Interestingly, research conducted in 2010 or earlier finds a positive correlation between having outstanding student debt and other debt (e.g., mortgage, vehicle, or credit card), when comparing graduates with and without debt (see, e.g., Fry, 2014). However, it appears that young adults are becoming more loan averse in the post–Great Recession era. Brown and Caldwell (2013) find that households with student debt had lower overall debt than households without student debt. They speculate that borrowers post–Great Recession have become less sure about the labor market, causing a drop in the demand for credit. In addition, lenders may have become more reserved about supplying loans to high-balance student borrowers in the tighter credit markets that followed the financial collapse. As a result, having student debt may further hinder young adults' ability to accumulate assets, thereby weakening the return on a college degree and reducing the ability of higher education to act as an equalizer in society.

The differences this research has begun to reveal are not just novel questions for analysts to pursue; they have tangible and often dramatic implications for a generation of Americans and, increasingly, the nation's collective future. Young adults who graduate with debt feel them, as do their families and people in their communities. Together, these differences result in a shift in how people view student loans and even how they view the value of attending institutes of higher education. For example, Walsemann, Gee, and Gentile (2014) find evidence of a negative association between student loans and mental health of young adults who were ages 25 to 31. Fry (2014) discovered that 18- to 39-year-olds with two- or four-year degrees who had outstanding student debt were less satisfied overall with their financial situations than similarly situated young adults without outstanding student debt (70 percent versus 84 percent, respectively). Further, he found that 18- to 39-year-olds with two- or four-year degrees who had outstanding student debt were less likely to perceive an immediate payoff from having gone to college than similarly situated young adults without outstanding student debt (63 percent versus 81 percent, respectively). More anecdotally, headlines proclaiming the student debt "crisis" and portending the "end of college" reflect this growing angst, born of the new calculus that has weakened the connection between financial aid, educational attainment, and later financial outcomes.

The Great Recession was the spark that helped ignite students to call for a revolution in how higher education is financed. Student activism on issues of inequality in the United States is certainly not a new phenomenon. However, growing dissatisfaction with the cost of higher education has captured the attention of established student organizations and spawned the development of new movements. Energized by the support of key political figures and buttressed by the reach and agile responsiveness of social media, these organizations seek to educate and motivate the American public toward an overhaul of higher education financing. What started as protests against tuition increases has grown into an issue of such national significance that every major political candidate in the 2016 presidential election developed a plan for dealing with student debt. The details varied, ranging from assisting students with loan payments to offering entirely free higher education, but the underlying consensus is that the time for normal science has passed. The United States is ready for a financial aid revolution. The Corinthian 15 (later called the Corinthian 100) is an example of a student activist group fighting against what they perceive as an unjust student debt system. They came together as a result of the forced closing of the for-profit Corinthian Colleges. The colleges were forced to close by the

U.S. Department of Education due to accusations of fraud and predatory lending practices (Kamenetz & O'Connor, 2014). Despite forcing Corinthian Colleges to close, the U.S. Department of Education continued to attempt to collect debt owed by students who attended the colleges. So, while Corinthian Colleges had the opportunity to be freed from huge amounts of liability and the new owners of the campuses were able to purchase them at a discounted rate, the students were left strapped with debt (Nasiripour, 2015). This prompted a group of students, initially called the "Corinthian 15" but later the "Corinthian 100," to join together and refuse to make payments on their loans.

Another activist organization heavily involved in the Corinthian dispute is "Strike Debt," which started as an offshoot of the Occupy Wall Street movement. They started a program in 2012 called Rolling Jubilee, which raises money to purchase bundled debt for pennies on the dollar. Rather than going after the debtors like other purchasers, Rolling Jubilee just pays off the debt, be it medical or other personal debt. In May 2014, Rolling Jubilee purchased nearly $4 million in debt for students of Everest College for just $106,709; a few months later, they purchased the remaining $13.4 million in Everest College debt. Because there is no secondary market for student loans, Rolling Jubilee paid "unpaid tuition receivables," not the Genesis loans themselves. Nor was this activist group the only entity to flag the lending practices of Corinthian Colleges—the parent corporation of Everest College—as harmful. In September 2014 the Consumer Financial Protection Bureau announced that it was suing Corinthian Colleges for predatory lending. Likely invigorated by legislative support for the victims of Corinthian Colleges and with support from Strike Debt's Debt Collective, on February 23, 2015, 15 students who had attended Everest College launched a debt strike, refusing to meet their debt obligations. Shortly after, an editorial in the *New York Times* by an author who touted his decision to default on his student loans attracted significant attention (Siegel, 2015). The narrative was shifting, and student loans were increasingly viewed not as beneficent financial aid or even benign financial products but as threats to American young adults' futures. Even so, these organizations and advocates on the front lines of the student debt movement are constrained in their use of innovative tactics by the peculiar nature of the student loan instrument and often judged through a lens still largely debt-centric (see Jackson, 2015). Even the flagrantly unethical practices of actors like Corinthian Colleges did little to shake the student loan foundation, as interests such as the U.S. Department of Education continued to use regulatory and judicial avenues to curtail relief for student debtors (Kitroeff, 2015). Largely stymied through traditional channels, then, activism and protest gained ground. In order to assist students with federal student loan debt, Rolling Jubilee evolved into the "Debt Collective" to more specifically focus on student debt, using direct action and other high-profile approaches.

Other student activist movements have developed in response to student debt. Riding the wave of success from marchers demanding increases in the minimum wage and motivated by attention to this issue in the 2016 presidential race, the Million Student March held on November 12, 2015, was an effort to push for cancellation of all student debt, debt-free college, and a $15 minimum wage for all student workers. Further fueling this growing militancy is the growing acceptance of formerly radical ideas in the political mainstream. Notable evidence of this is Bernie Sanders's presidential platform. For example, in a June interview with Katie Couric on Yahoo! News, just months after announcing his candidacy for president, Mr. Sanders outlined five solutions to the lack of upward mobility in the United States. In addition to a tax on Wall Street speculation, Sanders called for free college. He further stated that the only way these changes will happen is if millions of Americans are involved in the political process and, specifically, "if a million young people march on Washington and say you better vote to deal with student debt." Students' commitment to this cause is reinforced by their sense that the American dream of opportunity is slipping out of their grasp, as their willingness to use confrontational approaches is bolstered by victories on other fronts, as in recent minimum wage increases in communities around the country.

Other student movements have been galvanized by support from other key legislators, such as Congresswoman Maxine Waters (D-CA) and Senator Elizabeth Warren (D-MA). In 2009, Waters helped pass SAFRA—the Student Aid and Fiscal Responsibility Act, geared toward helping families and students pay for college. A longtime critic of predatory lending, she has remained a champion for students, working on legislation to protect veterans from predatory lending practices and protect all students from predatory credit card accounts. Congresswoman Waters has also been a vocal proponent of the investigation into for-profit Corinthian Colleges by the Consumer Financial Protection Bureau and has introduced several pieces of legislation to provide additional protections to students and to ensure their ability to seek future legal action.

Elizabeth Warren is also a longtime advocate for students in higher education. Although Corinthian Colleges officially shut its doors in April 2015, and, with legislative pressure, the U.S. Department of Education agreed to relieve the federal student debt of the displaced students, Senator Warren led the efforts to encourage a formal process of debt relief and protect these students from additional requirements to prove the legitimacy of their claim and taxation on the balance of the canceled debt.

In recognition of the true nature, scope, and gravity of the student loan problem, student activists have suggested we must begin to imagine meaningful alternatives. Their voices are amplified by analysis and commentary that insist that our financial aid system perform up to the standards of our American values, which hold that only effort expended and innate ability possessed should determine one's relative outcomes. The United States invests in education—particularly higher education—as the principal path to prosperity, the royal road to economic mobility. These potential outcomes cannot be realized without a financial aid system that enhances, rather than compromises, education's potency as an equalizer. Confronted with the impending loss of this route to financial well-being and true opportunity, students and parents and policymakers and pundits are increasingly demanding policies that will restore education as an equitable ladder to the American dream.

Most of the time people work within existing paradigms. Every once in a while, though, there are people who will dare to challenge the world as it is and imagine a radically different "truth." Their minds, then, are freed to think about the issues they face in ways that were not previously possible. As we seek to find alternatives to the current financial aid paradigm, we should not lose sight of these moments in our collective history when we have dared to dream and, as a result, were able to leap forward. The race to the moon was just such a moment. In the early 1960s we were "pushed" by the Russian entrance into space. Before this, we were constrained by our own imaginations about what is possible and, as a result, we fell behind the rest of the world. To move away from a debt-dependent financial aid system, we once again need to imagine the possibilities and dare to reach for what might seem to many to be the stars.

Conclusion

The architects of NDSL did not know that they initiated a period of normal science in financial aid that would extend through the Great Recession. During this period student loans became the primary mechanism policymakers would have to expand access to college. As indicated by Morse (1977) and the *U.S. News & World Report* article discussed at the beginning of this section, student loans represented an innovation in financial aid in 1958 that both liberals and conservatives could see as an acceptable compromise. This would not have been possible without the external push that the Soviet Union's entrance into space provided. Sputnik ushered in concerns over the Soviet Union's growing military might and intensified fears of communism overtaking the United States and its way of life. Once ensconced as a key component of the U.S. financial aid system, it is no surprise that each time student loans were challenged, people thought, "But what could they possibly be replaced with?" As a result, American policy ended up considering tweaks to the existing program that were meant to maintain it, rather than fundamentally change it. According to Kuhn (1962), periods of normal science persist until the current paradigm becomes increasingly less able to solve a growing number of the problems or when external events provoke a clamor for a different vision: a revolution. The Great Recession provided the conditions by which it is becoming increasingly clear that student loans are failing to solve the problems facing society—and may exacerbate or even create problems. Therefore, a fundamental reconsideration of how best to finance higher education is needed. Chapter 2 discusses some of these tweaks to the student loan program that have been initiated in hopes of sustaining it through this current period of revolution.

References

Adamson, M. (2009). The financialization of student life: Five propositions on student debt. *Polygraph, 21*, 97–110.

Akers, B. (2014). *How much is too much? Evidence on financial well-being and student loan debt.* Washington, DC: American Enterprise Institute.

American Student Assistance (2013). *Life delayed: The impact of student debt on the daily lives of young Americans.* Washington, DC: American Student Assistance.

Archibald, R. B. (2002). *Redesigning the financial aid system: Why colleges and universities should switch roles with the federal government.* Baltimore, MD: The Johns Hopkins University Press.

Baum, S., & O'Malley, M. (2003). College on credit: How borrowers perceive their education debt. *Journal of Student Financial Aid, 33*(3), article 1. Retrieved from http://publications.nasfaa.org/jsfa/vol33/iss3/1

Baum, S., & Schwartz, S. (1988). *The impact of student loans on borrowers: Consumption patterns and attitudes towards repayment—Evidence from the New England Student Loan Survey.* Boston, MA: Massachusetts Higher Education Assistance Corporation.

Boshara, R., & Emmons, W. (2013). *After the fall: Rebuilding family balance sheets, rebuilding the economy.* St. Louis, MO: Federal Reserve Bank of St. Louis. Retrieved from http://www.stlouisfed.org/publications/ar/2012/pages/ar12_2a.cfm

Bricker, J., Kennickell, A., Moore, K., & Sabelhaus, J. (2012). Changes in U.S. family finances from 2007 to 2010: Evidence from the survey of consumer finances. *Federal Reserve Bulletin, 98*(2), 1–80. Retrieved from http://www.federalreserve.gov/Pubs/Bulletin/2012/articles/scf/scf.htm

Brown, M., & Caldwell, S. (2013). *Young adult student loan borrowers retreat from housing and auto markets* (pp. 1–21). New York: Federal Reserve Bank of New York.

Brown, M., Haughwout, A., Lee, D., Scally, J., & van der Klaauw, W. (2015). Looking at student loan defaults through a larger window. Retrieved from http://libertystreeteconomics.newyorkfed.org/2015/02/looking_at_student_loan_defaults_through_a_larger_window.html#.VttP5ObzNPA

Burd, S. (2013). *Undermining Pell: How colleges compete for wealthy students and leave the low-income behind.* Washington, DC: New America.

Carrns, A. (2014). Save for retirement first, the children's education second. Retrieved from http://www.nytimes.com/2014/03/01/your-money/save-for-retirement-first-the-childrens-education-second.html

Cervantes, A., Creusere, M., McMillion, R., McQueen, C., Short, M., Steiner, M., & Webster, J. (2005, November). Opening the doors to higher education: Perspectives on the Higher Education Act 40 years later. TG Research and Analytical Services, Texas Guaranteed Student Loan Corporation.

Cooper, D., & Wang, C. (2014). Student loan debt and economic outcomes. *Current Policy Perspectives* (Washington, DC). Retrieved from http://www.bostonfed.org/economic/current-policy-perspectives/2014/cpp1407.htm

Dew, J. (2008). Debt change and marital satisfaction change in recently married couples. *Family Relations, 57*(1), 60–71.

Dynarski, S., & Scott-Clayton, S. (2013). Financial aid policy: Lessons from research. *Future of Children, 23*(1), 67–91.

Edmiston, K. D., Brooks, L., & Shepelwich, S. (2013). *Student loans: Overview and issues (update)*. Kansas City, MO: Federal Reserve Bank of Kansas City. Retrieved from https://www.kansascityfed.org/PUBLICAT/reswkpap/pdf/rwp%2012-05.pdf

Education Amendments of 1980, 20 U.S.C. (1980). Public Law 96–374.

Egoian, J. (2013, October 23). 73 will be the retirement norm for millennials. *Nerdwallet.* Retrieved from http://www.nerdwallet.com/blog/investing/2013/73-retiremen t-norm-millennials/

Elliott, W., & Lewis, M. (2015). *The real college debt crisis: How student borrowing threatens financial well-being and erodes the American dream.* Santa Barbara: Praeger.

Elliott, W., & Nam, I. (2013). Is student debt jeopardizing the long-term financial health of U.S. households? *Review, 95*(5), 1–20. Retrieved from https://www.stlouisfed.org/

household-financial-stability/events/20130205/papers/
Elliott.pdf

Emmons, W. R. (2012). *Don't expect consumer spending to be the engine of economic growth it once was.* St. Louis, MO: Federal Reserve Bank of St. Louis. Retrieved from http://www.stlouisfed.org/publications/re/articles/?id=2201

Fry, R. (2014). Young adults, student debt and economic well-being. Pew Research Center's Social and Demographic Trends Project, Washington, DC.

Fuller, Matthew B. (2014). A history of financial aid to students. *Journal of Student Financial Aid, 44*(1), 42–68.

Geiger, R. L., & Heller, D. E. (2012). Financial trends in higher education: The United States. *Educational Studies, 2012*(3), 5–29.

General Accounting Office. (2003, October). *Student loan programs: As federal costs of loan consolidation rise, other options should be examined.* Washington, DC: Author. Retrieved from http://www.gao.gov/assets/250/240559.pdf

Gicheva, D. (2011). *Does the student-loan burden weigh into the decision to start a family?* University of North Carolina at Greensboro. Retrieved from http://www.uncg.edu/bae/people/gicheva/Student_loans_marriageMarch11.pdf

Goldrick-Rab, S., Kelchen, R., & Houle, J. (2014). *The color of student debt: Implications of federal loan program reforms for black students and historically black colleges and universities.* Retrieved from https://news.education.wisc.edu/docs/WebDispenser/news-connections-pdf/thecolorofstudentdebt-draft.pdf?sfvrsn=4

Gomme, P., & Rupert, P. (2004). *Measuring labor's share of income.* Cleveland, OH: Federal Reserve Bank of Cleveland.

Greene, K. (2012, October 26). New peril for parents: Their kids' student loans. *Wall Street Journal.* Retrieved from

http://online.wsj.com/article/SB100008723963904440242
04578044622648516106.html

Greenstone, M., Looney, A., Patashnik, J., & Yu, M. (2013).
Thirteen economic facts about social mobility and the role
of education. The Brookings Institution, Washington, DC.
Retrieved from http://www.brookings.edu/research/reports/
2013/06/13-facts-higher-education

Hartman, R. R. (2013, May 23) Who makes money off
your student loans? You might be surprised. *Yahoo
News*. Retrieved from http://news.yahoo.com/blogs/
the-lookout/makes-money-off-student-loans-mi
ght-surprised-093332073.html

Heller, D. (2011). The financial aid picture: Realism,
surrealism, or cubism? In Michael B. Paulsen (Ed.), *Higher
education: Handbook of theory and research* (pp. 125–160).
New York: Springer.

Heller, D. E. (2002). *Condition of access: Higher education for
lower income students.* Westport, CT: American Council on
Education/Praeger.

Heller, D. E. (2008). The impact of student loans on college
access. In S. Baum, M. McPherson, & P. Steele (Eds.), *The
effectiveness of student aid policies: What the research tells us*
(pp. 39–68). New York: College Board.

Herr, E., & Burt, L. (2005). Predicting student loan default
for the University of Texas at Austin. *Journal of Student
Financial Aid, 35*(2), 27–49.

Hershbein, B. (2016). A college degree is worth less if you
are raised poor. Retrieved from http://www.brookings.edu/
blogs/social-mobility-memos/posts/2016/02/19-college-
degree-worth-less-raised-poor-hershbein

Hiltonsmith, R. (2013). At what cost: How student debt
reduces lifetime wealth. Washington, DC: Demos.

Hochschild, J., & Scovronick, N. (2003). *The American dream
and the public schools.* New York: Oxford University Press.

Hoxby, C. M. (2004). *Economics of where to go, when to go, and how to pay for it*. Chicago, IL: University of Chicago Press.

Huelsman, M., Draut, T., Meschede, T., Dietrich, L., Shapiro, T., & Sullivan, L. (2015). Less debt, more equity: Lowering student debt while closing the black-white wealth gap. Washington, DC: Demos. Retrieved from http://www.demos.org/publication/less-debt-more-equity-lowering-student-debt-while-closing-black-white-wealth-gap

Jackson, A. (2015, June 15). Guy who suggested you default on your student loans: "I'm crucified by the pampered elite media." *Business Insider*. Retrieved from http://www.businessinsider.com/lee-siegel-says-hes-being-crucified-by-the-elite-media-2015-6

Jackson, B., & Reynolds, J. (2013). The price of opportunity: Race, student loan debt, and college achievement. *Sociological Inquiry, 83*(3), 335–368.

Johnstone, D. B. (1977). Federally sponsored student loans: An overview of issues and policy alternatives. In L. D. Rice (Ed.), *Student loans: Problems and policy alternatives* (pp. 16–47). New York: College Entrance Examination Board.

Kamenetz, A., & O'Connor, J. (2014). The collapse of Corinthian colleges. Retrieved from http://www.npr.org/blogs/ed/2014/07/08/329550897/the-collapse-of-corinthian-colleges

Keppel, F. (1987). The higher education acts contrasted, 1965–1986: Has federal policy come of age? *Harvard Educational Review, 57*(1), 49–67.

Kiley, K. (2013). Merit consideration. Inside Higher Ed. Retrieved from https://www.insidehighered.com/news/2013/05/08/merit-aid-makes-college-more-expensive-low-income-students-report-finds

Kitroeff, N. (2015, October 14). Obama administration hits back at student debtors seeking relief. *Bloomberg News*. Retrieved from http://www.bloomberg.com/news/articles/2015–10–14/obama-administration-hits-back-at-student-debtors-seeking-relief

Kuhn, T. S. (1962). *The structure of scientific revolutions*. Chicago, IL: University of Chicago Press.

Lovenheim, M. (2011). The effect of liquid housing wealth on college enrollment. *Journal of Labor Economics, 29*(4), 741–771. Retrieved from http://www.jstor.org/stable/10.1086/660775Lumina Foundation & Institute for Higher Education Policy. (2014). Where financial aid began: Partnering with campuses and states. Retrieved from https://www.luminafoundation.org/resources/where-financial-aid-began

Mann, H. (1848). *Twelfth annual report of the Board of Education*. Boston, MA: Dutton and Wentworth.

McCann, C. (2015). Student loan programs. Retrieved from http://www.edcentral.org/edcyclopedia/federal-student-loan-programs-history/

McClure, S. E. (1983). The National Defense Education Act, Interview #4. Retrieved from http://www.senate.gov/artandhistory/history/resources/pdf/McClure4.pdf

Mendoza, P. (2012). The effect of debt and working while enrolled on baccalaureate completion: A counterfactual analysis. *Journal of Student Financial Aid, 42*, 25–59.

Mettler, S. (2014). *Degrees of inequality: How the politics of higher education sabotaged the American dream*. New York, NY: Basic Books.

Middle-Income Student Assistance Act, 20 U.S.C. (1978). Public Law 95–566.

Miller, B. (2014). *The student debt review: Analyzing the state of undergraduate student borrowing*. Washington, DC: New America.

Mishel, L., Bivens, J., Gould, E., & Shierholz, H. (2013). *The state of working America*, 12th ed. Ithaca, NY: Economic Policy Institute Book, Cornell University Press.

Morse, J. F. (1977). How we got here from there—A personal reminiscence of the early days. In L. D. Rice (Ed.), *Student loans: Problems and policy alternatives* (pp. 16–47). New York: College Entrance Examination Board.

Mumper, M. (1996). *Removing college price barriers: What government has done and why it hasn't worked.* New York: State University of New York Press.

Nasiripour, S. (2015). Education Department Steers Corinthian Colleges Students to Other Troubled For-Profits. *Huffington Post.* Retrieved from http://www.huffingtonpost.com/2015/04/28/corinthian-education-department_n_7166562.htmlNational Association of State Student Grant and Aid Programs. (2001). 31st Annual Survey Report, 1999-2000 Academic Year. New York, NY: State Higher Education Services Corporation.

Nixon, R. (1972). Statement on signing the education amendments of 1972. Retrieved from http://www.presidency.ucsb.edu/ws/?pid=3473

Ratcliffe, C., & McKernan, S. (2013). *Forever in your debt: Who has student loan debt, and who's worried?* Washington, DC: Urban Institute.

Rodriguez, F., & Jayadev, A. (2010). *The declining labor share of income.* Human Development Reports, Research Paper. United Nations Development Programme.

Rothstein, J., & Rouse, C. E. (2011). Constrained after college: Student loans and early-career occupational choices. *Journal of Public Economics, 95*(1–2), 149–163.

Schenet, M. (1993). *Recent changes in federal student aid.* CRS Report for Congress. Congressional Research Service, Library of Congress, Washington, DC.

Schorn, D. (2006). Does the lender's success come at too step a cost to students and taxpayers? Retrieved from https://web.archive.org/web/20110203142613/http://www.cbsnews.com/stories/2006/05/05/60minutes/main1591583.shtml

Selingo, J. (2001). Questioning the merit of merit scholarships. *Chronicle of Higher Education, 47*(19), A20–A22.

Siegel, L. (2015, June 6). Why I defaulted on my student loans. *New York Times*. Retrieved from http://www.nytimes.com/2015/06/07/opinion/sunday/why-i-defaulted-on-my-student-loans.html?_r=0

Tedeschi, B. (2009). College tuition not on the house. Retrieved from http://www.nytimes.com/2009/04/05/realestate/05mort.html

Urahn, S.K., Currier, E., Elliott, D., Wechsler, L., Wilson, D., and Colbert, D. (2012). *Pursuing the American dream: Economic mobility across generations.* Washington, DC: Economic Mobility Project, the Pew Charitable Trusts.

U.S. Congress (1978). *Middle Income Student Assistance Act.* Washington, DC: U.S. Government Printing Office.

U.S. Department of the Treasury. (2006, March). *Lessons learned from the privatization of Sallie Mae.* Washington, DC: Author. Retrieved from https://www.treasury.gov/about/organizational-structure/offices/Documents/SallieMaePrivatizationReport.pdf

Walsemann, K.M., Gee, G.C., & Gentile, D. (2014). Sick of our loans: Student borrowing and the mental health of young adults in the United States. *Social Science & Medicine, 124*(2015), 85–93.

Wei, C.C., & Skomsvold, P. (2010). *Borrowing at the maximum: Undergraduate Stafford Loan borrowers in 2007–2008.* Washington, DC: National Center for Education Statistics.

Woo, J. H., & Choy, S. P. (2011). Merit aid for undergraduates: Trends from 1995–96 to 2007–08. In Thomas Weko (Ed.), *Stats in brief (NCES 2012-160)*. Washington, DC: National Center for Education Statistics. Retrieved from http://nces.ed.gov/pubs2012/2012160.pdf

Zumeta, W. (2001). State policy and private higher education. In M. B. Paulsen & J. C. Smart (Eds.), *The finance of higher education: Theory, research, policy, and practice* (pp. 396–416). New York: Agathon Press.

2 Problems, Controversies, and Solutions

Introduction

When a prospective college student is presented with a financial aid "package" that includes student loans, this debt is treated as though it was just another form of financial assistance, analogous to grants, scholarships, or work-study arrangements. In truth, student loans have more in common with other consumer debt products than with educational benefits. They carry significant risks of future delinquency and default (New America, 2015), with their attendant consequences for borrowers' financial positions, outcomes not contemplated for those receiving non-debt financial aid. Indeed, even compared to some other types of loans, student borrowing can exert effects somewhat less benign, particularly when it comes to long-term economic consequences from nearly inescapable debt burdens. Here, some of the controversies in today's student debt landscape are discussed, organized into three categories. First, there are the ways in which student debt is serviced, including the general prohibition on discharge in bankruptcy and the use of regulatory mechanisms to garnish benefits and wages to secure collections. Second, there are policy "innovations" that seek to ameliorate some of the problems associated with student loans, while preserving their central role in the financial aid

---

A protester dressed as the "Master of Degrees," holds a ball and chain representing his college loan debt, during Occupy DC activities in Washington, D.C. While college graduates still fare better in the labor market than those without postsecondary titles, many students feel that their futures are constrained by the debts they carry. (AP Photo/Jacquelyn Martin)

system. These include various income-contingent loan schemes, of which government income-based repayment (IBR) is the most prominent. These deals exchange some reduction in borrowers' monthly obligations for an often much-longer period of indebtedness. Also included in the category of seemingly novel approaches are loan repayment programs that condition eligibility on specifically prescribed employment agreements, as well as policy proposals to shift risks more firmly onto borrowers' shoulders, as in calls to institute loan underwriting standards and expect students to make more "informed" choices. Finally, there are some signs that policy will concede the dangers associated with at least some forms of student borrowing and, then, impose limits, by lowering loan caps, limiting borrowing by graduate students and/or parents, and/or restricting borrowing at some types of institutions. While this latter category is distinguished by its potential to truly reduce some of the harm wrought by student debt, in the absence of other viable financial aid alternatives, there is also the danger that it may preclude access to college for those without the wealth required to confront high costs. This is perhaps the most controversial of all aspects of today's student loan debate, then. When preserving the viability and perceived acceptability of student borrowing as the centerpiece to the U.S. financial aid system is exalted above ensuring that such a system really serves students' education financing needs, all Americans should be on alert.

Standing in sharp contrast to these approaches are robust, equitable financial aid solutions that provide students with meaningful options, augment their abilities, and facilitate the realization of their educational aims. Properly conceived and adequately executed, these policies would include both long-term shifts toward asset-based financial aid, which helps families accumulate resources to finance college while also cultivating greater educational expectations (see Elliott, 2013b) and, then, greater achievement, and some financial reparation for those whose lives have already been adversely affected by the inherent failings of our debt-dependent model. In the United States, which has positioned educational attainment as the primary mechanism for upward mobility, financial aid should offer more than a promissory note. Students' higher education plans should hinge on their aspirations, not their contemplated balance sheets, and graduates' social media updates should feature career advancement more prominently than questions about deferment and forbearance options. As a consensus emerges about the problems with student loans, we need to harness this momentum to pivot more boldly to a new direction.

Following Borrowers, Protecting Creditors

Much is made of the fact that, unlike many other forms of debt, student loans are "unsecured," not backed by an asset that can be recouped in the event of a borrower's failure to repay. A closer look at servicing arrangements underscores the considerable protections available to creditors, however. Indeed, while student loans are not secured by reclaimable property, there is considerable security for creditors concerned about their interests. First, there is the unique prohibition against discharging student loans in bankruptcy. While U.S. bankruptcy laws provide general relief for those debtors who fall into unfortunate circumstances and are unable to repay their obligations, federal student loans have been excluded from bankruptcy protection since the 1970s. The Higher Education Amendments Act of 1976 established that borrowers had to wait five years from loan initiation before filing for bankruptcy. However, in the 1990s there were rising concerns by lenders about graduates walking away from their debt obligations shortly after graduating. For example, Balli (1998) wrote an article titled "U.S. Clamps Down on Loans to 'Deadbeat' Doctors" for the *Los Angeles Times*. In response to these concerns, the Higher Education Amendments Act of 1998 established that borrowers could no longer discharge student loans through bankruptcy, with very few exceptions. As part of bankruptcy reform in 2005, private student loans were extended the same treatment, even though private lenders can incorporate accounting for default risk into the terms offered (Darolia, 2015), making such protections less necessary for these entities. There are student loan hardship exceptions in the bankruptcy law; indeed, some analysis suggests that exceptions claimed are relatively frequently approved (Iuliano, 2012). Still, current bankruptcy law places student debt in the same category as debts for child support/alimony, tax claims, and criminal penalties (Demos, 2015), an odd standard for debt accrued in pursuit of education. In addition, the process by which borrowers can claim this consideration or appeal adverse decisions has been criticized as arbitrary, difficulty to navigate, and requiring often-expensive legal assistance (Pardo & Lacey, 2009).

In sum, then, bankruptcy considerations markedly differentiate student loans from other debt instruments, a distinction that also sends an important signal to students about their options and what the future may hold.

There is sparse fiscal rationale for this strict treatment of student loans, since allowing bankruptcy discharge is estimated to cost only approximately 3 percent of the total amount of student loans issued annually, far less than other measures to assist distressed borrowers (Demos, 2015). Instead, the exception is defended as a guard against morally hazardous borrowing, even though analysis has failed to find evidence that student borrowers "opportunistically default" on a wide scale (Darolia & Ritter, 2015). As would be expected, despite this scant evidence for widespread, legitimate need for these lender protections, discussions about reducing individuals' ability to discharge student debt in bankruptcy are often greeted by opposition from lenders. And student borrowing is big business; private loans made up $150 billion of the $1.1 trillion student loan market in 2012 (Hartman, 2013). One of the unintended consequences of student loan policy is that it created incentives for banks and other financial institutions to act to protect the student loan program from any potential threats to its survival. As Mettler (2014) explains, "Then in turn, the profitability of the enterprise led the banks to engage in rent-seeking behavior, mobilizing to protect the student loan system and to make its terms all the more favorable to them" (54).

Unlike in regard to other loan instruments, however, lenders and their advocates can couch their self-defense in language emphasizing educational opportunity, rather than profit calculus. Specifically, those advancing the lender position have alleged that ending these protections could harm disadvantaged students by reducing access to financing and, then, to higher education. For example, during a hearing about student loan reform, Congressman Steve Cohen (R-TN) said (emphasis added), "If we make student loans unconditionally dischargeable we will encourage abuse, increase the interest rates students pay on their loans, and *dry up the flow of capital into the student lending market. This will either decrease access to higher education* or create a vacuum the Federal Government will have to fill again at taxpayer expense" (Government Printing Office, 2009). The debate becomes, then, not about what financial aid policy would best serve students' needs, or even how to best structure student loans so that they exert positive rather than predatory force on students' outcomes, but, instead, about whether imposing any restrictions on lenders will inevitably harm the students whose futures depend on the availability of educational loans.

Nonetheless, as repayment difficulties mount and consumer protections in federal direct loans are enhanced, without corollaries in the private loan market, greater regulation in this arena seems on the horizon, at least for those private loans that do not offer repayment modifications. At present, this would implicate most of the private student loan market, since few today offer IBR options, forgiveness procedures, or anything more expansive than short-term forbearance allowances, even though these measures have proven feasible and useful in the arena of federal student loans. In October 2015, the U.S. Department of Education entered the fray, calling for regulatory reform and highlighting the inequities faced by borrowers in the federal and private student loan markets. The report issued positioned student loans within the larger financial aid system and framed the challenges as those of college afford-ability and expansion of opportunity (U.S. Department of Education, 2015). Such articulation underscores the particular functions of student loans in the U.S. economic opportunity structure. Student debt is, at its core, a deal between students and lenders—whether the federal government or private equity holders—that finances a broader and more fundamental bar-gain: that education will pay rewards commensurate with stu-dents' expense of effort and ability. It is often the only available bridge that students in today's education financing landscape have, by which to access higher education; students, therefore, come to the exchange at a distinct disadvantage. Where this contract has broken down—illustrated most dramatically in bankruptcy—borrowers deserve to emerge with the potential, still, to climb.

Questionable servicing practices are seen not only at the extreme end, where borrowers are in true financial ruin. At ear-lier points, as well, borrowers who find themselves delinquent are often dismayed by creditors' powers to recoup their invest-ments. Creditors and those acting on their behalf have access to significantly intrusive methods and can exert themselves even to extents that substantially compromise borrowers' financial security. While these servicing approaches unfold against the backdrop of very limited bankruptcy recourse, seldom are such dire measures explicitly invoked. Far more common than bank-ruptcy are experiences of student loan default and, especially, delinquency, the latter of which befalls almost two in five stu-dent borrowers (Brown, Haughwout, Donghoon, Scally, & van der Klaauw, 2015). Even as these adverse occurrences become relatively commonplace, they exact considerable financial and mental tolls on borrowers. First, all protections and accommo-dations extended to borrowers are revoked in the case of a stu-dent loan default, which often means that the loan becomes due in its entirety. Student loan servicing agreements also include significant fees and collection costs (as high as 40 percent for

Perkins loans and 24 percent for Stafford, PLUS, and consolidation loans) which, when added to the principal and interest, can dramatically increase the total obligation (Mayotte, 2015). Student borrowers failing to comply with their education debts have nowhere to hide from their creditors. In addition to the lack of bankruptcy protection, student lenders have the ability to garnish up to 15 percent of borrowers' wages, claim tax refunds, and even recover debts from Social Security and other government benefits. Unlike for many other types of loans, these collection efforts are backed by the regulatory might—and long enforcement reach—of the federal government, and they are not without costs, itself an important point of controversy in today's financial aid environment. Many are frustrated by the U.S. Department of Education's investment of, for example, $1.4 billion to pay collection agencies to track down borrowers who were delinquent or in default in 2011 (Martin, 2012), a particularly substantial expenditure within the context of declines in the value of need-based financial aid and budget peril in other programs.

Defining the "Problem" as One of Repayment Strain Leads to Narrowly Focused "Solutions"

With rising delinquency and default rates in the headlines and a majority of Americans who relied on student loans dissatisfied with how they financed their educations (Vien, 2015), the student loan system is in need of a transformation. Instead of an overhaul, however, what student borrowers have mostly seen is an image makeover, with some tweaks around the margins in order to preserve the core of debt-dependent financial aid. In this vein are loan modification approaches such as IBR and Pay-As-You-Earn (PAYE), as well as calls to improve student borrowing decisions. Even public and private loan forgiveness measures often have more rhetorical than tangible value, particularly where eligibility criteria and/or limited geographic or industry scope means that relatively few borrowers qualify for assistance, even as headlines trumpet their generosity (see Mayotte, 2016). Critique of the modesty and, in some cases, disingenuousness of these measures is not to suggest that they are entirely without merit. Some bring real relief to short-term finances, and some—in the case of student loan forgiveness that incentivizes graduates' work in underserved industries, populations, or localities—serve other legitimate public policy aims. However, some of the loan modifications may also erode borrowers' ultimate financial positions and distort education and career decisions. Emphasizing borrowers' responsibility for their own outcomes can lead to harmful victim-blaming. And all of these attempts to soften student borrowing's rough edges fail to address the underlying premise that predicating access to higher education on a debt-ridden foundation may, indeed, be a bad idea.

IBR, a particular example of income-contingent loans, has grown dramatically in popularity in recent years, fueled by regulatory changes that have extended its availability (Inside Higher Ed, 2015) and by a perception that *the* problem with student loans occurs when a given student's educational "bet" fails to pay off in immediately higher earnings, resulting in a cash crunch (Dynarski, 2016). IBR caps student loan payments between 0 and 10 percent of borrowers' incomes, with loan forgiveness after 10 years for those working in government or nonprofit sectors and 20 years for other borrowers whose loans have not been fully discharged by that time (Delisle, 2013). If the only aim is to reduce delinquency and default— so that individual borrowers feel better and the student loan problem appears less severe—then IBR seems largely success-ful. To initiate an IBR plan, borrowers have to request it. As publicity of the provisions rise alongside borrowers' difficulties with student loan repayment, more and more borrowers are asking for these modifications. According to a GAO (2014) report, 51 percent of direct loan borrowers were eligible for IBR in September 2012, but only 13 percent had enrolled as of 2014. Then, enrollment grew in IBR by 368 percent in just two years as debtors flocked to the program (Mitchell, 2015b). Others report even higher rates of enrollment into IBR plans. For instance, in 2013, IBR programs accounted for 6 percent of borrowers in repayment, a figure that had grown to nearly 11 percent by 2014 (Delisle, 2014) and 20 percent by 2016 (White House Council of Economic Advisors, 2016). Furthermore, these programs account for almost 22 percent of the direct loan portfolio in repayment (Delisle, 2014), and growth is expected to continue as the student loan landscape expands and more borrowers become aware of the short-term repayment relief income-contingency offers.

While increasingly popular among borrowers, IBR is certainly not an entirely benign development. Indeed, use of IBR may be contributing to one of the starkest trends in student borrowing: the growing length of time needed to repay student loans. Akers and Chingos (2014) found that the mean period of repayment had grown to more than 13 years in 2010, from approximately 7.5 years in 1992. Of course, as anyone who has completed an introductory financial education class has learned, the total cost of financing usually increases with an extension of the period of indebtedness. IBR works similarly to a consumer's use of credit cards to finance large purchases he/she cannot afford all at once; in exchange for agreeing to pay on the debt for a longer period, the amount exacted in every repayment is reduced. In student borrowing, the time it takes to pay off loans is only likely to grow as income-driven repayment plans are promoted as a way to increase affordability. While the trend in student loan policy in recent years has been to rely on income-based programs as a way of addressing the problems of affordability and borrowers' cash crunches, there are growing signs that this might only be magnifying the student debt crisis to come.

As borrowers' incomes are diverted over this increasingly longer period away from asset accumulation and toward debt management, the negative association of student debt with long-term financial well-being may intensify as well (Elliott &

Lewis, 2015). Further, correctly calibrating IBR agreements is complicated by insufficient understanding of how much constitutes a harmful amount of debt—on a monthly basis, as well as in the aggregate. For example, Baum and Schwartz (2005) estimated that the recommended cutoff for unmanageable student debt was between 8 or 10 percent, a figure that may sound reasonable yet does not hold up in other analyses. Egoian (2013), for example, found that four-year college graduates with median debt of $23,300 had $115,096 less in retirement savings than four-year college graduates with no student loans by the time they reach age 73. Critically, Egoian's (2013) estimates assumed that 7 percent of an indebted college graduate's earnings go toward yearly loan repayments. That is, he found substantial, long-term, negative effects that kick in even at levels of indebtedness lower than 10 percent. However, 10 percent is the figure currently used for IBR payment plans, with an associated assumption that it represents a debt obligation less likely to cause harm to borrowers. Egoian's findings are even more alarming given that he based his estimates on relatively small amounts of debt—$23,000—while many borrowers owe far more, and that his estimates assumed that households would pay off their student debt in 10 years, while, as described earlier, the average student debtor now holds his or her debt 13 years. IBR plans' ability to ward off adverse financial effects of student debt will, of course, be compromised by incorrect parameters for calculating debt obligations. In this light, analysis to date suggests, at the least, that the use of 10 percent of a borrower's income as being not harmful to the borrower seems to be questionable.

One of the early perceived advantages of student debt, in contrast to grants or scholarships, is the relatively low cost to taxpayers (see Morse, 1977). The thinking is that student loans are cheaper for the public because most of the investment is repaid, unlike grants or scholarships, which are clearer transfers from public coffers to individuals. While this may have been the case initially, as the number of people who have debt has grown over time, the costs associated with the student debt system have grown significantly, as well. As the nation considers our collective financial aid policy, we should also reassess the fiscal assumptions on which these policies rest and explicitly test the common wisdom about the student loan "bargain." The costs of the student loan system have grown administratively, as more students apply and must be processed, although these would be growing costs in other financial aid arrangements, as well. Student lending also incurs costs due to the expanding apparatus needed for collection; notably, these are not costs that have any residual educational value, but merely represent expenditures to try to make student lending "work" as designed. Student loan costs have also increased because of programs like IBR that are needed to mitigate the harm that having student debt can inflict on the postcollege financial health of students. This means that student loans are having to function less like the loans intended, in order to avoid some of the negative effects that would otherwise result. For instance, evidence suggests that the sizable student debts owed by many Americans are simply not dischargeable at the lower payment levels negotiated in IBR schemes. This accounting makes debt forgiveness is relatively commonplace and, then, IBR expensive. Currently, IBR costs an estimated $11 billion per year, most of that in loan forgiveness (Delisle, 2015). As a greater percentage of those eligible for IBR take the government up on this offer, these costs are likely to continue to rise. When student loans are forgiven, the cost is often greater than for direct grants, since the former requires long periods of loan servicing before reaching forgiveness. In addition, loan forgiveness is seldom well targeted to those students who most need aid in order to access higher education (Delisle, 2015), compromising IBR's efficiency, as well.

Students in income-contingent repayment plans whose incomes are low enough that the required monthly payments do not cover the interest on the loan experience negative amortization (Equal Justice Works, 2015). The loan balance then continues to grow, as the payments are insufficient to pay all of the exacted interest or the original principal. This represents another limitation and risk of IBR, which may not help students get out from under their education debt at all. While it is mitigated somewhat by today's low interest rates, the variability of student loan interest raises the specter of even greater problems in IBR mechanisms in the future. From the 1960s through 1992, interest rates on student loans were fixed (i.e., do not change over the life of the loan) and ranged between 6 and 10 percent (New America Foundation, 2012). In 1992 Congress enacted variable rates that were set once a year based on the interest rates on short-term U.S. Treasury securities plus 3.1 percentage points, capped at 9 percent (New America Foundation, 2012). In 2006, this changed back to a fixed rate at 6.8 percent. In 2013, new legislation tied student loan interest rates to the financial market; while each loan's interest rate is fixed, a student with loans originating over the course of his or her college education may have loans with several different interest rates. In considering borrowers' experiences with student loans, interest rates matter. In an article in *The Columbus Dispatch*, Riepenhoff and Wagner (2012) reveal how student loan debt can double due to compounding interest and debt-collection fees. They examined a random sample of 394 cases from nearly 16,000 lawsuits filed by the U.S. government and found these interest and fee effects in 40 percent of defaulted student loan debtors. Private loan interest rates are even more disadvantageous to borrowers than are federal loans, even as they provide lenders with very favorable terms. This accounting underscores the imbalance in the risks and rewards the student loan market offers to borrowers and lenders, respectively. Within the student debt debate, interest rates have become prominent talking points. Senator Elizabeth Warren from Massachusetts has led the charge on reducing interest rates as a solution to the student debt crisis (Dash, 2015), flagging as unfair deals where student loan giant Sallie Mae, for example, lends money to students at interest rates up to 40

times the rate the company pays to borrow its initial capital
(see Nasiripour, 2015). Senator Warren has proposed allowing
existing borrowers to refinance their loans from the 6.8 percent to 3.8 percent. The new REPAYE (Pay As You Earn) plan
also attempts to address the problem of compounding interest
by reducing the amount of interest the borrower is charged to
50 percent of the unpaid interest (Equal Justice Works, 2015).
While popular among student borrowers, however, some argue
reducing interest rates will do little to help those most in need
pay back their student loans (James, 2015), even if such action
would reduce the overall cost of college financing somewhat.
Certainly, the interest rate debate does not address the core
challenge of providing meaningful financial aid alternatives to
aspiring college students. At any rate above zero, student debt
still costs students and still has the potential, then, to interfere
with the benefits and returns (Elliott & Lewis, 2015; Hiltonsmith, 2014) higher education is supposed to provide. Particularly because the incidence of student borrowing is distributed
highly unequally among American young people (Huelsman,
2015), this is a far greater threat than manipulations of interest
rates can ameliorate.

IBR is more than a payment schedule, then; often, it is an
acknowledgment of the unaffordable nature of a borrower's
obligation. Many students are unable to pay back their loans
with the smaller payments allowed under IBR. Some may even
intentionally use IBR to postpone the inevitable, buying time
until—at 10, 20, or 25 years, depending on one's particular
circumstances—the federal government forgives the remaining
balance. These scenarios have not gone unnoticed as, significant
for the fortunes of individual students and the evolving political
debate, IBR plans have been framed as a type of student loan
bailout or giveaway (Dorfman, 2014; Matthews, 2012). The
increasing frequency of the end result of loan forgiveness has
led some to contend that the existence of IBR further distorts
not only financial aid decisions at the individual level, but the
aggregate context of tuition pricing as well. According to this

reasoning, IBR plans make it so that it does not matter how much students borrow or schools charge; borrowers and institutions alike know that students need only to make minimal payments in an IBR plan in order to secure debt forgiveness in the end. Tamanaha (2012) provides the following example of a hypothetical IBR arrangement. "A student who owes $130,000 will pay exactly the same amount over the 20 years as a student who owes $200,000 (assuming the same income)." These discussions seldom note that the forgiven debt is treated as taxable income, a reality that may result in sizable payments to the IRS after students' loans are forgiven, depending on the amount forgiven and their economic situations at the time of forgiveness. These distortions are undeniable; indeed, there is even evidence that, in an attempt to game the system, some schools have gone as far as to tell students that they will make their IBR payments for them (Tamanaha, 2012). To prevent these types of abuses, the REPAYE plan limits the amount that can be forgiven. Other restrictions may be forthcoming in response to concerns about abuses. Those who focus on the moral hazards of IBR loan forgiveness may be missing the rhetorical forest for the trees, however. The growth in the number of students who cannot discharge their debts after years of timely repayment likely signifies something important about the heavy debt burdens with which many leave college and the relatively low earnings that often follow even college completion. If IBR is not working as intended, to support student borrowers through a smooth process of affordable repayment, perhaps that says more about the nature of student borrowing than the need to further modify this particular escape hatch.

Some voices in the student loan policy dialogue contend that the costs of IBR are growing not only in an absolute sense (i.e., dollar amount), but also that they disproportionately benefit those who owe the most, who may not be those in greatest need of government support for education financing (Delisle, 2013). IBR benefits accrue disproportionately to those who have high debts, often because they attended expensive colleges and/or obtained advanced degrees (Delisle, 2013), because these very large balances are more difficult to fully repay on the affordable scale that IBR outlines. While overrepresented among IBR beneficiaries, however, these borrowers are, in many cases, not those most harmed by their student loans, at least in terms of default rates (Dynarski, 2016). At the same time, student financial aid is somewhat of a zero-sum game, and the money invested in relief for these heavily indebted borrowers necessarily impairs efforts to construct more equitable policy solutions, including those that might disproportionately aid disadvantaged students impaired by even relatively small loan balances. This is not to suggest that a narrative that blames those seeking advanced degrees or attending prestigious institutions for the problems in the current student loan system or, certainly, for the barriers that some students face in seeking to access higher education, is accurate or productive. Indeed, such a framing is potentially dangerous, as it takes focus off the root problem, which is financing higher education with loans, and puts forward an argument that student behavior, rather than institutional failing, is at fault. It also may help to further promote a rationale that only certain students can afford to pursue certain types of degrees or to study at certain institutions, a logic that runs directly counter to the role of higher education as a great equalizer in the American economy. This narrative also perpetuates the idea that default rates are the most important measure of how well borrowers are doing, a flawed metric that obscures the greatest failings of our dependence on student debt. Again, when the student loan policy conversation is contorted in order to preserve an undeserved place for student debt in financial aid, these convolutions should signal distress and the need for more substantial reforms.

There is evidence that student loans may be affecting not just who attends higher education—and where—but also what students study, and what courses their lives and careers later take. Indeed, to the extent to which the specter of student debt, and sometimes, the promise of forgiveness, can influence choice of degree programs and careers (see Field, 2009; Rothstein & Rouse, 2011) for those without other financing options, student borrowing may exacerbate the lopsided nature of higher education, effects that may be magnified by the mercurial and sometimes illogical parameters of loan modification and forgiveness programs. Today, the federal government is not the only actor in the debt forgiveness game. Employers are also acutely aware of the pressure that student indebtedness places on workers—particularly recent college leavers—and some are attempting to use employee benefits to position themselves for competitive advantage. While only 3 percent of employers report offering student loan repayment as a benefit to employees (Greenfield, 2015), as the labor market recovers post-recession (Cohen, 2016), more companies may utilize this approach to recruit and retain quality talent. While these measures can provide significant assistance to troubled borrowers, the proverbial devil is in the details. In particular, debt forgiveness that requires extended periods of employment before benefits are extended, that fails to protect borrowers from tax implications (LaPlante, 2015; Lieber, 2012), or that constrains career advancement may reduce the value of the benefit or, again, introduce additional elements of inequity. Any time that a student chooses a particular school or major, or a college graduate takes a particular job or stays in a particular community, solely because of the student loan terms associated with such a decision, debt-dependent financial aid's effects are rippling throughout the U.S. educational and economic systems, with consequences that deserve our attention. What these loan modifications all share, of course, is a seeming commitment to maintaining the institution of student debt by making the terms more manageable, rather than addressing the problems at their foundation.

Tweaks around the Margins Rather Than Fundamental Reconsiderations

That student loans are a big business should be no surprise. This debt instrument has been crafted so that taxpayers and financial institutions are protected against the risk of default by rules that forbid students from discharging their student loans through bankruptcy and that allow repayment to be collected through such means as garnishing tax refunds, wages, and even Social Security benefits. Few other loans come with terms as favorable for lenders, an accounting that has helped to attract creditors to the marketplace and that looms over the government's involvement in the student loan enterprise, as well. The Congressional Budget Office (CBO) reported that the federal government stood to make a profit of $50 billion from student loans in 2013 (as reported in Jesse, 2013). Nor is the government the only entity enriched by student loans; collection agencies, for example, make large profits servicing student loans (Lorin, 2015), and others have carved out industries peddling financial guidance for student borrowers or offering products that trade on families' student debt anxiety.

The inclusion of such an overt profit motive has created a type of perverse incentive system. As a result, groups that profit within the student loan industry often fight to maintain it and to maximize the profits their stakeholders receive. For example, Sallie Mae spends millions of dollars lobbying Congress each year. Gupta (2013) reports that from 1998 to 2012, Sallie Mae spent about $37.5 million on lobbying activities in efforts to block bills like the Private Student Loan Bankruptcy Fairness Act of 2013 and the Fairness for Struggling Students Act of 2013. In addition to hiring lobbyists in an attempt to influence the political system, many of these actors have also been found to engage in "unfair and deceptive" practices by, for example, failing to provide service members with a 6 percent interest rate cap on their student loans (Bidwell, 2014). They have also been accused by several of their own employees of providing misleading or incomplete information to borrowers, including inappropriately steering students toward forbearance or even putting them into forbearance without their knowledge in order to keep default rates low (PBS, 2009). Others have accused Sallie Mae of providing subprime loans to low-income students attending for-profit colleges in order to gain a larger share of this very lucrative market. These practices are unfair in intention and disproportionate in effect, particularly since low-income and otherwise disadvantaged students are concentrated in this sector of the higher education system (IHEP, 2010). For example, Burd (2012) reports that,

> Sallie Mae agreed to provide funds for private student loans, with interest rates and fees totaling more than 20 percent per year, to low-income and working class students at these schools who normally wouldn't qualify for them because of their poor credit records. Sallie Mae apparently viewed these loans as "loss leaders," meaning that the company was willing to make these loans, many of which were likely to go into default, in exchange for becoming the exclusive provider of federal loans to the hundreds of thousands of students these huge chains collectively serve.

Such institutional profit-seeking, even contrary to established financial practices, eerily parallels the predatory behavior within the mortgage loan sector, widely credited with contributing to the housing market collapse in 2007 (see Rugh & Massey, 2010). While the outcomes in the student loan context are far from ensured, there would seem to be adequate cause for parties from many quarters to take a close look at the activities of student lenders.

Information as the Answer

Some of the efforts to limit the damage wrought by student borrowing seek to intervene not with the loan instruments themselves, but at the level of the borrower, instead. In an approach perhaps analogous to improving population health by disseminating information, some have argued for policies to deliver more information to prospective borrowers at the point of debt assumption in order to presumably assist them in navigating financing choices. Some of these proposals aim to arm students with better information about repayment schedules, institutional performance, and projected earnings, supposedly to help them make wiser decisions about when, where, and how much to borrow. This was the intention, for example, of the Empowering Students through Enhanced Financial Counseling Act, passed by the U.S. House of Representatives in a 405–11 vote in July 2014. This vote suggests relative unanimity on the issue of whether such measures are advisable. Indeed, it may appear, at first glance, that there is nothing very contentious about providing more frequent and comprehensive entrance and exit counseling for student borrowers and requiring institutions to annually project expected total student debt. The extraordinary thing about this apparently innocuous proposal, however, is where it locates responsibility for fixing the student debt problem: not with the financial aid system, policymakers, or even educators, but with students themselves. Therefore, while more information may be, on its face, a good—or at least harmless—thing, expecting that students can educate themselves to better outcomes without providing them with any improved options from which to choose their financing path completes the shift toward individual responsibility for higher education toward which we have been inching for decades. Examining these proposals through this lens reveals their impracticality and, perhaps even more profoundly, their cynicism. Even if it was possible for students to make, at age 18 or 19, an informed decision about their projected educational returns in an uncertain labor market several years later, there is something disturbing about asking American young people to set aside emotionally charged aspirations and, instead, coolly calculate whether college is really in their best financial interest (see discussion in Elliott & Lewis, 2015). Legislation cannot be expected to "empower students" if they lack avenues by which to pursue meaningful choices. Indeed, absent viable alternatives to loans, this information provision could even backfire, increasing disadvantaged students' loan aversion (see Perna, 2000 re: loan

aversion), sending damaging messages about the risks associated with financing college, and widening the gap in educational attainment by socioeconomic status. Although providing
more accurate information about the outcomes delivered by
a given institution may facilitate better selection, such counseling cannot likely overcome the forces that conspire to push
disadvantaged students to precisely the schools least equipped
to facilitate their success (see Giancola & Kahlenberg, 2016;
Hoxby & Avery, 2013). Fundamentally, we cannot reasonably
expect to solve the student-debt problem by simply informing
students of how problematic their debt is likely to be.

Building on the "information as prevention" approach are
proposals to underwrite student loans to more comprehensively account for students' likely outcomes and, then, cred-
itworthiness, before extending credit (see Akers, 2014). Such
a policy, if adopted, would be a dramatic departure in student
loan practices. By explicitly accounting for the risks presented
by particular borrowers, this approach would also directly con-
tradict the rationale that, today, justifies the preferential treatment student loans receive in the financial marketplace. While
the specific parameters are unclear, student loan underwriting
guidelines would likely include an assessment of the institution, including its cohort default and graduation rates and
alumni labor market outcomes, as well as an analysis of the
individual student and his or her plans. The latter component
is the most controversial, since it would likely preclude borrowing entirely by some students, disqualified because their past
academic track records do not bode well for future progress,
their occupational plans are deemed unrealistic, their financial backgrounds are assumed to warrant lender caution, or
some combination of these factors. Of course, these guidelines
would not treat all students equally, nor would the resulting
decisions be equitably distributed in the population of aspiring
college students. Even a casual observer of education statistics
can see patterns that would likely influence the underwriting
decisions of student lenders, who might decide, for example,

that nontraditional students enrolling in for-profit or two-year colleges with relatively low graduation and high default rates (see Looney & Yannelis, 2015) are risks they prefer not to take.

If the financial aid landscape presented students with a wide range of potential financing options, cautiously considering whether student loans are a "good bet" for a given student may be a wise approach. If borrowers judged "poor risks" would be offered non-loan financial aid instead of debt packages, such a shift could significantly improve student loan performance and, most importantly, student outcomes. Today, however, most students are choosing not between student loans and non-debt alternatives but, instead, between borrowing to go to college and not going at all. That means that the denial of student loans to those who cannot meet GPA or other requirements without providing any replacement financial aid (see Mitchell, 2015a) could pull more rungs out of the higher education ladder, compounding the injustices of unequal academic preparation and leaving millions of aspiring college students with few options for continuing their educations.

Putting a Lid on Student Borrowing— Is "Nothing" Better Than Student Debt?

A frame that views aggregate debt levels as the real student loan problem naturally sees limits on student debt as the best possible solution. Some policy proposals, then, have sought to simply reduce the availability of student loans, a blunt response with tremendous potential to alter the higher education experience, even as it does inevitably constrain debt assumption. In addition to influencing students' decisions to borrow, through the provision of information and other approaches, some advocate loan reforms that make it impossible for students to access larger lines of credit. Graduate students have been particularly targeted for these loan restrictions, including elimination of loan forgiveness programs (Lanza, 2015) in an effort to deter borrowing. These cutbacks have come even though graduate school is increasingly important for occupational success in many sectors (Pappano, 2011) and even though graduate students of color are especially dependent on borrowing (see Elliott, Lewis, & Johnson, 2014). Graduate students are not the only ones possibly affected by these trends, however. Across-the-board loan caps, intended to limit debt exposure, may hit low-income students disproportionately, given their relatively greater reliance on student borrowing (Huelsman, 2015) to finance living expenses, in addition to tuition and fees (Krupnick, 2015). Even with today's relatively easy access to student loans, many disadvantaged students face significant unmet need (Engle & Tinto, 2008). This gap between available resources—including student loans—and college costs can prevent enrollment and completion, a dynamic that would likely intensify if loan limits are lowered. A final type of proposal to restrict student borrowing relates to the types of institutions where federal student loans, at least, can be used. On the one hand, such a policy could incentivize improved performance by schools currently failing their mostly low-income and first-generation students (see TICAS, 2015). However, such a measure could also limit access to the very institutions most open to underserved students, an outcome that could hinder these students' progress toward their intended degrees. Critically, such standards might also obscure the differential role of various types of institutions within the stratified U.S. higher education system (Carnevale & Strohl, 2013). In some cases, the comparatively poor performance of some educational institutions could stem as much from their larger numbers of disadvantaged students, as from actual failures (Cielinski, 2015). If schools that struggle to support marginal students through graduation and to equip them for postcollege success are then penalized for lagging behind institutions without such a steep hill to climb, the effect may paradoxically be to further deny equitable opportunities. Yes, the students whose student borrowing is thwarted by these stricter loan guidelines may owe less in student debt, but, without viable options for securing advanced education, it would be difficult to argue that they were any the better for the policy change.

Channeling Momentum for Good

In today's context, the fear of taking away student loans without pivoting to an alternative approach is a powerful current constraining pursuit of meaningful changes. Because "financial aid" so often means student debt, it can be difficult to imagine another way. As discussed earlier, making changes to student borrowing without offering alternatives may indeed have the effect, particularly in the short term, of reducing access to higher education among those who currently depend on debt. Without asset-based alternatives or, at least, more robust need-based grants, to fill the resulting chasm, pivoting away from reliance on student debt blocks some students' educational attainment altogether. These potential harms are not merely theoretical. Historically black colleges and universities, for example, reported reductions in enrollment following the imposition of stricter lending guidelines for Parent PLUS loans, which now consider prospective borrowers' credit histories (Wang, 2013). This does not mean that student loans are the best we can do, however, or that a generation of American young people can afford for our collective imagination to be so shackled by the confines of the status quo. As the history traced in Chapter 1 underscores, there have been times in the relatively recent past when financial aid meant something far different from a loan package. The future, too, can hold real alternatives. Here, in today's student loan policy dialogue and, especially, in the growing calls for debt relief and education reform, are the seeds of promise and the first rumblings of revolution. Directing such energies toward the most productive channels requires beginning with a clear assessment of the harms rendered by student debt dependence and the criteria by which to judge a different approach, a superior one. There is a need for this analysis within each of the policy avenues contemplated earlier. Perhaps nowhere is a clarity of purpose and commitment to equity more critically needed than in the conversation about the pros and cons of the policy cause *du jour*: "free college."

Free College?

Making college free is not without problems. While free college proposals have the singular purpose of making college accessible to all, they fail to consider that middle-income and high-income students are considerably more likely to attend and graduate from college in the first place (Bailey & Dynarski, 2011), which means they would benefit first and, perhaps, most, from reductions in tuition prices. Without addressing these disparities throughout the education pipeline, making college free at the point of enrollment would likely do relatively little to upend higher education's reinforcement of racial and class stratification (see Carnevale & Strohl, 2013; Fischer, 2016)—a task that financial aid should be charged to accomplish. The United States needs a 21st-century financial aid system that works in concert with early education efforts to reduce the gaps in achievement so more children—including those currently disadvantaged—are prepared to attend college. American schools, from kindergarten to postgraduate, need financing mechanisms that serve to increase children's expectations of what they can accomplish and incentivize their engagement and achievement. And we need education financing that communicates a clear, communal, commitment to making education a viable conduit to equitable opportunity and shared prosperity. Free college, while inherently appealing to a tuition-fatigued public, is an expensive endeavor that nonetheless falls short on those essential fronts (Ready, 2015). It would not diverge from the status quo that, today, considers early education, higher education, and economic mobility policies separately, a false dichotomy that leaves too many gaps where too many children fall.

Any offer of "free college" is limited by its narrow focus on cost constraints only at the point of enrollment. Just as in the domains described earlier, however, policies for free college are not all created equal. Many of these distinctions are substantive, likely to result in considerable differences in outcomes for particular groups of students. For example, proposals to make only two-year colleges free may further ensconce a two-tiered system wherein low-income and minority students are disproportionately steered into these colleges because of their financial constraints, even when their effort and ability might suggest they would benefit more from a more selective four-year university (see Harnisch & Lebioda, 2016). These risks are exacerbated by some of the features of free community college plans, which in some cases cover only tuition and not living expenses or reduce state spending on other financial aid programs in order to finance the two-year college subsidy (Harnisch & Lebioda, 2016). Already today, students who have few family resources to finance college often choose two-year schools for affordability when they might otherwise have been qualified for and selected a higher-status four-year school, while more economically advantaged students continue to select a school based on the best educational fit (Bastedo & Flaster, 2014). By increasing the cost differential between two- and four-year institutions and, in some cases, cannibalizing financial aid programs that students can carry to their institution of choice, investment in free two-year college may intensify existing inequality, particularly because students who attend two-year colleges are, on average, less likely to graduate from college and earn less than students who attend more selective institutions (Looney & Yannelis, 2015).

Proposals to make college entirely free, as advanced prominently by Democratic presidential nominees and advocated by many student and activist groups, are less likely than two-year-only offers to exacerbate current inequality, but they are still problematic. Significantly, free college proposals may not even make much of a dent in student debt and may not, then, substantially change the accounting children face as they contemplate college. For example, in Sweden where tuition is currently free, about 85 percent of students leave with debt that averages around $19,000 (Phillips, 2013). This is because tuition is not the only costs students face. They also must pay for things like rent, transportation, fees, and food, costs particularly acute for economically disadvantaged students. "Free college" does not reduce costs for all of those other essentials. As with policies to make two-year colleges free, some proposals for free college would finance the high price tag by eliminating existing financial aid programs and redirecting those dollars, a move that could make it more difficult for low-income students to finance their educations.

Understanding the potential and limitations of making college tuition free requires considering the myriad of factors that facilitate and constrain the educational attainment of American students today, and the ways in which existing inequalities contribute to unequal patterns of achievement. This more comprehensive lens views financial aid as more than just a way to confront tuition costs and reimagines these resources as tools with which to restore higher education as a potent catalyst of equitable opportunity. This broader vision for financial aid begins long before and continues long after the point of college enrollment. Inequity does not begin in college; instead, achievement gaps persist throughout the educational pipeline (Pell Institute & PennAHEAD, 2015). More recently, research has revealed that even college graduation does not create a truly level-playing field. Even among graduates of similar institutions, returns are unequal. For those who do manage to graduate from a four-year college, the Federal Reserve Bank of St. Louis finds that Hispanic ($68,379 income/$49,606 net worth) and black American students ($52,147 income/$32,780 net worth) receive less benefit from having obtained a degree than their white ($94,351 income/$359,928 net worth) and Asian ($92,931 income/$250,637 net worth) counterparts with regard to their 2013 annual median income and median net worth (Emmons & Noeth, 2015). These findings parallel those discussed in Chapter 1, which indicate that college graduates who grow up in families with incomes below 185 percent of the poverty level earn less over the course of their lives than those who grow up in families with incomes above 185 percent of the poverty level (Hershbein, 2016). These disparate outcomes are fueled by disparities in our labor and capital markets and magnified by differences in the resources with which students approach the educational system (Price, 2016). In the aggregate, these analyses suggest that strategies that focus *only* on college affordability may fail to achieve some of our most cherished aspirations for education. When it comes to investing in higher education as a path to the American dream of equitable opportunity for all, then, "free" is not exactly what children need.

How about a Bailout?

Some student groups and some other advocates have called for a "bailout" for student debtors, similar to what big banks received (e.g., Applebaum & StudentNation 2014). Others have suggested that a bailout would result in a moral hazard (i.e., rewarding imprudent behavior rather than punishing it, in ways that influence subsequent behavior) (Evans, 2012). Placing the responsibility for sage financial decisions on individual students, however, continues the flawed assessment that they are primarily to blame for the problematic student debt with which they are now shackled. This question of culpability is important, particularly because pinning responsibility often precedes the critical determination of who should pay. In the arena of student loans, there are many potential culprits, all of which possess more agency in regard to student

debt assumption than students themselves: lenders, government policymakers, and higher educational institutions, for
example. Because of the high stakes, considerations other than
actual assessment of contribution to the problem help to guide
determination of "guilt." In particular, eager to pin the blame
on entities presumed to be relatively amenable to government
intervention, many suggest universities should, at least in part,
be on the hook (see Dame, 2013). Certainly institutional
actions are implicated in families' increasing reliance on student aid and in the perpetuation of an explicit profit motive
in higher education. For example, some colleges leveraged the
shift toward merit aid to help them move up in the university
rankings to become an elite private school and openly did so
at the expense of low-income students by deliberately offering underfunded financial aid packages in order to discourage
them from enrolling (Burd, 2013).

These intentional policies not only limit the opportunities lower-income students had when making a decision of
where to attend college, but also forced students attending
these schools to finance more of their education using student loans. With such documented cases of duplicity by institutes of higher education, it is hard to argue that the schools
themselves are not also culpable and should share some of
the burden of paying off the debt. However, they are clearly
not alone; furthermore, understanding their role requires also
untangling the ways in which policymakers' actions—particularly at the state level, where public aid for higher education
has declined precipitously as a share of institutional budgets
(Hiltonsmith & Draut, 2014)—changed the options available
to university administrators. In addition, this text has highlighted some of the deceptive practices that private lenders like
Sallie Mae have used to increase the numbers of student with
debt, the amount of debt incurred, and how long it takes them
to pay off their loans and under what terms. The point is not
to list all of the potential groups who should help finance a

bailout, but, instead, to suggest that the current student debt crisis is not the fault of borrowers alone. If punishment is needed, then, it should not solely fall on the borrowers, and they are not the only entities who need inducement to change future behavior.

A bailout would not need to be an all-or-nothing proposition. It should, however, be an explicit policy choice, with clear rules for eligibility (Needham, 2014) and an official statement recognizing the need for a different direction. Even if it included a pivot away from future debt dependence, a student debt bailout would not correct every inequity in the higher education system. But it could make a substantial difference, not only in the overall well-being of American young people, but also in the relative positions of groups differently affected by student debt today. According to Demos and the Institute on Assets and Social Policy (2015), a student debt bailout for those making $50,000 or less would decrease the black-white wealth gap by nearly 37 percent among low-wealth households, and a policy that bails out those making $25,000 or less would decrease the black-white wealth gap by over 50 percent. However, policies that would bail out all students regardless of income would increase median net worth for all households, but would actually exacerbate wealth inequality, since white families have higher college attendance rates and greater aggregate debt in total dollars. Since higher education is understood to be the centerpiece of the U.S. economic mobility system, policies within this realm must be viewed through an equity lens. Within the domain of student loan bailouts, then, these findings suggest that a targeted approach would do more to reduce inequality than a policy that forgave all debt. When contemplating new directions and considerable investments in financial aid policy, it is not enough that everyone is better off. The nation needs policies that erode inequality and give all Americans a real chance at upward mobility.

Outlining a strategic—rather than an absolute—bailout makes such a policy more fiscally manageable and potentially politically feasible, as well. At the least, such a bailout needs to be on the metaphorical table of considered policy options, because, even if bailing out every student debtor is likely unworkable, reflexively claiming "moral hazard" to avoid addressing the real hardship experienced by millions who did exactly what policy and our ethos of the American dream encouraged—borrowed to finance an education that was supposed to pay dividends, for them and for us all—is indefensible. Significantly, analysis of the repayment realities realized by borrowers in IBR plans reveals that many of the scenarios that unfold resemble a bailout (Kadlec, 2014). Creation of a policy whereby borrowers can have their loans forgiven in full after 10 or 20 years, regardless of their incomes or the progress they have made toward paying down their loan balances, and the ascendance of this policy in the student loan landscape, reveals the considerable appetite for a bailout in fact, if not in rhetoric. However, this type of bailout disproportionately benefits the most sophisticated and most indebted students, many of whom were already advantaged in their pursuit of higher education (Delisle & Holt, 2013). Indeed, today we may have the liability of a bailout, including the significant costs (Kadlec, 2014) and potential for distortion of behavior, without the benefits, including relief for the most struggling borrowers (Kelly, 2014) or the collective accounting of student loans' failures.

Constructing the right policy levers within a bailout hinges, of course, on correctly understanding the causes of greatest hardship for student borrowers. It demands clarity on the vision of higher education as a conduit of mobility and central to Americans' expectations about how they are supposed to be able to leverage their effort and ability for a real chance of success. It requires moving past alarmist rhetoric about high absolute balances and beyond the crushingly low expectations to which many hold student loans today to instead demand that the pursuit of higher education—for future generations of students, and for those who have already completed their studies—should not mean a lifetime of compromised financial well-being, but instead a sound investment in their productive future. As part of a pivot away from our largely failed experiment with student loans, a large-scale but well-targeted student loan bailout is entirely consistent with our national objective to build a more financially capable future. Our governmental systems are more than capable of approaching student loan bailout with some nuance, directing relief at those who, evidence suggests, are struggling the most, including those who never earned a degree despite costly attempts (Kelly, 2014). Too many student borrowers have been harmed as a result of their belief in the American dream. They deferred wages to attend higher educational institutions that were supposed to prepare them for better jobs. They vested their hopes in an education system that was supposed to deliver real opportunity, if only they were bright enough and worked hard enough. Instead, with crushing frequency, they find themselves worse off, at least in terms of wealth accumulation, in what has now become known as an "education paradox" (Pew Charitable Trusts, 2014, p. 3). When our policy bargains fail to this extent, we must intervene decisively. It is a policy intervention for a new day, springing from a different paradigm, and it would stand as a bold but commonsense response to the true challenges we confront. It would mark, then, a break with our recent past, but a reconnection with our historic foundation and an affirmation of our shared future.

Conclusion

Today's student debt dialogue is a policy conversation characterized by near-consensus that there is a problem but considerable difference of opinion about its precise nature and, in particular, the most salient indicators that evidence the problem's magnitude and scope. The overarching feature of this debate, however, is the near-absence of broad, comprehensive solutions, widely regarded as true alternatives to the debt-dependent status quo. This is what the country needs, in regard to student debt: a reason to believe that something really different is possible, and a path forward, toward what all would consider at least a better future. In other words, not just nicer, fairer, or even fewer, student loans, but their converse: an asset-empowered counterpoint. Such a path would ensure that more American students could climb the ladder that higher education is supposed to represent. It is still a route that requires lots of hard work, but instead of attempting the journey shackled by rising debt loads and increasingly discouraged by the bleak prospects ahead, students can count on critical tools for their treks. Instead of lugging the burden of frightening and confusing promissory notes, young people would be equipped with wealth transfers at critical stages along the way and guided into constructive relationships with institutions—educational and financial—that support the realization of their aspirations. Nor is the difference between such an asset-empowered future and today's debt-dependent reality only seen on the balance sheet. This path also carries different expectations of future educational attainment, cultivates different capacities that equip children to achieve, and promises a payoff more consistent with what we think of as success. For most Americans, asset empowerment is an illusion, or, at best, a distant hope. Instead, debt is seen as inevitable, and the stage is set for a lifetime of resulting disadvantages. This is where reimagining financial aid could be a lever to greater opportunity and equity, for generations of Americans to come. The mechanics of ensuring that all American children have savings accounts from which to pay for college and infusions of wealth into them can seem daunting. The prospect of pulling away from the student loan shore without being able to clearly see the way to paying for college from assets instead can appear scary. But the impact it could make in pulling the United States out from under that $1.3 trillion of debt, one savings account at a time, could be huge. And the effect on educational attainment—itself critical to the United States' future competitiveness and to the viability of the American ideal of equal opportunity—could be transformative. As described in this overview of the controversies at the edges of student loan reform today, we have reached the limits of what policy modifications can do for American higher education. It is time for a more decisive break with the failed policies of the past.

In *The Structure of Scientific Revolutions* Thomas Kuhn (1962) discusses how periods of normal science are interrupted by periods of revolutionary science. Kuhn suggests that during periods of normal science, researchers identify questions to investigate based on existing knowledge. The insights gained from these analyses are constrained by the limits of the prevailing paradigm, such that resulting changes tend to mostly comprise tweaks around the margins, rather than fundamental reconsiderations. Periods of normal science persist until the current is no longer able to solve a growing number of the problems, or when external events provoke a clamor for a different vision, *a revolution*. The U.S. financial aid model has been in a period of normal science for far too long. The goal of financial aid has been narrowly framed as only helping young adults pay for college, a low bar that completely ignores its potential to have a positive influence on early education, college completion, and postcollege financial health. Proposed changes have focused primarily on making financial aid better suited to this very modest objective, then, with the unsurprising result that the underlying problems go unresolved. It is a model in need of revolution. Revolutions seldom start without a spark. Today, policy innovation in asset-based financial aid—in the form of children's savings accounts, modified "Promise" programs, and calls for substantial wealth transfers—provides the tinder from which such a spark can be ignited. It would not be the first such dramatic departure in U.S. policy history.

The GI Bill made higher education and housing possible for millions of veterans. Although the expense may have seemed unthinkable to many in a country recovering from war spending, it not only improved millions of lives, but within eight years of the bill's signing, it had returned every dollar invested in education nearly seven-fold in economic output and federal tax revenue, according to a congressional cost-benefit analysis (Subcommittee on Education and Health, 1988). Returning veterans represented a crisis to the postwar economy, and revolution was necessary. The GI Bill was instrumental, providing educational opportunity to individual veterans and equipping Americans with the skills and knowledge to carry the nation into postwar recovery. It was also revolutionary, because it helped a generation understand that a timely wealth transfer that aligns with the American belief in rewarding effort and ability can spur economic growth and strengthen the American way of life. One generation later, however, that lesson was all but lost, as the student loan business began ratcheting up. Fueled by growing strains on the individual and collective levels in the intervening decades, again today, as murmurs intensify about the failures of higher education to deliver on the American dream of equitable opportunities for all, a period of scientific revolution appears to be looming. The student loan paradigm is in crisis: our debt-dependent system discourages low-income loan-averse students from enrolling in college (Perna, 2000), reduces completion rates among students who make it to college, distorts career choices (Rothstein & Rouse, 2011), delays building homes and families (Gicheva, 2013), and lowers the return on a degree by reducing retirement savings and overall net worth (Hiltonsmith, 2013).

In recognition of the true nature, scope, and gravity of the student loan problem, we must begin to imagine meaningful alternatives, and to insist that our financial aid system perform up to the standards of our American values, which hold that only effort expended and innate ability possessed should determine one's relative outcomes. The United States invests in education—particularly higher education—as the principal path to prosperity, the royal road to economic mobility. These potential outcomes cannot be realized without a financial aid system that enhances, rather than compromises, education's potency as an equalizer.

Children's savings accounts or CSAs may be one such intervention. Typically started at birth or kindergarten, families' investments are leveraged with an initial deposit and matching donor funds usually at a 1:1 ratio. Unlike student debt, CSAs have the potential to work on multiple dimensions—early education, affordability, completion, and postcollege financial health—to improve outcomes and catalyze opportunity.

With regard to early education, an experimental test of CSAs finds infants who were randomly assigned to receive a CSA demonstrated significantly higher social-emotional skills at age four than their counterparts who did not receive a CSA (Huang, Sherraden, Kim, & Clancy, 2014). These effects are strongest among low-income families, suggesting that such interventions can be forces for equity within the educational system. Children with improved social and emotional skills display attitudes, behavior, and academic performance that reflect an 11 percentile-point gain in achievement, compared to controls (Durlak, Weissberg, Dymnicki, Taylor, & Schellinger, 2011). CSAs may improve children's social-emotional skills by giving parents new hope for their children's future educational attainment, which in turn may change how they interact with them.

With regard to enrollment and graduation, the term "wilt" refers to the sizable number of minority and low-income students who fail to transition to college despite having the desire and ability (Elliott & Beverly, 2011). CSAs may reduce wilt by helping students form a *college-saver identity* (Elliott, 2013a). Students who form a college-saver identity expect to go to college *and* have identified savings as a strategy to pay for it. From this perspective, it is not enough for a student to have big dreams for his or her future; he or she has to have a tangible reason to believe that there is actually a way to get there. This is what asset empowerment looks like in the life of a young scholar.

However, it is perhaps in the *postcollege period* that CSAs rise highest above other forms of financial aid, even today's populist proposals for "free college." Evidence suggests that CSAs may be a gateway not only to greater educational attainment, itself a conduit of economic mobility, but also a more diversified asset portfolio that may result in greater asset accumulation in other forms such as stocks, retirement accounts, and real estate (Friedline & Elliott, 2013; Friedline, Johnson, & Hughes, 2014). Contrast this to the strained financial fortunes of indebted recent college graduates (Elliott & Lewis, 2015) and the growing doubts about whether college is really a path to prosperity (see Long, 2015).

Looking at financial aid as more than just paying the tuition bill reveals the full measure of the "crisis," and the true stakes in this coming revolution. Disadvantaged students need the bargaining power to make institutions augment their own efforts. However, part of changing bargaining power is changing the distribution of resources in society. Given the distribution of wages today and the divergence of income and productivity (Mishel, 2012), this essential redistribution of resources is unlikely to happen without a wealth transfer. CSAs provide a vehicle for such wealth transfers, in addition to facilitating families' own savings. Though branded as un-American, as formulated here, the idea of a wealth transfer is completely consistent with American history and with our collective narrative of individual effort. It is about equipping all children with tools that complement their own contributions, as "American" as the plow, the automobile, or the iPhone. We are no strangers to wealth transfers; before the GI Bill there was the Homestead Act, similarly envisioned as an agreement between the government and individuals, in pursuit of economic gains for both parties. As would CSAs, which include an expectation that families make some contribution to their children's accounts, these wealth transfers required considerable individual effort,

yet offered real promise to change the distributional consequences of existing systems—property ownership, on the one
hand, and higher education, on the other—in ways that helped
to transform power and pathways to prosperity, for generations.
In the 21st century there has yet to be such a wealth transfer,
although the need has never been more urgent.

Is a financial aid revolution imminent? Most of the time
people work within existing paradigms. Every once in a while,
though, there are people who will dare to challenge the world
as it is and imagine a radically different "truth." Their minds,
then, are freed to think about the issues they face in ways that
were not previously possible. As we seek to find alternatives to
the current financial aid paradigm we should not lose sight of
these moments in our collective history when we have dared
to dream and, as a result, were able to leap forward. The race
to the moon was just such a moment. In the early 1960s we
were pushed by the Russian entrance into space. Before this,
we were constrained by our own imaginations about what is
possible and, as a result, fell behind the rest of the world. To
move away from a debt-dependent financial aid system in favor
of an asset-empowered one, we once again need to imagine the
possibilities and dare to reach for what might seem to many to
be the stars.

Perhaps the reason that the United States has not seen the
level of student and allied activism on the issue of student
debt witnessed in other countries (see, among many others,
Hackett, 2016)—sporadic revolts and online unrest notwith-
standing—is that this country has yet to contemplate an alternative capable of capturing their imaginations and warranting
the sweat. Better servicing terms, lower interest rates, more
affordable monthly payments, even a chance to borrow only
to pay for living expenses instead of the entire cost of attendance—none of these are policy issues worthy of the real revolution. But a grand wealth-building program, on the scale of
the Homestead Act or the GI Bill, that would equip all young
people with assets from which to control their own destinies is

revolutionary, indeed. It is time for such a bold new direction. It is worth the fight. If foundations transform their scholarship programs into asset investments, if the Pell Grant can be reimagined as an early commitment to children's futures, if the money and rhetorical energy spent servicing and defending student loans can be channeled instead into building a structure of universal asset accounts currently inconceivable to most economically disadvantaged Americans, then we will have cut ourselves lose from the dominant paradigm that sees only student loans 2.0 as the "future" of financial aid. Changing our national culture so that we think about financing college when children are born, not when they graduate, will not be simple. Redefining financial aid to mean financing that really helps students, instead of an offer to trade paying tomorrow for paying today, will not be easy. However, these tasks do not seem as daunting as flying to the moon must have seemed to people in 1961, or even as challenging as girding a nation for success in a radically transformed postwar economy. This revolution can be realized. We only must be willing to free our minds, so that we can dare to make a better future for our children.

References

Akers, B. (2014). *How much is too much? Evidence on financial well-being and student loan debt.* Washington, DC: American Enterprise Institute.

Akers, B., & Chingos, M. (2014). Is a student loan crisis on the horizon? Washington, DC: Brookings Institution. Retrieved from http://www.brookings.edu/~/media/research/files/reports/2014/06/24-student-loan-crisis-akers-chingos/is-a-student-loan-crisis-on-the-horizon.pdf

Applebaum, R., & StudentNation. (2014). Forgive student loan debt: Five year on: The founder of StudentDebtCrisis.org. reflects on the state of student deb crisis. Retrieved from http://www.thenation.com/article/forgive-student-loan-debt-five-years/

Bailey, M., & Dynarski, S. (2011) Gains and gaps: Changing inequality in U.S. college entry and completion. Working Paper. Washington, DC: The National Bureau of Economic Research. Retrieved from http://www.nber.org/papers/w17633

Balli, C. (January 21, 1998). U.S. clamps down on loans to 'deadbeat' doctors. *Los Angeles Times.* Retrieved from http://articles.latimes.com/1998/jan/21/news/mn-10669

Bastedo, M. N., & Flaster, A. (2014). Conceptual and methodological problems in research on college undermatch. *Educational Researcher, 43,* 93–99.

Baum, S., & Schwartz, S. (2005). How much debt is too much? Defining benchmarks for manageable student debt. Commissioned by the Project on Student Debt and the College Board, Washington, DC.

Bidwell, A. (2014). Justice department takes action against Sallie Mae. Retrieved from http://www.usnews.com/news/articles/2014/05/13/sallie-mae-must-pay-service-members-60-million-for-student-loan-violations

Brown, M., Haughwout, A., Donghoon, L., Scally, J., & van der Klaauw, W. (2015). Looking at student loan defaults through a larger window. *Liberty Street Economics.* New York: Federal Reserve Bank of New York. Retrieved from http://libertystreeteconomics.newyorkfed.org/2015/02/looking_at_student_loan_defaults_through_a_larger_window.html#.VpVJeStGmKz

Burd, S. (2012). An unsettling settlement in class action lawsuit challenging Sallie Mae's subprime lending practices. Retrieved from https://www.newamerica.org/education-policy/an-unsettling-settlement-in-class-action-lawsuit-challenging-sallie-maes-subprime-lending-practices/

Burd, S. (2013). Undermining Pell: How colleges compete for wealthy students and leave the low-income behind. *New America* (Washington, DC). Retrieved from http://

education.newamerica.net/sites/newamerica.net/files/
policydocs/Merit_Aid%20Final.pdf

Carnevale, A., & Strohl, J. (2013). Separate and unequal:
How higher education reinforces the intergenerational
reproduction of white racial privilege. Washington, DC:
Center on Education and the Workforce. Retrieved from
https://cew.georgetown.edu/wp-content/uploads/2014/11/
SeparateUnequal.FR_.pdf

Cielinski, A. (2015). Using post-college labor market
outcomes: Policy challenges and choices. Washington, DC:
Center on Law and Social Policy. Retrieved from http://
www.clasp.org/resources-and-publications/publication-1/
Using-Post-College-Labor-Market-Outcomes.pdf

Cohen, P. (2016, January 8). Robust hiring in December
caps solid year for U.S. jobs. *New York Times*. Retrieved
from http://www.nytimes.com/2016/01/09/business/
economy/jobs-report-hiring-unemployment-december.
html?_r=0

Dame, J. (2013, December 7). 42% of Millennials blame
colleges for rising student debt. *USA Today*. Retrieved from
http://www.usatoday.com/story/news/nation/2013/12/07/
millennials-student-debt-blame/3896623/

Darolia, R. (2015, September 29). Should student loans be
dischargeable in bankruptcy? *Brown Center Chalkboard*.
Washington, DC: Brookings Institution. Retrieved from
http://www.brookings.edu/blogs/brown-center-chalkboard/
posts/2015/09/29-student-loan-bankruptcy-darolia

Darolia, R., & Ritter, D. (2015, September). Do student
loan borrowers opportunistically default? Evidence
from bankruptcy reform. *Working Paper No. 15–17/R*.
Philadelphia, PA: Federal Reserve Bank of Philadelphia.

Dash, S. (2015). Senator Warren's fierce advocacy for student
loan reform. Retrieved from http://www.huffingtonpost.
com/stephen-dash/senator-warrens-fierce-ad_b_7623884.
html

Delisle, J. (2013). Beware savvy borrowers using Income-Based Repayment. *Ed Central.* Washington, DC: New America. Retrieved from http://www.edcentral.org/beware-savvy-borrowers-using-income-based-repayment/

Delisle, J. (2015). What does income-based repayment for student loans cost? *Ed Central.* Washington, DC: New America. Retrieved from http://www.edcentral.org/income-based-repayment-cost/

Delisle, J., & Holt, A. (2013). Beware savvy borrowers using income-based repayment. *Ed Central.* Washington, DC: New America. Retrieved from http://www.edcentral.org/beware-savvy-borrowers-using-income-based-repayment/

Demos. (2015). No recourse: Putting an end to bankruptcy's student loan exception. Washington, DC: Author. Retrieved from http://www.demos.org/publication/no-recourse-putting-end-bankruptcy%E2%80%99s-student-loan-exception

Demos and Institute on Assets and Social Policy. (2015). Less debt, more equity: Lowering student debt while closing the black-white wealth gap. Retrieved from https://iasp.brandeis.edu/pdfs/2015/lessdebt.pdf

Dorfman, J. (2014, June 19). Here comes the student loan forgiveness. *Forbes.* Retrieved from http://www.forbes.com/sites/jeffreydorfman/2014/06/19/here-comes-the-student-loan-forgiveness/#12d81ccb3d67

Durlak, J. A., Weissberg, R. P., Dymnicki, A. B., Taylor, R. D., & Schellinger, K. B. (2011). The impact of enhancing students' social and emotional learning: A meta-analysis of school-based universal interventions. *Child Development, 82*(1), 474–501.

Dynarski, S. (2016, January 7). The trouble with student loans? Low earnings, not high debt. *Evidence Speaks.* Washington, DC: The Brookings Institution.

Egoian, J. (2013, October 23). 73 will be the retirement norm for millennials. *Nerdwallet.* Retrieved from http://www.nerdwallet.com/blog/investing/2013/73-retirement-norm-millennials/

Elliott, W. (2013a). Can a college-saver identity help resolve the college expectation-attainment paradox? St. Louis, MO: Center for Social Development, Washington University. Retrieved from https://csd.wustl.edu/Publications/Documents/FS13-30.pdf

Elliott, W., ed. (2013b). Building expectations, delivering results: Biannual report on the assets and education field. Lawrence, KS: Assets and Education Initiative. Retrieved from https://aedi.ku.edu/sites/aedi.ku.edu/files/docs/publication/CSA/reports/Full-Report.pdf

Elliott, W., & Beverly, S. (2011). The role of savings and wealth in reducing "wilt" between expectations and college attendance. *Journal of Children and Poverty, 17*(2), 165–185.

Elliott, W., & Lewis, M. (2015). *The real college debt crisis: How student borrowing threatens financial well-being and erodes the American dream.* Santa Barbara: Praeger.

Elliott, W., Lewis, M., & Johnson, P. (2014). Unequal outcomes: Student loan effects on young adults' net worth accumulation. Lawrence, KS: Assets and Education Initiative. Retrieved from http://www.save2limit debt.com

Emmons, W., & Noeth, J. (2015). Why didn't higher education protection black and Hispanic wealth? St. Louis, MO: Federal Reserve Bank of St. Louis. Retrieved from https://www.stlouisfed.org/publications/in-the-balance/issue12-2015/why-didnt-higher-education-protect-hispanic-and-black-wealth

Engle, J., & Tinto, V. (2008). Moving beyond access: College success for low-income, first-generation students. Washington, DC: Pell Institute.

Equal Justice Works. (2015). Love and student debt: How the new REPAYE plan could affect marriages. Retrieved from http://www.huffingtonpost.com/equal-justice-works/love-and-student-debt-how_b_8647204.html

Evans, K. (2012). Student loans: The next bailout? Retrieved from http://www.cnbc.com/id/47171658

Field, E. (2009). Educational debt burden and career choice: Evidence from a financial aid experiment at the NYU Law School. *American Economic Journal: Applied Economics, 1*(1), 1–21.

Fischer, K. (2016, January 17). Engine of inequality. *The Chronicle of Higher Education*. Retrieved from http://chronicle.com/article/Engine-of-Inequality/234952

Friedline, T., & Elliott, W. (2013). Connections with banking institutions and diverse asset portfolios in young adulthood: Children as potential future investors. *Children and Youth Services Review, 35*(6), 994–1006.

Friedline, T., Johnson, P., & Hughes, R. (2014). Toward healthy balance sheets: A savings account as a gateway to young adults' asset diversification and accumulation? Federal Reserve of Boston.

Fry, R. (2014). Young adults, student debt and economic well-being. Pew Research Center's Social and Demographic Trends Project, Washington, DC. Retrieved from http://www.pewsocialtrends.org/files/2014/05/ST_2014.05.14_student-debt_complete-report.pdf

GAO. (2014). Federal student loans: Education could do more to help ensure borrowers are aware of repayment and forgiveness options. Retrieved from http://www.gao.gov/assets/680/672136.pdf

Giancola, J., & Kahlenberg, R. D. (2016). *True merit?* Landsdowne, VA: Jack Kent Cooke Foundation. Retrieved from http://www.jkcf.org/assets/1/7/JKCF_True_Merit_Report.pdf

Gicheva, D. (2013). In debt and alone? Examining the causal link between student loans and marriage, *Working Paper*, University of North Carolina at Greensboro.

Government Printing Office. (2009). "An undue hardship? Discharging educational debt in bankruptcy." Hearing before the Subcommittee on Commercial and Administrative Law of the Committee on the Judiciary. House of Representatives. 111th Congress, First Session. Retrieved from https://www.gpo.gov/fdsys/pkg/CHRG-111hhrg52412/html/CHRG-111hhrg52412.htm

Greenfield, R. (2015, December 7). The hot, new company benefit: Student debt repayment. *Bloomberg Business.* Retrieved from http://www.bloomberg.com/news/articles/2015–12–08/the-hot-new-company-benefit-student-debt-repayment

Gupta, S. (2013). Sallie Mae's profits soaring at the expense of our nation's students. Retrieved from http://billmoyers.com/groupthink/what-to-do-about-student-loans/sallie-maes-profits-soaring-at-the-expense-of-our-nation%E2%80%99s-students/

Hackett, D. (2016, April 7). University students asked to leave Legislative Assembly Thursday. *CBC News.* Retrieved from http://www.cbc.ca/news/canada/new-brunswick/u-de-m-protest-student-debt-1.3525645

Harnisch, T. L., & Lebioda, K. (2016). The promises and pitfalls of state free community college plans. Washington, DC: American Association of State Colleges and Universities. Retrieved from http://www.aascu.org/policy/publications/policy-matters/freecommunitycollege.pdf

Hartman, R. R. (2013). Who makes money off your student loans? You might be surprised. Retrieved from http://news.yahoo.com/blogs/lookout/makes-money-off-student-loans-might-surprised-093332073.html;_ylt=AwrTcc1IIutWWTwAE60nnIlQ;_ylu=X3oDMTEybDg3MTJ1BGNvbG8DZ3ExBHBvcwMxBHZ0aWQDQjE3MThfMQRzZWMDc3I-

Hershbein, B. (2016). A college degree is worth less if you are raised poor. Retrieved from http://www.brookings.edu/blogs/social-mobility-memos/posts/2016/02/19-college-degree-worth-less-raised-poor-hershbein

Hiltonsmith, R. (2013). At what cost: How student debt reduces lifetime wealth. Washington, DC: Demos.

Hiltonsmith, R., & Draut, T. (2014). The great cost shift continues: State higher education funding after the recession. Washington, DC: Demos. Retrieved from http://www.demos.org/publication/great-cost-shift-continues-state-higher-education-funding-after-recession

Hoxby, C., & Avery, C. (2013). The missing "one-offs": The hidden supply of high-achieving, low-income students. *Brookings Papers on Economic Activity.* Washington, DC: The Brookings Institution. Retrieved from http://www.brookings.edu/~/media/Projects/BPEA/Spring-2013/2013a_hoxby.pdf

Huang, J., Sherraden, M., Kim, Y., & Clancy, M. (2014). Effects of child development accounts on early social-emotional development: An experimental test. *Journal of American Medical Association Pediatrics, 168*(3), 265–271.

Huelsman, M. (2015). The debt divide: The racial and class bias behind the "new normal" of student borrowing. Washington, DC: Demos. Retrieved from http://www.demos.org/publication/debt-divide-racial-and-class-bias-behind-new-normal-student-borrowing

IHEP. (2010). A portrait of low-income young adults in education. Washington, DC: Author. Retrieved from http://www.ihep.org/sites/default/files/uploads/docs/pubs/brief_a_portrait_of_low-income_young_adults_in_education.pdf

Inside Higher Ed. (2015, October 28). Obama's income-based repayment expansion finalized. Washington, DC: Author. Retrieved from https://

www.insidehighered.com/quicktakes/2015/10/28/
obamas-income-based-repayment-expansion-finalized

The Institute for College Access & Success. (2015).
National policy agenda to reduce the burden of
student debt. Retrieved from http://ticas.org/initiative/
student-debt-policy-agenda#psat

Iuliano, J. (2012). An empirical assessment of student loan
discharges and the undue hardship standard. *American
Bankruptcy Law Journal, 495*(86).

James, K. (2015). Lowering rates isn't the answer: Student
loan borrowers need program reform to get out of
debt. Retrieved from http://www.usnews.com/opinion/
knowledge-bank/2015/03/24/focus-on-reform-not-lower-
rates-to-help-student-loan-borrowers

Jesse, D. (2013, November 25). Government
books $41.3 billion in student loan profits.
USA Today. Retrieved from http://www.
usatoday.com/story/news/nation/2013/11/25/
federal-student-loan-profit/3696009/

Kadlec, D. (2014, April 24). The next massive bailout:
student loans. *Time*. Retrieved from http://time.
com/72786/the-next-massive-bailout-student-loans/

Kelly, A. (2014, June 30). Who's struggling to pay back
their student loans? (Hint: It's not who you think).
Forbes. Retrieved from http://www.forbes.com/sites/
akelly/2014/06/30/whos-struggling-to-pay-back-their-
student-loans-hint-its-not-who-you-think/

Krupnick, M. (2015). Low-income students struggle to pay
for college, even in rare states that offer help. *Hechinger
Report*. Retrieved from http://hechingerreport.org/low-
income-students-struggle-to-pay-for-college-even-in-rare-
states-that-offer-help/

Kuhn, T. S. (1962). *The structure of scientific revolutions*.
Chicago, IL: University of Chicago Press.

Lanza, A. (2015, March 11). Graduate school loan borrowers may face reduced forgiveness options. *U.S. News & World Reports*. Retrieved from http://www.usnews.com/education/blogs/student-loan-ranger/2015/03/11/graduate-school-loan-borrowers-may-face-reduced-forgiveness-options

LaPlante, J. A. (2015). Congress's tax bomb: Income-based repayment and disarming a problem facing student loan borrowers, 100 *Cornell L. Rev.* 703. Retrieved from http://scholarship.law.cornell.edu/clr/vol100/iss3/4

Lieber, R. (2012, December 14). For student borrowers, relief now may mean a big tax bill later. *New York Times*. Retrieved from http://www.nytimes.com/2012/12/15/your-money/for-student-borrowers-a-tax-time-bomb.html

Long, H. (2015, December 9). Is going to college worth it? Goldman Sachs says maybe not. *CNN Money*. Retrieved from http://money.cnn.com/2015/12/09/news/economy/college-not-worth-it-goldman/

Looney, A., & Yannelis, C. (2015). A crisis in student loans? How changes in the characteristics of borrowers and in the institutions they attended contributed to rising loan defaults. Washington, DC: The Brookings Institution. Retrieved from http://www.brookings.edu/about/projects/bpea/papers/2015/looney-yannelis-student-loan-defaults

Lorin, J. (2015, December 11). Who's profiting from $1.2 trillion of federal student loans? *Bloomberg News*. Retrieved from http://www.bloomberg.com/news/articles/2015–12–11/a-144–000-student-default-shows-who-profits-at-taxpayer-expense

Martin, A. (2012, September 9). Debt collection agencies cashing in on student loans. *New York Times*. Retrieved from http://www.nytimes.com/2012/09/09/business/once-a-student-now-dogged-by-collection-agencies.html?pagewanted=all

Matthews, C. (2012). The people's bailout: Occupy Wall Street wants to forgive your debt. Retrieved from http://business.time.com/2012/11/12/the-peoples-bailout-occupy-wall-street-wants-to-forgive-your-debt/

Mayotte, B. (2015). 4 states that offer generous loan forgiveness programs. *U.S. News & World Reports*. Retrieved from http://www.usnews.com/education/blogs/student-loan-ranger/articles/2016–05–04/4-states-that-offer-generous-student-loan-forgiveness-programs

Mayotte, B. (2016). Understand the consequences of student loan default. *U.S. News & World Reports*. Retrieved from http://www.usnews.com/education/blogs/student-loan-ranger/2015/03/04/understand-the-consequences-of-student-loan-default

Mettler, S. (2014). *Degrees of inequality: How the politics of higher education sabotaged the American dream*. New York: Basic Books.

Mishel, L. (2012). Understanding the wedge between productivity and median compensation growth. *Economic Policy Institute* (Washington, DC). Retrieved from http://www.epi.org/blog/understanding-wedge-productivity-median-compensation/

Mitchell, J. (2015a, December 6). Should anyone be eligible for student loans? *Wall Street Journal*. Retrieved from http://www.wsj.com/articles/should-anyone-be-eligible-for-student-loans-1449436508

Mitchell, J. (2015b, November 20). U.S. student loan-forgiveness program proves costly. *Wall Street Journal*. Retrieved from http://www.wsj.com/articles/u-s-student-loan-program-proves-costly-1448042862

Nasiripour, S. (2015, December 31). How Elizabeth Warren beat a student loan giant. *Huffington Post*. Retrieved from http://www.huffingtonpost.com/entry/elizabeth-warren-student-loan-giant_us_568412fbe4b06fa68881b03f

Needham, V. (2014). Lawmakers push for clearer student loan forgiveness rules. *The Hill*. Retrieved from http://thehill.com/policy/finance/206380-lawmakers-push-for-clearer-rules-on-forgiving-student-loans-for-borrowers-in

New America. (2015). The problems with debt—Default rates, collection. Washington, DC: Author. Retrieved from http://atlas.newamerica.org/federal-student-loan-default-rates

Pappano, L. (2011, July 22). The master's as the new bachelor's. *New York Times*. Retrieved from http://www.nytimes.com/2011/07/24/education/edlife/edl-24masters-t.html

Pardo, R. I., & Lacey, M. R. (2009). The real student-loan scandal: Undue hardship discharge litigation. *American Bankruptcy Law Journal, 83*(1).

The Pell Institute and PennAHEAD. (2015). Indicators of higher education equity in the United States. College Station, PA: Authors. Retrieved from http://www.pellinstitute.org/downloads/publications-Indicators_of_Higher_Education_Equity_in_the_US_45_Year_Trend_Report.pdf

Perna, L. W. (2000). Differences in the decision to attend college among African Americans, Hispanics, and Whites. *Journal of Higher Education, 71*(2), 117–141.

Pew Charitable Trusts. (2014). A new financial reality: The balance sheets and economic mobility of Generation X. *Pew Charitable Trusts* (Washington, DC). Retrieved from http://www.pewtrusts.org/~/media/Assets/2014/09/Pew_Generation_X_report.pdf

Phillips, M. (May 31, 2013). The high price of a free college education in Sweden. *The Atlantic*. Retrieved from http://www.theatlantic.com/international/archive/2013/05/the-high-price-of-a-free-college-education-in-sweden/276428/

Price, C. (2016). Fixing inequality of opportunity. *Spotlight on Poverty*. Retrieved from http://spotlightonpoverty.org/spotlight-exclusives/fixing-inequality-opportunity/

Public Broadcasting Service. (2009). Lawsuits against Sallie
    Mae. Retrieved from http://www.pbsnow.shows.org/525/
    sallie-mae-law-suits.html

Ready, T. (2015, June 24). Free college is not enough:
    The unavoidable limits of the Kalamazoo Promise.
    Social Mobility Memos. Retrieved from http://
    www.brookings.edu/blogs/social-mobility-memos/
    posts/2015/06/24-kalamazoo-promise-college-ready

Riepenhoff, J., & Wagner, M. (2012). Investigation:
    Federal student loans become constant burden. Retrieved
    from http://www.dispatch.com/content/stories/
    local/2012/12/16/constant.html

Rothstein, J., & Rouse, C. E. (2011). Constrained after
    college: Student loans and early-career occupational
    choices. *Journal of Public Economics, 95*(1–2), 149–163.

Rugh, J. S., & Massey, D. S. (2010). Racial segregation and
    the American foreclosure crisis. *American Sociological
    Review, 75,* 629–651, doi:10.1177/0003122410380868.

Subcommittee on Education and Health. (1988).
    A cost-benefit analysis of government investment in
    post-secondary education under the World War II
    GI Bill. Retrieved from http://www.jec.senate.gov/
    reports/100th%20Congress/Improving%20Access%20
    to%20Preschool%20and%20Postsecondary%20
    Education%20%281480%29.pdf

Tamanaha, B. (2012). The problem with IBR. Retrieved from
    http://www.nationaljurist.com/content/problem-ibr

U.S. Department of Education. (2015). Strengthening
    the student loan system to better protect all borrowers.
    Washington, DC: Author. Retrieved from http://www2.
    ed.gov/documents/press-releases/strengthening-student-
    loan-system.pdf

Vien, C. L. (2015, July 1). 68% of Americans with student
    loans are unhappy with how they financed college.

Journal of Accountancy. Retrieved from http://www. journalofaccountancy.com/issues/2015/jul/college- financing-student-loans.html

Wang, H. L. (2013). Student loan changes squeeze historically black colleges. *National Public Radio*. Retrieved from http://www.npr.org/ sections/codeswitch/2013/09/26/226552999/ student-loan-changes-squeeze-historically-black-colleges

White House Council of Economic Advisors. (2016). Investing in higher education: Benefits, challenges, and the state of student debt. Washington, DC: Authors. Retrieved from https://www.whitehouse.gov/sites/default/files/page/ files/20160718_cea_student_debt.pdf

3 Perspectives

Introduction

This chapter compiles short essays from different voices in and around our student debt debate. As the nation stands at a crossroads, considering its higher education financing options at this pivotal moment, the perspectives shared here reflect different views and would lead to distinct directions. Some offer advice to individual students contemplating their own use of student loans and the potential implications for their futures. Some call for a fairly dramatic departure from the debt-dependent status quo, in pursuit of much lower student tuition and/or an asset alternative to student borrowing. Some examine the peculiar nature of the student loan instrument and the rationale for its construction and protection, while one shares a student's personal experience with student debt, as a reminder of the very real people behind the statistics. This collection is certainly not meant to be definitive; indeed, readers could likely offer their own perspectives, illuminating various aspects of the student loan landscape and contributing to the dialogue the country sorely needs. In pursuit of a more informed discussion on one of the most critical policy issues facing a generation, these individuals—experts by training, organizational affiliation, and/or personal witness—offer their takes on student debt, including how we got here, what it means, what options we have, and what tomorrow could hold.

President Barack Obama signs a presidential memorandum on reducing the burden of student loan debt in Washington, D.C., on June 9, 2014. Recent congressional and administrative actions on student debt have brought some relief to student borrowers. (AP Photo/Jacquelyn Martin)

Student Debt: How Did We Get Here and Why Should We Worry?
Mark Huelsman

College has long held a special place in the American mind. From the energy of alumni and football fans on fall Saturdays to the chatter in high school hallways when seniors are just starting to decide their futures, the very thought of going to college holds a sense of excitement and idealism that few other American institutions evoke.

In recent years, though, the excitement about college has been paired by something else: anxiety about the cost of college and the prospect of student loan debt. Back in the early 1980s, students could easily pay for tuition and fees with a part-time, minimum-wage job; however, today's students are staring at the prospect of tens of thousands of dollars for a single year of school (U.S. Department of Labor, 2009). Parents, who could once count on a little bit of savings to cover a large portion of college bills, now have to watch as their children take on debt to attend even public schools. While we still have football, basketball, computer labs, clubs, and quads, one thing is for sure: this isn't your parents' college experience.

So what happened? How did college simultaneously become more important and more financially out-of-reach? How did we go from a system in which college—tuition, fees, room, and board—could be paid for through part-time summer employment to one where students would have to work full-time for more than a year to cover just one year's worth of college expenses (see College Board, 2015)?

There are many complicated reasons why college costs have risen so far, so fast. But perhaps the biggest reason is that while states used to generously fund their public colleges and universities—including community colleges—they've stopped doing so over a period of three decades. Back in the late 1980s, states picked up most of the cost of educating students at public colleges because state leaders believed that people should have easy pathways to education. After all, higher levels of education in a region were associated with higher incomes, greater health outcomes, lower crime, greater rates of voting and community service, and lower reliance on other government services—which could save the state money in the long term (IHEP, 2005). And states, along with the federal government, were willing to collect tax money in order to keep college affordable. Unfortunately, state leaders gradually reduced funding for education and directed funds to other areas that required immediate attention. Starting in the 1980s, states were confronted with other costs, including the cost of delivering healthcare, elementary and secondary education, and greater spending on prisons (even as crime had dropped nationally) (CBPP, 2015; Mitchell & Leachman, 2014). This coincided with an antitax movement that swept over many states; lower taxes meant that states could spend less on public services, including higher education ("Tax Revolts: Some Succeed, Some Don't," 2009). Meanwhile, the federal government did not so much reverse these trends, but allowed grant and scholarship aid—including the Pell Grant, which is directed to low-income students—to fall in value relative to rising cost of college (Huelsman, 2015). So as state funding dropped and federal funding remained the same, tuition and fees began to climb, and students were inevitably forced to take on more student loans to pursue a college education.

As a result, there is around four times as much student debt as there was a decade or so ago—total debt rose from around $364 billion in 2004 to $1.2 trillion in 2015 (Bricker, Brown, Hannon, & Pence, 2015). The average debt upon graduation went from around $9,500 in 1993 to nearly $30,000 just two decades later (Huelsman, 2015). At the same time, household incomes for the vast majority of families have stayed the same or declined, when the cost of living is taken into account (Desilver, 2014). Only a small slice of wealthy families have seen their incomes go up, particularly since the beginning of this century.

Student Debt: Why Worry?

Certainly, the very idea of rising debt makes a lot of people uneasy—particularly since the trillions of dollars in loan bills will come due someday. Nonetheless, college is still a good investment for most students—and for society. In addition to all of the benefits to the general public that were previously mentioned—better health, more civic participation and volunteerism, lower crime—those who attend college are much more likely to earn more throughout their lifetimes than if they had not attended (Pew Research Center, 2014). Therefore, if a college degree is still very valuable, should we really be that concerned that most students are graduating with debt?

From my perspective, the answer to this question is a resounding "yes." In fact, rising student debt is a serious concern because all students should have the opportunity to attend college as a means to better their socioeconomic well-being. Student debt places barriers in front of students' economic mobility in the form of: (1) access to education, (2) college completion, (3) post-collegiate opportunities, and (4) racial and economic inequality.

Access: Who Gets to Go?

The first reason to be concerned about rising college costs and student debt is simple: It may be preventing some people from going to college at all. And certainly, there's now worry that college is seen as too expensive and is preventing students from attending, even if they have the grades and qualifications (ACSFA, 2013). For instance, the prospect of seeing financial aid not come close to meeting the cost of attending college may discourage lower-income and working-class students from attending college. Most research shows that lowering the price that students pay for college increases the likelihood that they will attend (Elliott & Lewis, 2015). Unfortunately, our trends have been going in the opposite direction; college is getting more expensive, not less.

Completion: The Smoker's Dilemma

College is a time for optimism. No one who goes to college thinks "I'm probably not going to graduate." Unfortunately, many students do not end up completing college, and many take far longer than four years to complete a bachelor's degree (and longer than two years to complete an associate degree) (NCES, 2013).

Not finishing college used to be no big deal; all it meant was that instead of earning money from a job, a student spent a couple extra years in school instead. But now, not finishing college increasingly means that a student leaves school with no diploma but lots of debt. In other words, we as a society have increased the risk of going to college and not completing a degree. And while most people with student debts can eventually pay it off—especially those who graduate—we should be worried about putting additional risk onto today's students. Think of this like smoking; most smokers don't end up dying of lung cancer, but smoking increases the risk of getting sick, and there's a general benefit to society if we limit the number of people who smoke regularly.

After College: What Good Is More Money if It's Just Paying Off Loans?

For students who do graduate from college, we should be worried about what the additional monthly loan payment is doing to their ability to save money while they are young. Some are worried that the rise in student debt means that today's generation of young people is less likely to buy houses—which is important, because owning a home is the biggest way that families build more wealth and maintain a comfortable lifestyle (Brown, Caldwell, & Sutherland, 2014).

But maybe today's students are less interested in owning a home and might be more interested in renting and enjoying life in the city. So long as young people are able to build up savings in other ways, perhaps student debt is not as big a deal as some fear. Unfortunately, we have plenty of evidence that student debt is preventing young people from saving—for a rainy day or a potential emergency, or even for their eventual retirement. Young families with student debt have far less in retirement savings than those who left college debt-free (Huelsman, 2015). Furthermore, students are taking around 13 years to pay off their loans, which is almost twice as long as those who took on debt just 20 years ago (Akers & Chingos, 2014). As a society, we should be worried that even if most students can make their monthly payments, student debt is holding them back from being able to put away money for the future.

Inequality: Our Generation's Challenge

When it comes to student debt, not all student debt is created equal. In recent years, our country has been grappling with the troubling fact that inequality—simply, the gap between wealthy and the non-wealthy—has grown substantially (McKernan, Ratcliffe, Steuerle, Kalish, & Quakenbush, 2015). What's worse, we know that wealth is something that often has a color; white families own nearly $16 for every $1 owned by black families, and $13 for every $1 owned by Latino families. Despite our country's progress in overcoming some of the nastiest examples of racism, the gaps are true for young families and older families alike (Huelsman, 2015). Not only should this offend our American notions of fairness and equal opportunity, but it's not good for our economy. If many families are unable to spend or save money, fewer people are contributing to businesses and society. As a country, we run the risk of having fewer entrepreneurs and inventors and of having a far less productive country.

Unfortunately, student debt could be a contributor to inequality. We have found that students from lower-income households are more likely to borrow for a degree than their wealthier student counterparts, and black students are far more likely than white students to graduate with debt (Huelsman, 2015). In turn, young black households are more likely to have student debt after college, and far less wealth and savings than young white households (Huelsman et al., 2015). And the longer we go without addressing this problem, the worse the situation may become: those who have wealth—from a home, investments, or savings—are more likely to pass it onto their children, who in turn probably will not have to borrow for college.

Conclusion

Student debt may be the most important economic issue facing young people today. Most students now must borrow for a college degree, and there is evidence that it is putting pressure on young households in ways that our parents, and older generations, never experienced. Without addressing the rise in student debt, we may have several generations who cannot adequately save for retirement or a rainy day, or fully participate in the economy. And it may prevent some students from going to college at all and ensure that black and Latino students who do go begin their careers behind the starting line of those who did not have to take on debt. It's a big problem that calls for big solutions.

References

Advisory Committee on Student Financial Assistance Access Matters: Meeting the Nation's College Completion Goals Requires Large Increases in Need-Based Grant Aid, Table 1-C, 2013. Retrieved from http://www2.ed.gov/about/bdscomm/list/acsfa/accessmattersspring2013.pdf

Akers, Beth, & Chingos, Matthew. (2014, June). Is a student loan crisis on the horizon? Brookings Institution.

Retrieved from http://www.brookings.edu/research/
reports/2014/06/24-student-loan-crisis-akers-chingos

Bricker, J., Brown, Meta, Hannon, Simona, & Pence,
Karen. (2015). How much student debt is out there?
Board of Governors of the Federal Reserve System.
Retrieved from http://www.federalreserve.gov/econresdata/
notes/feds-notes/2015/how-much-student-debt-is-out-
there-20150807.html

Brown, M., Caldwell, Sydnee, & Sutherland, Sarah. (2014,
May 13). Just released: Young student loan borrowers
remained on the sidelines of the housing market in 2013.
Federal Reserve Bank of New York. Retrieved from
http://libertystreeteconomics.newyorkfed.org/2014/05/
just-released-young-student-loan-borrowers-remained-
on-the-sidelines-of-the-housing-market-in-2013.html#.
Vms6qEorLBS

Center on Budget and Policy Priorities. (2015, April 14).
Policy basics: Where do our state tax dollars go?
Retrieved from http://www.cbpp.org/research/
policy-basics-where-do-our-state-tax-dollars-go

College Board. (2015). *Trends in college pricing.* Retrieved
from https://trends.collegeboard.org/college-pricing

Desilver, Drew. (2014, October). For most workers, real
wages have barely budged for decades. Pew Research
Center. Retrieved from http://www.pewresearch.org/fact-tank/
2014/10/09/for-most-workers-real-wages-have-barely-
budged-for-decades/

Elliott, W., & Lewis, M. (2015). *The real college debt crisis:
How student borrowing threatens financial well-being and
erodes the American dream.* Santa Barbara: Praeger.

Huelsman, M. (2015). The debt divide: The racial and
class bias behind the new normal of student borrowing.
Retrieved from http://www.demos.org/publication/

debt-divide-racial-and-class-bias-behind-new-normal-student-borrowing

Huelsman, M., Draut, T., Meschede, T., Dietrich, L., Shapiro, T., & Sullivan, L. (2015). Less debt, more equity: Lowering student debt while closing the black-white wealth gap. Washington, DC: Demos and the Institute for Assets and Social Policy. Retrieved from http://www.demos.org/publication/less-debt-more-equity-lowering-student-debt-while-closing-black-white-wealth-gap

Institute for Higher Education Policy. (2005). *The investment payoff: A 50-state analysis of the public and private benefits of higher education*. Washington, DC: Authors. Retrieved from http://www.ihep.org/sites/default/files/uploads/docs/pubs/investmentpayoff.pdf

McKernan, Signe-Mary, Ratcliffe, C., Steuerle, C. E., Kalish, E., & Quakenbush, C. (2015, February). Nine charts about wealth inequality in America. The Urban Institute. Retrieved from http://apps.urban.org/features/wealth-inequality-charts/

Mitchell, Michael, & Leachman, Michael. (2014, October). Changing priorities: State criminal justice reforms and investments in education. Center on Budget and Policy Priorities. Retrieved from http://www.cbpp.org/research/changing-priorities-state-criminal-justice-reforms-and-investments-in-education

National Center for Education Statistics, Digest of Education Statistics, Table 326.10. Graduation rates of first-time, full-time bachelor's degree-seeking students at 4-year postsecondary institutions, by race/ethnicity, time to completion, sex, and control of institution: Selected cohort entry years, 1996 through 2006. Retrieved from https://nces.ed.gov/programs/digest/d13/tables/dt13_326.10.asp

Pew Research Center. (2014). The rising cost of not going to college. Pew Research Center. Retrieved from http://

www.pewsocialtrends.org/files/2014/02/SDT-higher-ed-FINAL-02–11–2014.pdfTax revolts: Some succeed, some don't. (2009, April 15). *New York Times*, Room for debate. Retrieved from http://roomfordebate.blogs.nytimes.com/2009/04/15/tax-protests-that-changed-history/?_r=0

U.S. Department of Labor. (2009). History of Federal Minimum Wage Rates Under the Fair Labor Standards Act, 1938–2009. Retrieved from http://www.dol.gov/whd/minwage/chart.htm

Mark Huelsman is a senior policy analyst at Demos, a public policy organization focused on addressing economic and political inequality. He is an expert on college affordability, student debt, and higher education policy.

Student Loans and Bankruptcy in the United States
Rajeev Darolia

Introduction

As a growing number of borrowers have difficulty repaying their student loan debt in the United States, the treatment of educational debt in bankruptcy proceedings has become an increasingly salient policy issue. Currently, debtors retain their obligation to service student loan debt after filing bankruptcy barring exceptional circumstances. This is because of laws that were enacted in response to concerns that student loan debtors have an incentive to abuse the bankruptcy system. If such abuse is widespread, credit would likely be less accessible and more expensive for many who are seeking to borrow money for college. Nondischargeability policies are controversial, however, because they can impede a debtor's ability to rebuild after facing financial hardship.

Bankruptcy Reform and Student Loan Debt

There are two major types of personal bankruptcy: Chapter 7, commonly referred to as liquidation, and Chapter 13, considered reorganization. Under Chapter 7, debtors surrender assets to pay secured debts, while unsecured debts (where borrowers do not place collateral against the loan) are typically discharged. Under Chapter 13, filers can choose to retain their assets but pledge future income to pay back a portion of their obligations.

Prior to bankruptcy reforms, debtors could generally clear their student loan debt by choosing to file Chapter 7 bankruptcy and surrendering their assets. However, new college graduates typically have few assets to give up. Therefore, strategic students could run up large debts that they never plan to repay, even if they have a sufficiently high income, because they can declare bankruptcy on the eve of lucrative careers. This led to concern that the easy discharge of educational loans in bankruptcy would reduce student loan credit availability, raise prices for those who borrow, and "bring discredit on the operation of the bankruptcy laws" (Commission on Bankruptcy Laws of the United States, 1973, p. 95). In response, lawmakers passed laws to protect against this moral hazard, starting with federal student loan debt in the late 1970s and extending to private student loan debt in 2005. The goal of these laws is to prevent fraud and to preserve educational credit availability, and as a result, most student loan borrowers cannot enjoy the full extent of relief from bankruptcy.

An important distinction relevant to the treatment of student loan debt in bankruptcy is the type of student loan debt, federal or private, the borrower intends to discharge. The private student loan market, in particular, has been the focus of legislative roll-back efforts. Private lenders can arguably incorporate risk associated with the bankruptcy discharge into the terms of their loans. Federal student loan debt has been a less popular target, because federal student loan programs are subsidized by taxpayers and because the public is on the hook for costs associated with default on this debt.

Student Debt Nondischargeability Laws: Costs and Benefits

While the theoretical arguments for why student loan debtors have incentive to abuse the bankruptcy system are established, evidence of such strategic behavior beyond anecdotes is sparse. Critics of nondischargeability laws point to a 1978 report by what was then called the Government Accounting Office that did not support claims of widespread abuse by opportunistic student loan borrowers. More recently, Darolia and Ritter (2015) analyzed millions of anonymized credit bureau records to examine whether bankruptcy filing behavior changed following the 2005 law that made private student loan debt nondischargeable. While they do not rule out the possibility that some filers were gaming the bankruptcy system, these authors do not find evidence that suggests widespread opportunistic behavior by private student loan borrowers before the policy change.

There are exceptions to nondischargeability laws for reasons such as undue hardship, disability, and military conscription. However, the standards being used to prove undue hardship in the appeals process have been criticized for being unduly stringent and inconsistently applied (Melear, 2011; Salvin, 1996). Moreover, the appeals process can be expensive and arduous for debtors who may not have access to the resources necessary to file such appeals. These conditions have led to court cases pleading for clearer or less stringent discharge standards (Kitroeff, 2015) and legislative proposals that attempt to roll back nondischargeability (see, for example, Durbin, 2013).

Although nondischargeability laws may harm those who need relief from student loan debt, there is also evidence that they help others by making credit available to them. The price and availability of credit are likely to vary with the lenders' expected recovery in the case of default, and expected recovery is negatively related to the ease with which debtors can file bankruptcy and the financial incentives of doing so (White, 1998). Ang and Jimenez (2015) analyzed administrative data from nine large private student loan lenders and found that after the 2005 bankruptcy reform, these lenders expanded credit supply and were more likely to extend credit to relatively less creditworthy borrowers.

Conclusion

A robust educational credit market can lead to a vast array of benefits that are enjoyed by both students and society (Avery & Turner, 2012). However, as long as student debt is restricted from being discharged in bankruptcy, it will carry with it amplified financial risk since struggling students may not be able to obtain the "fresh start" the bankruptcy system aims to provide. This risk is particularly acute since those that are most likely to default on their student loans are relatively vulnerable: they are more likely to be from low-income families and live in poorer neighborhoods and are less likely to complete their postsecondary programs and gain a well-paying job (Looney & Yannelis, 2015). Therefore, policymakers need to weigh the burden that nondischargeability policies impose on struggling debtors against the incentives to abuse the bankruptcy system and the increased availability of student loan credit that accompanies nondischargeability.

References

Ang, Xiaoling, & Jimenez, Dalie. (2015). Private student loans and bankruptcy: Did four-year undergraduates benefit from the increased collectability of student loans? In Brad Hershbein and Kevin Hollenbeck (Eds.), *Student loans and the dynamics of debt*. Kalamazoo, MI: W.E. UpJohn Institute for Employment Research.

Avery, Cristopher, & Turner, Sarah. (2012). Student loans: Do college students borrow too much—or not enough? *Journal of Economic Perspectives, 26*(1), 165–192.

Commission on the Bankruptcy Laws of the United States. (1973). Report of the commission on the bankruptcy laws of the United States. *Business Lawyer, 29*(1), 75–116.

Darolia, Rajeev, & Ritter, Dubravka. (2015). Do student loan borrowers opportunistically default? Evidence from bankruptcy reform. Federal Reserve Bank of Philadelphia Working Paper No. 15–17/R.

Durbin, Dick. (2013). As student loan debt surpasses $1 trillion, senators introduce legislation to address crisis. Press release, January 1. Retrieved from http://www.durbin.senate.gov/newsroom/press-releases/as-student-loan-debt-surpasses-1-trillion-senators-introduce-legislation-to-address-crisis.

Kitroeff, Natalie. (2015, October 8). This court case could unshackle Americans from student debt. *Bloomberg Business*. Retrieved from http://www.bloomberg.com/news/articles/2015–10–08/this-court-case-could-unshackle-americans-from-student-debt

Looney, Adam, & Yannelis, Constantine. (2015). A crisis in student loans? How changes in the characteristics of borrowers and in the institutions they attended contributed to rising loan defaults. *Brookings Papers on Economic Activity* Conference Draft.

Melear, Kerry Brian. (2011). *The devil's undue: student loan discharge in bankruptcy, the undue hardship standard, and the Supreme Court's decision in* United Student Aid Funds v. Espinosa. IHELG Monograph 11–01. Houston, TX: Institute for Higher Education Law and Governance.

Salvin, Robert. (1996). Student loans, bankruptcy, and the fresh start policy: Must debtors be impoverished to discharge student loans? *Tulane Law Review, 71*(1996), 139–202.

White, Michelle. (1998). Why it pays to file for bankruptcy: A critical look at the incentives under U.S. personal bankruptcy law and a proposal for change. *University of Chicago Law Review, 65*(Summer 1998), 685–732.

Rajeev Darolia is an assistant professor of public affairs and of education at the University of Missouri. He is also a visiting scholar at the Federal Reserve Bank of Philadelphia. His research interests include education policy and household finance, with recent projects focusing on higher education regulation, student borrowing, and government-sponsored consumer credit programs. Dr. Darolia holds a PhD in public policy, a master's degree in economics, and a bachelor's degree in finance.

Advice from Our Side of the FAFSA
Scott and Mandy Sponholtz

As financial aid professionals, we regularly encounter families trying to navigate the complicated question of "How do I pay for college?" As parents, we're struggling with that same question ourselves. The cost alone is intimidating. For 2015–2016, the average sticker price is $19,550/year for tuition and room and board for an in-state student at a public four-year school or more than double that amount for a private four-year school (College Board, 2016). These costs come at a time when many families are trying to recover financially from the economic crisis of the mid-2000s.

Moreover, the current personal savings rate in the United States of around 5 percent (see NerdWallet, 2015) suggests that these families are struggling to save enough money for basic personal needs (e.g., emergencies or retirement) and have very little left over for educational expenses.

In addition, some adults have returned to college themselves and now face their own student loan payments for the next 10–30 years.

Based on our professional knowledge (and personal experience), we offer the following advice to reduce debt before, during, and after a student finishes college.

Have Honest Conversations about College Options

When we went to college (we won't say how long ago), our parents had frank conversations with us about cost. Scott considered attending some schools out of state instead of the flagship university in his own backyard. But he thought about his majors—political science and communication studies—and realized they were not specialized enough to justify the added expense of an out-of-state school. Mandy's parents stated upfront they would help cover the costs of any in-state, public school. But, if she wanted to go to a private school or out-of-state, she had to get a "full ride." There was a four-year university about 30 minutes from her hometown that offered her a modest scholarship, but she didn't feel like it was the right fit. She ended up attending a public, four-year liberal arts school three hours away that was in-state, meeting her parents' criteria.

Here's the secret about choosing a school: most students are happy with their college choice, even if that school is not their first choice. For instance, Mandy wanted to go to a four-year university, but there were only seven schools available in-state. Even though her options were more limited, she maintains unequivocally that her choice was the right one. Similarly, Scott's options were more open, but he ended up satisfied attending his hometown school. Each student needs to take steps to make on-campus connections with other students, faculty, and staff.

When thinking about a school, families need to know what they can afford. This isn't just a discussion for dependent students and their parents, but it also applies to students who are living independently. When considering schools, look carefully at the family or the individual's budget and then start looking at schools that meet those criteria. Research (Hoover, 2010) (as well as our own personal experience) shows that you'll likely be very happy with your choice.

Work, Work, Work

So what do you do if your child's college fund or your paycheck does not allow you to pay the necessary expenses, even after grants and scholarships? Help your student write a resumé! There are a myriad of employers that provide part-time positions for college students. Some employers are even conveniently located on-campus. Numerous studies show positive benefits for students working 10–20 hours a week (especially on-campus) (see, for example, Orszag, Orszag, & Whitmore, 2001). These benefits include higher grades, lower risk of dropout, and increased graduation rates. Many colleges also participate in Federal Work-Study, a program for students with financial need that makes it easier for them to work on-campus (or some community positions) and earn a paycheck. Just be aware that working too much can become detrimental to your studies. The threshold for "working too much" while in school varies from student to student, but research shows that more than 20 hours per week seems to be a popular tipping point.

Students Control Borrowing, Not Schools

The daily news is replete with stories about student debt levels. Their stories contain sound bites such as "My school made me borrow the money." We understand that, for some students, loans are the only option available. You might think that the amount on your award notification is what you must borrow, but that may not be the case. You, the student, control how much you borrow for your educational expenses.

According to the U.S. Department of Education, "Schools cannot engage in a practice of originating Federal Student Aid (FSA) Loans only in the amount needed to cover the school charges" (U.S. Department of Education, 2015–2016, p. 3). This means that schools must allow a student to borrow up to annual loan limits, regardless of what the student actually needs for educational expenses. As outlined in the Higher Education Act, schools may only limit the amount of money a student borrows in very extreme and documented cases. For example, a school may refuse to let a student borrow money if he or she signs a statement saying he or she will not repay the loan. Or in another case, a school may reduce the amount a student may borrow if he or she documents that he or she will not use excess loan funds for legitimate educational expenses (e.g., books or housing), but instead will go on a ski trip with his or her friends.

In short, schools must offer you the maximum loan amount available. The flipside of that coin means that you must control your debt level.

When calculating your eligibility for student loans, schools must account for various educational expenses. Some expenses directly relate to your program of study, such as tuition, fees, books, and supplies. Others are indirect costs that all adults have, such as housing, food, and transportation expenses. If you are able to cover these indirect costs through other means (such as through wages from employment), then you do not need to borrow money for these expenses. If you calculate that you need enough money only to cover the direct costs, and the loan offered by the school is more than that amount, find out how to reduce the amount on your award notification. A school must honor a request to reduce your loan amount—in some cases even after you receive the loan funds (U.S. Department of Education, 2015–2016).

If you must borrow loans that accrue interest, such as an unsubsidized loan, you can reduce the interest that accrues while you are in school. For every $1,000 you borrow, $42.90 in interest accrues annually. When you receive a quarterly statement of interest that has accrued on your loan from your loan servicer, you can (but are not required to) pay off that interest. This can save hundreds or thousands of dollars of interest while you are completing your degree.

Borrowing Doesn't Have to Be Scary

Is it possible to be debt free when you graduate college? Yes. Is it feasible for everyone? Not necessarily. Please don't let the desire to be debt free scare you away from your educational goals. You have control over the amount you borrow. Exercise that control by the choices you make: what school you will attend, how much you will work, and your lifestyle while in college. This is where your financial aid office can help. Financial aid administrators, like us, can help you develop a budget, locate loans with the lowest interest rates, and determine an appropriate amount of loan payments when you graduate.

Once you determine how much you need to borrow to fund your education, make sure your expected salary will support a reasonable student loan payment. Experts agree that your student loan payment should not be more than 10–15 percent of your annual salary. Or stated another way, keep the total amount you borrow to no more than what you expect to make your first year after graduation (Edvisors, undated).

Students who borrow loans directly from the U.S. government have a number of benefits. First, the loans have a fixed interest rate, which makes payment amounts predictable. Next, depending on the amount of debt, there are a variety of repayment plans available. Some, like the 10-year standard repayment plan, are designed to reduce the total amount of principal and interest paid. On the other hand, income-driven repayment plans (IDR) were created for students whose monthly student loan payments were too high based on the student's salary. These IDR plans limit monthly student loan payments to 10–20 percent of a student's available income. Your financial aid office or loan servicer can help you review the options that best suit your financial situation.

Putting It All Together

Funding a college degree takes communication, planning, research, and hard work. In spite all of these efforts, we know that many students and parents must borrow in order to finance a student's education. We've seen students and parents take on more debt than they can handle, but we've also seen students manage the debt they accrue quite well by selecting an affordable school and by working part-time to reduce the amount of money they need to borrow. Financial aid administrators, like us, are available and want to help guide families through every step of the financial aid process: (1) developing a budget, (2) securing a loan, and (3) finding a repayment plan that meets the student's income and life goals.

References

College Board. (2016). *Trends in college pricing.* Retrieved from https://trends.collegeboard.org/college-pricing/ figures-tables/average-net-price-over-time-full-time-students-sector

Edvisors. (undated). Responsible student loan borrowing. Retrieved from https://www.edvisors.com/college-loans/ choosing-loans/responsible-borrowing/

Hoover, E. (2010, November 1). The science of student satisfaction. *The Chronicle of Higher Education.* Retrieved from http://chronicle.com/blogs/headcount/ the-science-of-student-satisfaction/27654

NerdWallet. (2015). *The American personal savings rate is not nearly high enough.* Retrieved from https://www.nerdwallet. com/blog/banking/american-personal-saving-rate/

Orszag, J. M., Orszag, P. R., & Whitmore, D. M. (2001). *Learning and earning: Working in college.* Brockport, NY: SUNY. Retrieved from https://www.brockport.edu/ academics/career/supervisors/upromise

U.S. Department of Education. (2015–2016). *Federal student aid handbook.* Washington, DC: Author. Retrieved from https://ifap.ed.gov/ifap/byAwardYear.jsp?type=fsahandbook &awardyear=2015-2016

Scott and Mandy Sponholtz have over 30 years of combined experience in financial aid administration. Scott worked at three different financial aid offices, moving through the ranks to his current position as associate director of financial aid at the University of Kansas Medical Center where he helps future dentists, doctors, nurses, and pharmacists finance their educations. Mandy worked in two aid offices, but also spent time training and providing policy guidance to schools on how to interpret the thousands of rules and regulations. She currently serves as a policy analyst for the National Association of Student Financial Aid Administrators, which is an advocacy and training organization to support aid administrators in colleges and universities. As Scott tells it, the two "fell in love over a FAFSA." Now married, they have two daughters, ages eight and two, and have the same teaching moments as many parents: money doesn't magically appear in our wallets, don't scratch your armpit with your fork, and we love you no matter what.

Developing a Mind-Set for Paying Off Student Debt
Phil Schuman

Teaching Financial Education Is Fun

I've often wondered why I have so much fun teaching financial education. In part, I think it's because it's such a relatively new field in higher education that there's an opportunity to teach it the way I want, meaning I get to apply my educational background (BA psychology, MBA) into my design. Another thing that makes financial education so fun to teach is that I can see real changes in how my students think about their own debt. They not only acquire a more profound understanding of their own college loan debt, but they also have more optimism about paying off their debts after they graduate. In this essay, I focus specifically on how students are learning about financial education at Indiana University, and I explain how this system of financial education helps students get a handle on their student loan debts during and after college.

Debt Letters and Financial Education at Indiana University

One of the key features of financial education at Indiana University is that all student borrowers receive a "debt letter" every year they attend. These letters detail a student's cumulative debt total in his or her academic career and his or her projected monthly payment, and are designed to raise awareness about how debt will impact life during and after college. One of the main reasons we chose to implement the "debt letter" is because we discovered that students were unaware of how much debt they had and/or if they had any debt at all.

This awareness of debt is the first step of a student getting a handle on it. The debt letter attempts to help students control their debt situations by creating both reactive and proactive behaviors:

- reactive because students can now see how their loans add up and can begin to understand the impact of student loans on graduation;
- proactive because by knowing the loan totals, students can make future borrowing decisions that take into account their current financial status.

The student borrowing data at Indiana University suggest that the debt letters are leading to positive changes in students' financial behaviors. Since the implementation of the debt letter in the fall of 2012, Indiana University has seen a 16 percent decrease in borrowing ($44 million) across all of its campuses (Indiana University, 2015), a clear sign that a little bit of communication can go a long way in helping students to get a handle on their debt.

Developing a Mind-Set of Control

Knowing the numbers isn't the only step in getting a handle on debt. In fact, developing the right attitude toward getting rid of debt is also extremely important. While I will never disagree that it stinks to have loans to pay back immediately after graduation—my wife and I had $110,000 of cumulative debt after we graduated—the mind-set that a graduate has regarding his or her control over student loans will ultimately determine how efficiently he or she pays them off.

The psychological term "locus of control" refers to "how strongly people believe they have control over the situations and experiences that affect their lives" (The Great Schools Partnership, 2013). People with an external locus of control choose to believe that what happens to them is largely out of their control. In contrast, those with an internal locus of control believe they have a direct influence over the events in their lives; they believe that if something is wrong, they are the one who can fix it. My favorite example to use is the difference between my brother and I when we (attempt to) play golf. My brother tends to have the external locus, meaning that when he hits a bad shot, he often attributes it to things such as the wind, the ground, or something being askew with the putting green. Essentially, he is saying that poor play was a result of something beyond his control, and there's nothing he can do to fix it. By having an internal locus of control, I attribute my poor play to my swing, my concentration, or something else that has to do with how I approach the game. The internal locus of control allows me to say to myself that because my faults are due to me, I have the ability—should I choose to put in the effort—to fix it.

This is why we want students to learn to develop an internal locus of control mentality with their loans. We want students to avoid placing blame on external factors for "causing" them to have student loans because the moment they start looking to externalize the blame and responsibility is the moment they lose their drive to tackle repayment. Having an internal locus of control means that the student understands that he or she is responsible for his or her loans and he or she can decide how fast he or she wants to tackle getting rid of them. We tell our students to be mad at their debt, to be mad that it's there, but, at the same time, to be aware that the debt was incurred so that they could build a better future. If students can develop a healthy anger at their debt and couple it with the internal locus of control, it will increase the likelihood that they will seek out financial education and work toward developing a plan that will get rid of the debt as fast as they possibly can.

Options for Paying Back Student Loans

When students do choose to start paying back their loans, how they approach the repayment is also key. When I talk to students about their debt, I tell them they have three options with repayment: focus on the interest rates of the loans, focus on the balances of the loans, or just apply some extra money to whatever loans they want. This last option of throwing extra money at their debt with no real strategy is the option I always tell students to avoid. While it's nice that they are applying extra money to their loans, the lack of planning in how they're tackling the repayment increases the likelihood that they could just end up running in circles with their debt and taking a longer-than-necessary time to pay the debt off.

Should the student have good self-control and discipline, we would recommend paying off according to the interest rates. In this situation, the student would organize his or her loans from highest interest rate to lowest—with no focus on the balances—and would pay the minimum on every loan except for the one with the highest interest rate. On that loan, he or she would apply whatever extra funds he or she has toward it. However, this method can be challenging because it's easier to get discouraged when your extra effort every month doesn't show a lot of relative gain. And if you do end up getting discouraged, you're much less likely to continue placing extra effort on those loans, leading to a longer life with debt.

The last method involves lining up the balances of your loans from lowest to highest and paying extra on the loans with the lowest balances in order to eliminate them more quickly. In most cases, I recommend this method to students because it is the one that is most likely to generate the momentum that will help them continue to tackle their debt. By focusing on the lowest balances, students will see their loans disappear faster initially, which is more likely to generate a feeling of progress and will make them more likely to continue to tackle their debt at an increasing rate. Each time a loan is paid off, the money that was used to pay that loan can be applied to be the next loan, and so on until all of their loans are gone.

Conclusion

And that moment when a person pays off his or her loans is going to be a phenomenal one. His or her dedication to confronting the debt amount he or she has accumulated, framing his or her mind to take responsibility for the debt that is there, and utilizing a repayment strategy that generates a feeling of momentum will allow him or her to be more diligent with their finances than those who didn't have to take out debt. This is another reason why I have so much fun teaching financial education to students: I get to be a part of their success many years after they graduate.

References

The Great Schools Partnership. (2013). The glossary of education reform. Retrieved from http://edglossary.org/locus-of-control/.

Indiana University. (2015). IU leader testifies about success of university's financial literacy efforts. Bloomington, IN: Author. Retrieved from http://news.iu.edu/releases/iu/2015/06/financial-literacy-testimony.shtml

Phil Schuman is the director of Financial Literacy, Indiana University.

Education: Still Valuable, Just Not Equitable
Melinda Lewis

While much has been made recently of disparities in earnings by field of study (see, for example, Fuller, 2015), there is a significant return on higher education for the average college graduate. For example, Carnevale, Rose, and Cheah (2011) found that average lifetime earnings are $1,547,000 for an adult with a high school diploma compared to $2,268,000 for an adult with a college degree. Furthermore, while anxiety whether college is still a "good deal" has captured media attention, a degree remains one of the few viable paths to prosperity in the United States. Urahn et al. (2012) found that children who are born into the bottom family income quintile and attain a college degree are three times more likely to make it to the top quintile as adults than those who do not earn degrees. Beyond the merely economic, higher education is associated with positive outcomes in health (Cutler & Lleras-Muney, 2006; Hernandez-Murillo & Martinek, 2011) and other dimensions of well-being, such as marital satisfaction (Tampieri, 2010).

Since college is still worthwhile for most would-be students, what explains headlines calling it "a ludicrous waste of time and money" (Reich, 2014)? The anxieties fueling such judgments likely stem from concerns about college costs and inadequate financial aid, both real threats. For those contemplating college, how "worth it" a degree is may hinge largely on how much one has to pay. The truth is that two students, both bright and hard-working, will likely have very different experiences preparing for, attending, and profiting from their educations, depending on how family wealth or, conversely, student indebtedness, facilitates their academic pursuits (see Elliott & Lewis, 2015b). Yes, those who borrow to pay for their higher education are still "better off" than those without any college at all, but young Americans contemplating their futures are right to wonder whether that is really the best standard to use. Anyone who has seen hopes of homeownership or other measures of financial security evaporate in the face of student loan payments (Elliott & Lewis, 2013; Hiltonsmith, 2013) can quickly understand the difference between what they "got" for their degrees in comparison to those able to finance college debt-free. Nor are higher education's inequities limited only to return; reliance on debt-dependent financing has altered the entire trajectory, widening the gaps that separate privileged and disadvantaged students. Anyone who has seen dreams of attending an elite institution wither in the face of harsh economics (Kahlenberg, 2004) or whose college preparation has "melted"

(Castleman & Page, 2014) despite his or her best efforts can see through assurances that higher education is equally accessible to all. Education is still resoundingly important to American young people, but their chances of attaining it are, by some measures, more unequal than ever (Nellum & Hartle, 2015).

This is the real crisis in U.S. higher education: inequity. To confront it, Americans must resist both empty assurances that college is still a good idea and misguided chatter (see Kaufman, 2015) questioning whether college is still relevant. Instead, data underscoring economic and social advantages enjoyed by those with degrees should fuel a redoubling of our commitment to policies that facilitate equitable outcomes in such attainment, starting with the way we pay for it. The value of higher education is precisely why it matters so much that educational attainment correlates more strongly with socioeconomic status than with student aptitude (Bailey & Dynarski, 2011). Today, the lowest-achieving children from high-income families attend college at roughly the same rate as the highest-achieving children from low-income families (ACSFA, 2010), a pattern repeated for college completion (Mettler, 2014). It is because education is so determinant of later outcomes that Americans—particularly those contemplating college—must demand a financial aid system that facilitates fair chances to reap these fruits. If institutional aid practices effectively block access to some disadvantaged students (Burd, 2015; Golden, 2006), we need a new model. If reliance on student loans compromises some students' ability to realize the potential gains (Fry, 2014, among others) that college is supposed to confer (in predictably inequitable patterns; Huelsman, 2015b), it is time for a new standard. To construct a financial aid system for the 21st century, we must examine how approaches fare in increasing preparation, equalizing access, improving completion, and supporting postcollege financial well-being. That begins with an examination of the disparate educational paths of economically privileged and disadvantaged children.

Parallel Tracks and Different Journeys

Shaped by messages that emphasize education as the path to prosperity, American parents overwhelmingly hope that their children will go to college (Pew Research Center, 2012). However, children's actual experiences diverge sharply. Some walk into a pattern of expected attainment, living out plans their parents have made and fulfilling social roles that fit their visions of themselves (see Elliott & Lewis, 2015b). Others must swim against the figurative tide, battling institutions that fail to support their aspirations and overcoming accumulated disadvantages associated with: (1) inferior quality schools (Sacks, 2007), (2) poorer academic preparation (Farkas, 2003), (3) first-generation student status (Engle & Tinto, 2008), and (4) limited information about how college works (Caspar, 2014/2015). The former have stronger "parachutes" to catch them if they falter (Collins, 2013) and a far greater likelihood of success (Pell Institute & University of Pennsylvania, 2015), while the latter have to beat literal odds to convert hopes into accomplishments. These two types of students—the privileged and the disadvantaged—have vastly different journeys, shaped at every turn by their access to or lack of financial resources.

For example, even when they score competitively on entrance exams, low-income students are more likely to study in two-year or unselective four-year schools than elite colleges (Carnevale & Strohl, 2013), while those no smarter—but definitely wealthier—attend schools that provide distinguished faculty, more support services, and better facilities (Marcus & Hacker, 2015). Privileged students are bolstered by financial aid that augments their effort and ability, including "merit" awards that disproportionately benefit the wealthy (Heller, 2006) and institutional incentives designed to lure them (Burd, 2015). Often, they can avoid external financial aid altogether, relying instead on family assets. When they use loans, they can employ them strategically, including to facilitate particular enrollment decisions. Disadvantaged students, in contrast, often have only inadequate (Huelsman, 2015b) need-based aid (where awards are determined by financial need) and the specter of considerable student debt. In total, financial aid serves as much to reinforce inequities in educational attainment as to strengthen education's equalizing power. As a dominant force in the financial aid landscape, student borrowing is indicted in this assessment.

For Many Students, "College" Means "Debt"

Who has to borrow for college—and how much—shapes every aspect of higher education today. Among young adults with an associate degree or some college, 50 percent report having outstanding loans; this figure is 66 percent for those with bachelor's degrees and 78 percent for those with a graduate degree (Elliott, Lewis, & Johnson, 2014). Debt levels are smaller than newspaper headlines suggest but nonetheless significant; on average, students with an associate degree or less have $8,148 of outstanding debt, bachelor's degree holders have $21,433 of outstanding debt, and graduate degree holders have $55,716 of outstanding debt.

Institution type affects assumption of student debt (Institute for Higher Education Policy, 2011). Specifically, students at for-profit colleges are most likely to borrow, at least for associate and bachelor's degrees, where 76 percent and 84 percent of completers, respectively, have student loans. Students of color and those economically disadvantaged are more likely to borrow than privileged students. Elliott, Lewis, and Johnson (2014) found that 82 percent of blacks and 77 percent of Hispanics with bachelor's degrees borrow compared with 64 percent of whites and 59 percent of Asians; 76 percent of low-income and 53 percent of high-income individuals with bachelor's degrees have student loans (Elliott, Lewis, & Johnson, 2014). The amount of debt varies by socioeconomic status, too. Even though they are concentrated in less-expensive institutions, low-income students may need to rely on loans for a larger percentage of their expenses (Huelsman, 2015a), including not only tuition and fees but also housing, food, transportation, and other costs (Krupnick, 2015).

If financial aid options were really created equal, then patterns of debt assumption would be only of academic interest. Indeed, that is what some discussion of financial aid presents: that it really does not matter whether one finances college with grants or loans or family wealth, as long as the degree is earned (see Rose, 2013). Seen through another lens, however, differences in student borrowing reveal serious inequities in the higher education system. When one considers financial aid as not just a tool for paying tuition but a catalyst of prosperity, student debt's failings come into stark relief.

Student Borrowing: Unequal Erosion of Return on Degree

For most students, pursuit of higher education is not simply an intellectual exercise but a deliberate attempt to secure economic gains. Critically, then, reliance on debt compromises some students' ability to fairly reap the financial rewards of their studies, primarily by diverting the income earned by college graduates away from asset accumulation and toward debt maintenance, particularly during the early years in an individual's career. These effects may last well into adulthood, especially as debt shadows students into middle age. Spurred in part by expansion of income-based repayment (IBR) programs that exchange longer repayment periods for more manageable monthly bills, the average time that it takes to repay student loans grew from about 7 years in 1992 to a little more than 13 years in 2010 (Akers & Chingos, 2014). Still, more than one in five student borrowers use deferment or forbearance to avoid delinquency (Cunningham & Kienzl, 2011), a tactic that not only masks some evidence of the student debt crisis but also may make it harder for borrowers to build an asset base. As use of IBR grows in response to troubling figures on delinquency and default, these terms may only lengthen, and the longer that student debt "sticks" with a borrower, the longer it exerts a corrosive influence on financial well-being.

Research on student loans suggests that student borrowing is at least partly responsible for the growing wealth gap. For instance, Hiltonsmith (2013) found that households with four-year college graduates and outstanding student debt had $70,000 less in home equity than similar households without student debt. Similarly, Elliott, Grinstein-Weiss, and Nam (2013) found that families with outstanding student debt had 52 percent less in retirement savings than those without student debt, and Elliott and Nam (2013) found that families with college debt have 63 percent less net worth than those without student debt.

While we do not yet fully understand the ripple effects of this debt, they are likely to be profound, affecting not just balance sheets but the very foundation of the "deal" that defines the American dream: seeing your children do better, as the fruit of your labors. Generation Xers—the first to weather debt-intensive higher education—earn more than their parents but have less wealth and struggle to move up the ladder. Economic analysis suggests this paradoxically cruel trend can be mostly attributed to greater debt loads (Pew Charitable Trusts, 2014). Debtors will struggle to leverage wealth to secure educational opportunities for their own children (see Johnson, 2006, for example). Unable to save equitably for their futures or those of the next generation, today's student borrowers may become tomorrow's indebted parents (T. Rowe Price, 2015), relying on ever-greater debt to strive toward elusive economic well-being. Even worse, analysis suggests that loans fail to drive equitable outcomes on enrollment (Heller, 2008) and completion (see, among others, Kim, 2007; St. John, Andrieu, Oescher, & Starkey, 1994; Zhan, 2013), suggesting that debt may make it harder for some students to achieve in school. At every turn, then, debt-dependent financial aid misses opportunities to set

Americans on a path to success, precisely the role with which higher education is tasked. Dissatisfaction with this status quo is fueling momentum for policy change. In our zeal to do *something*, we must be careful to first accurately diagnose and then respond to the real problems posed by student debt.

Policy Reform Must Offer Meaningful Choices and Equitable Opportunity

Some of the proposed reforms could actually move policy in the wrong direction. Modifications like IBR that extend loan repayment prolong capital deferment, further severing the linkage between educational attainment and financial well-being. Initiatives to provide free two-year college (Perez-Pena, 2014) would likely intensify class divisions in institutional selection, as those who can afford other options would still choose colleges based on criteria such as selectivity and degree offerings. Other policies primarily repackage student debt. Pay-it-forward or income-share agreements, while not labeled "loans," still require students to exchange some future financial security for the chance to attend college. Regardless of their name, then, these measures would feel like student loans and likely have similarly corrosive effects on education's equalizing potency (see Goldrick-Rab, 2013, re: Pay-it-Forward).

Still other innovations, while offering some potential value, are infeasibly expensive while failing to solve the totality of the problems with debt. Most notable here are calls for "free college," which, despite costing billions, would still not address nontuition expenses that can be prohibitive for disadvantaged students (see Huelsman, 2015a). The promise of free college would not likely do much to increase the likelihood that a given student makes it to college or succeeds once there, while subsidizing the educations of those students equipped for college and likely to have attended anyway. Unique among "big ideas" to redesign higher education financing (Burke, 2015), asset-based financial aid has real potential to reimagine financial aid as the engine of our upward mobility system and, then, to move policy in the right direction.

Assets: A Real Alternative

Assets—including Children's Savings Accounts (CSAs)—evidence considerably stronger outcomes than student debt all along the educational trajectory. CSAs are typically designated for postsecondary education and are provided to children early on in life (i.e., at birth or kindergarten) in order to influence not only college affordability, but also college preparation (Elliott & Lewis, 2014).

CSAs leverage both parental deposits and additional transfers from public and/or private sources to build robust balances while cultivating a college-saver identity that is believed to explain how assets increase educational attainment (Elliott, 2013a), particularly among disadvantaged children. While research on CSAs is still evolving, evidence from a rigorous randomized control trial suggests that assets may be uniquely capable, among financial aid instruments, of affecting students' preparation for college. By improving young children's social/emotional functioning (Huang, Sherraden, Kim, & Clancy, 2014) and increasing maternal expectations (Kim, Sherraden, Huang, & Clancy, 2015), CSAs may position children to better engage with educational opportunities, thereby increasing achievement. Secondary data reveal further asset advantages on progress toward a degree (Elliott & Beverly, 2011), enrollment (Elliott, Song, & Nam, 2013), and college graduation (Elliott, 2013b).

CSAs' advantages are political and technical as well as functional. They are feasible, ideologically appealing, and scalable, making them immediately relevant as counterpoints to the debt-ridden status quo. CSAs could be provided at birth and seeded with $500, with a promise to match up to $500 of parental savings, for a first-year cost of only $3.25 billion (Cramer, 2006). They could be funded through transfers leveraged from repurposed Pell Grants (College Board, 2013), existing scholarship programs, and/or education tax incentives. Even today, communities around the country have put CSAs into practice. Currently, CSAs are provided to all kindergarteners in San Francisco schools (Phillips & Stuhldreher, 2011) and to all babies born as Maine residents (Clancy & Sherraden, 2014). Other initiatives surround families with asset building and the construction of college-going cultures (see Elliott & Lewis, 2015a for a discussion of Promise Indiana) and couple CSAs with parental savings accounts (New Mexico's Prosperity Kids). Collectively, these efforts are galvanizing constituencies to demand a financial aid system that succeeds where student borrowing is failing: restoring higher education as a viable pathway to the American dream of equitable opportunity.

Revolution in Financial Aid

While shifting from debt dependence to asset empowerment could transform children's outcomes and redeem the American dream for coming generations, even this dramatic change would do little for those already adversely affected by student debt. Here, our collective reckoning with the true costs of the student debt crisis should prompt not only a new direction for the future, but also an accounting for the past, including meaningful relief for those who bear the scars of their student loan "deal." By many measures, when held to any standard greater than just bridging college's immediate cost crunch, student loans are performing poorly. Individual borrowers are devastated by watching their investment of time and talent fail to deliver the returns that motivated their pursuit. It is this patently unfair outcome, multiplied by millions, that has called college into question, even if the diagnosis misses the mark. On the aggregate level, as millions of American youth and their families grapple with the dashing of their dreams against a mountain of debt or dodge that fate only to find that they have strayed from the one path most likely to lead ultimately to long-term financial well-being, student debt is a paradigm in obvious crisis. This is the moment, then, not to tinker around the edges, cling to the known in fear of what may come in its wake, or throw the proverbial "baby" (higher education) out with the student debt bathwater. Instead, Americans must insist on the financial aid system that this generation deserves and that their nation needs.

References

Advisory Committee on Student Financial Assistance. (2010). The rising price of inequality: How inadequate grant aid limits college access and persistence. Washington, DC: U.S. Department of Education.

Akers, B., & Chingos, M. (2014). Is a student loan crisis on the horizon? Washington, DC: Brookings Institution. Retrieved from http://www.brookings.edu/~/media/research/files/reports/2014/06/24-student-loan-crisis-akers-chingos/is-a-student-loan-crisis-on-the-horizon.pdf

Bailey, M., & Dynarski, S. (2011). Gains and gaps: Changing inequality in U.S. college entry and completion. *The National Bureau of Economic Research*. Retrieved from http://www.nber.org/papers/w17633

Burd, S. (2015). Out-of-state student arms race. Washington, DC: New America. Retrieved from https://www.newamerica.org/education-policy/out-of-state-student-arms-race/

Burke, A. (2015). 8 big ideas for reforming college. *Social Mobility Memos*. Washington, DC: The Brookings Institution. Retrieved from http://www.brookings.edu/blogs/brookings-now/posts/2015/11/8-big-ideas-for-reforming-college-in-the-us

Carnevale, A., Rose, S., & Cheah, B. (2011). The college payoff. Washington, DC: Georgetown University Center on Education and the Workforce.

Carnevale, A., & Strohl, J. (2013). Separate and unequal: How higher education reinforces the intergenerational reproduction of white racial privilege. Washington, DC: Georgetown University Center on Education and the Workforce.

Caspar, E. (2014/2015). A path to college completion for disadvantaged students. *Focus*. Madison, WI: Institute for Research on Poverty, University of Wisconsin-Madison. Retrieved from http://www.irp.wisc.edu/publications/focus/pdfs/foc312e.pdf

Castleman, B. L., & Page, L. C. (2014). *Summer melt: Supporting low-income students through the transition to college*. Cambridge, MA: Harvard University Press.

Clancy, M., & Sherraden, M. (2014). *Automatic deposits for all at birth: Maine's Harold Alfond College challenge*. St. Louis, MO: Washington University, Center for Social Development.

College Board. (2013). Rethinking Pell Grants. Washington, DC: College Board.

Collins, C. (2013, May 28). The wealthy kids are alright. *The American Prospect*. Retrieved from http://prospect.org/article/wealthy-kids-are-all-right

Cramer, R. (2006). Net worth at birth. Washington, DC: The New America Foundation.

Cunningham, A. F., & Kienzl, G. S. (2011). Delinquency: The untold story of student loan borrowing. Washington, DC: Institute for Higher Education Policy. Retrieved from http://www.ihep.org/assets/files/publications/a-f/delinquency-the_untold_story_final_march_2011.pdf

Cutler, D. M., & Lleras-Muney, A. (2006). Education and health: Evaluating theories and evidence. Working Paper No. 1235. Washington, DC: National Bureau of Economic Research.

Elliott, W. (2013a). Can a college-saver identity help resolve the college expectation-attainment paradox? St. Louis, MO: Washington University, Center for Social Development.

Elliott, W. (2013b). Small-dollar children's savings accounts and children's college outcomes. *Children and Youth Services Review, 35*(3), 572–585.

Elliott, W., & Beverly, S. (2011). The role of savings and wealth in reducing "wilt" between expectations and college attendance. *Journal of Children and Poverty, 17*(2), 165–185.

Elliott, W., Grinstein-Weiss, M., & Nam, I. (2013). Student debt and declining retirement savings. St. Louis, MO: Washington University, Center for Social Development.

Elliott, W. & Lewis, M. (2013). *Are student loans widening the wealth gap in America? It's a question of equity.* Lawrence, KS: Center on Assets, Education, and Inclusion (AEDI).

Elliott, W., & Lewis, M. (2014). Child Development Accounts (CDAs). In Cynthia Franklin (Ed.), *The encyclopedia of social work.* New York, NY: National Association of Social Workers Press and Oxford University Press.

Elliott, W., & Lewis, M. (2015a). *Transforming 529s into children's savings accounts (CSAs): The promise Indiana Model.* Lawrence, KS: Center on Assets, Education, and Inclusion (AEDI).

Elliott, W., & Lewis, M. (2015b). *The real college debt crisis: How student borrowing threatens financial well-being and erodes the American dream.* Santa Barbara: Praeger.

Elliott, W., Lewis, M., & Johnson, P. (2014). Unequal outcomes: Student loan effects on young adults' net worth accumulation. Lawrence, KS: Assets and Education Initiative (AEDI).

Elliott, W., & Nam, I. (2013). Is student debt jeopardizing the long-term financial health of U.S. households? *Review, 95*(5), 1–20. Retrieved from https://www.stlouisfed.org/household-financial-stability/events/20130205/papers/Elliott.pdf

Elliott, W., Song, H-a, & Nam, I. (2013). Small-dollar children's saving accounts and children's college outcomes by income level. *Children and Youth Services Review, 35*(3), 560–571.

Engle, J., & Tinto, V. (2008). Moving beyond access: College success for low-income, first-generation students. Washington, DC: Pell Institute.

Farkas, G. (2003). Racial disparities and discrimination in education: What do we know, how do we know it, and what do we need to know? *Teachers College Record, 105,* 1119–1123. Retrieved from http://www.hrpujc.org/documents/TCRecordFarkas.pdf

Fry, R. (2014). Young adults, student debt and economic well-being. Washington, DC: Pew Charitable Trusts.

Fuller, A. (2015, November 3). Parents' fears confirmed: Liberal arts students earn less. *Wall Street Journal.* Retrieved from http://www.wsj.com/articles/parents-fears-confirmed-liberal-arts-students-make-less-1446582592

Golden, D. (2006). *The price of admission how America's ruling class buys its way into elite colleges—and who gets left outside the gates.* New York: Broadway Books.

Goldrick-Rab, S. (2013, fall). Pay it forward is a step backward. *On Campus, 32*(1), pp. 10–11.

Heller, D. (2006). Merit aid and college access. Presentation to Symposium on the Consequences of Merit-Based Student Aid. Madison, WI: Wisconsin Center for the Advancement of Postsecondary Education. Retrieved from http://edwp.educ.msu.edu/dean/wp-content/uploads/2012/03/WISCAPE_2006_paper.pdf

Heller, D. E. (2008). The impact of student loans on college access. In S. Baum, M. McPherson, and P. Steele (Eds.), *The effectiveness of student aid policies: What the research tells us* (pp. 3–8). New York: College Board.

Hernández-Murillo, Rubén, & Martinek, Christopher. (2011, April). Which came first—Better education or better health? The Federal Reserve Bank of St. Louis. *The Regional Economist, 19*(2), 5–6.

Hiltonsmith, R. (2013). At what cost: How student debt reduces lifetime wealth. Washington, DC: Demos.

Huang, J., Sherraden, M., Kim, Y., & Clancy, M. (2014). Effects of child development accounts on early social-emotional development: An experimental test. *Journal of American Medical Association Pediatrics*, 168(3), 265–271.

Huelsman, M. (2015a, August 10). The case for debt-free college. Washington, DC: Demos. Retrieved from http://www.demos.org/publication/case-debt-free-college

Huelsman, M. (2015b). The debt divide: The racial and class bias behind the "new normal" of student borrowing. Washington, DC: Demos. Retrieved from http://www.demos.org/publication/debt-divide-racial-and-class-bias-behind-new-normal-student-borrowing

Institute for Higher Education Policy. (2011). Initial college attendance of low-income adults. Washington, DC: Author. Retrieved from http://files.eric.ed.gov/fulltext/ED521117.pdf

Johnson, H. B. (2006). *The American Dream and the power of wealth: Choosing schools and inheriting inequality in the land of opportunity*. New York: Taylor & Francis.

Kahlenberg, R. (2004). *America's untapped resource*. Washington, DC: The Century Foundation.

Kaufman, M. (2015). Is college still worth it? *Forbes*. Retrieved from http://www.forbes.com/sites/michakaufman/2015/03/20/is-college-still-worth-it/

Kim, D. (2007). The effects of loans on students' degree attainment: Differences by student and institutional characteristics. *Harvard Educational Review, 77*(1), 64–100.

Kim, Y., Sherraden, M., Huang, J., & Clancy, M. (2015). Child development accounts and parental educational expectations for young children: Early evidence from a statewide social experiment. *Social Service Review, 89*(1), 99–137.

Krupnick, M. (2015). Low-income students struggle to pay for college, even in rare states that offer help. *Hechinger*

Report. Retrieved from http://hechingerreport.org/low-income-students-struggle-to-pay-for-college-even-in-rare-states-that-offer-help/

Marcus, J., & Hacker, H. (2015). The rich/poor divide on America's college campuses is getting wider, fast. Washington, DC: The Hechinger Report. Retrieved from http://hechingerreport.org/the-socioeconomic-divide-on-americas-college-campuses-is-getting-wider-fast/

Mettler, S. (2014). *Degrees of inequality: How the politics of higher education sabotaged the American dream*. New York: Basic Books.

Nellum, C., & Hartle, H. (2015, winter). Where have all the low-income students gone? *The Presidency*. Washington, DC: American Council on Education.

Pell Institute and University of Pennsylvania. (2015). Indicators of higher education equity in the United States. Retrieved from http://www.pellinstitute.org/downloads/publications-Indicators_of_Higher_Education_Equity_in_the_US_45_Year_Trend_Report.pdf

Perez-Pena, R. (2014, February 4). Tennessee governor urges two free years of community college and technical school. *New York Times*. Retrieved from http://www.nytimes.com/2014/02/05/education/tennessee-governor-urges-2-free-years-of-community-college-and-technical-school.html?_r=0

Pew Charitable Trusts. (2014). A new financial reality: The balance sheets and economic mobility of Generation X. Washington, DC: Pew Charitable Trusts. Retrieved from http://www.pewtrusts.org/~/media/Assets/2014/09/Pew_Generation_X_report.pdf

Pew Research Center. (2012). Most parents expect their children to attend college. Washington, DC: Author. Retrieved from http://www.pewresearch.org/daily-number/most-parents-expect-their-children-to-attend-college/

Phillips, L., & Stuhldreher, A. (2011). Kindergarten-to-college. Washington, DC: New America Foundation. Retrieved from http://sfofe.org/wp-content/uploads/2011/10/K2C-Case-Study-Final.pdf

Reich, R. (2014, September 3). *College is a ludicrous waste of money*: Salon. Retrieved from http://www.salon.com/2014/09/03/robert_reich_college_is_a_ludicrous_waste_of_money_partner/

Rose, S. (2013, November–December). The value of a college degree. *Change: The Magazine of Higher Learning.*

Sacks, P. (2007). *Tearing down the gates: Confronting the class divide in American education.* Berkeley, CA: University of California Press.

St. John, E. P., Andrieu, S., Oescher, J., & Starkey, J. B. (1994). The influence of student aid on within-year persistence by traditional college-age students in four-year colleges. *Research in Higher Education, 35,* 455–480. Retrieved from http://www.jstor.org/discover/10.2307/40196136?uid=3739704&uid=2&uid=4&uid=3739256&sid=21102819913487

Tampieri, A. Sex and the Uni: Higher education effects in job and marital satisfaction. Working Paper 10/07. University of Leicester, United Kingdom. Retrieved from http://www.le.ac.uk/ec/research/RePEc/lec/leecon/dp10–07.pdf

T. Rowe Price. (2015). 2015 family financial trade-offs. Baltimore, MD: Author. Retrieved January from http://www.slideshare.net/TRowePrice/2015–03-final-tradeoff-deck

Urahn, S. K., Currier, E., Elliott, D., Wechsler, L., Wilson, D., & Colbert, D. (2012). *Pursuing the American Dream: Economic mobility across generations.* Washington, DC: Economic Mobility Project, the Pew Charitable Trusts.

Zhan, M. (2013). Youth debt and college graduation: Differences by race/ethnicity. St. Louis, MO: Washington University, Center for Social Development. Retrieved from http://csd.wustl.edu/Publications/Documents/WP13–08.pdf

Melinda Lewis is an associate professor of practice in the School of Social Welfare at the University of Kansas and assistant director of the School's Center on Assets, Education, and Inclusion. At AEDI, Ms. Lewis is responsible for helping to translate research into materials with direct policy implications, supporting the Center's scholarship in the areas of economic mobility and wealth creation, advancing the field of children's savings accounts (CSAs), crafting media pieces to highlight the Center's work, and helping to guide the Center's regional CSA research agenda. She recently coauthored the book The Real College Debt Crisis: How Student Borrowing Threatens Financial Well-Being and Erodes the American Dream *with Dr. Willie Elliott, AEDI's founding director.*

The College Conundrum—Does Student Debt Cancel Out the Value of Higher Education?
Aaron Conrad

I had just turned 40 years old when I decided that I needed to go back to school. After working for almost a decade in corrections, I realized that I wasn't really doing what I wanted. There was no future in my job, and there was no way to move up or on without getting at least a master's degree. I also decided that a career in social work was more in line with who I was and what I wanted to be doing with my life. The program in which I hoped to enroll required four semesters of coursework and substantial practicum hours to earn a Master of Social Work degree. I considered the possibility of going part-time and completing the degree over four years while continuing at my job. Career advisors and personal confidants both counseled against it, though, given my age and the fact that I was burned out and loathed my current job. I wanted to complete my advanced degree successfully and fairly quickly, which would require dedication and focus difficult to maintain while working full time. Instead, attending school full time and completing the degree in two years seemed to be the best course of action. This presented a challenge, however. In social work, going to school full time (coursework and practicum) would barely allow enough time per week for part-time employment; in the final year of my MSW, I would be in the field 24 hours per week and in class another 9 hours each week. It was hard to imagine how I could fit very much paid employment around those commitments and still keep up with homework. Also, there was no way I could save up enough money in the time before school started to afford even the first semester. Instate tuition for graduate students at the public institution where I enrolled was about $400 per hour, plus fees; I could expect to have to pay more than $6,500 per semester before even considering any living expenses. My only choice was to sign up for financial aid.

Applying for financial aid was something new for me. My parents had planned on me going to college as an undergraduate and saved enough to cover most of my expenses prior to my starting college as a freshman. As a result, when I graduated with my bachelor's degrees in psychology and criminology, the only debt in my name was a couple of credit cards that I had charged up on some junior- and senior-year excursions. My parents had always let me know that they assumed that I would go to college. They worked hard to ensure that they could finance my undergraduate education. They planned based on the world they knew and the one for which they wanted to prepare me. A bachelor's degree was all one needed to get a really good job when I was growing up in the 1970s and 1980s. Having to seek financial aid for my master's degree is not meant as a slight to them or to the amazing job they did planning for my undergraduate career as well as imbedding in my mind that college was essential. I can't imagine where I would be without their efforts. I can still remember an incident in the third grade where my pro-union, pro-blue collar, feminist teacher spent the afternoon telling us that jobs like being a teacher or a garbage man were important, necessary for society, and even had great benefits. That evening, over dinner, when I announced my intention to grow up and be a garbage man, the reaction of my parents was both swift and certain. After a brief moment of shocked silence, I was informed in no uncertain terms that I would not be a garbage man, that I was going to college, and that I would be doing great things that did not involve sanitation.

Those messages stayed with me. It was to those dinner-table conversations that I turned, a little more than 30 years later when I did not feel that I was doing great things. The opportunity to make a change and move toward my dreams now lay before me, but I couldn't afford any of it. Despite making mostly prudent financial decisions as an adult, I lacked the assets from which to finance the degree I needed. Financial aid was my only option for going back to school. In the spring of 2013 I filled out my Free Application for Federal Student Aid (FAFSA) for the first time and was subsequently awarded approximately $27,000 to go full time in the fall 2013 and spring 2014 semesters. I was awarded an additional $6,000 that summer for a study abroad course that moved me closer to graduation and, ultimately, helped to crystallize my career objectives as a social worker. The term "award" is a bit of a misnomer, however. While a small percentage of that money was in the form of scholarships that I had applied for or grants, the state in which I live gives out relatively few merit- or need-based grants, and graduate students are seldom eligible for sizable community- or institutional-based scholarships, either. Instead, the majority of what I received was unsubsidized federal loans. The "unsubsidized" qualifier is important. It meant that, even while I was in school, I was already accruing interest on those loans. In order to keep the interest tide at bay and try to head off the possibility of delinquency, I set up automatic payments to the loan accounts. This meant that I was now paying interest on the money I had borrowed with the money that I had borrowed, which is something no one with any financial sense recommends. It was my only choice, though, as I was now committed to graduation due to my financial aid debt.

When I was halfway through my MSW degree, I owed about $33,000. At that point, I realized that was also about half of what my house was worth. I had certainly never expected that pursuing a graduate degree would cut into my net worth to such an extent. That wasn't the only thing that didn't unfold as I had expected. The time that I had thought would be available for part-time employment was taken up by research I was doing for one of the scholarships I had won. It turns out that the vast majority of the practicum opportunities available to students are unpaid; students are usually even responsible for their own costs to commute back and forth, as well as any professional clothing required. Even borrowing more than I ever anticipated wasn't enough to meet all of my expenses. To make up the difference, I also received occasional help from my parents. Yes, I was 40-plus years old and my parents were sending me money. It was only when emergencies came up like unexpected car or house repairs, but those things definitely happened and continue to do so. I still need their financial help sometimes. Even with my qualms about this student borrowing growing, the next academic year I once again signed up for financial aid as I still had no other way to pay for school. I was awarded $30,000 for the fall and spring semesters, again mostly in unsubsidized loans. I also received an additional $4,500 for the summer semester so I could take the prerequisite statistics course prior to starting the PhD program.

Yes, the PhD program. Before graduating with my MSW in the spring of 2015, in the fall of 2014 I had applied for the PhD program in the School of Social Welfare. In part, I wanted to keep my options open after graduation. Primarily, though, I was motivated by the realization that if I returned to the workforce with my MSW I would likely return to doing something similar to the job that I left to go back to school. Inspired by my exposure to research, other scholars, and innovative programs, I wanted to do so much more. I was interested in conducting research and helping to create and affect policy. My mentors and professors convinced me that the PhD program was the way to do this, and they saw in me tremendous potential to make significant contributions to our field. It all felt right, to move toward a PhD, except for the financing.

The major problem weighing upon me, and the only thing that made me really pause and consider whether to apply for the PhD program, was the fact that I currently owed almost $68,000, or about what my house was worth. I say *my* house, but like almost everyone else out there I am making a mortgage payment. My home is an investment in my future and a statement of hope for financial security someday. I realized that going into the PhD program would require two more years of coursework. At that point I would owe twice what my house was worth, plus I would still have to figure out how to support myself the last two years of the PhD program while I was writing my dissertation. Ultimately what made my decision was reflecting on why I went back to school in the first place, which was my desire to do something greater to help others. I had witnessed during my MSW degree practica the frustration that the MSWs from whom I was learning experienced at having to deal with short-sighted or outdated policies. I realized my desire to change these things through research and advocacy would only be possible with a PhD. I decided it was worth the price—both financial and psychological.

I also considered that if I made this decision I would effectively be trapped by my debt. I would have no choice but to complete the degree and pray that I didn't get sick or have any major emergencies in the meantime. My interest payments had also increased, and I now had to spend even more money to pay the interest on the money that I had borrowed. Alongside this mounting debt obligation came a growing awareness that education, something my parents had sold me on, and I had always believed to be a sure thing and always beneficial, was now more of a gamble of questionable gain. Despite all of this, I committed to the PhD program in the spring of 2015 and signed up for another year of financial aid.

Common understanding is the first year of the social work PhD program is the toughest. For me, along with the stress of the increased demand in coursework and my graduate research assistant (GRA) position, there was the pressure of even more debt. This brings me to the current point in my academic career. I have finished my first year and a couple of summer school classes. I currently owe $96,000 in student loans and still have one more year of coursework to go. At the end of the second year of coursework, I'll owe approximately $118,000, the same as a decent home in the suburbs of a midwestern city and more than twice the median annual salary for an assistant professor of social work. One slightly positive development over the past year is that I now qualify for more subsidized loans, and the interest payments on those are waived until I graduate. Once I graduate, however, it will be game on. Currently, every buying decision I make is done within the context of my financial aid debt.

So what does student debt mean to me? One the one hand, student debt means opportunity, because there is no way that I could have completed my MSW or entered the PhD program without the option of getting student loans. I am certainly grateful for the opportunities that I have had, the knowledge I have gained, the places that I have traveled in my coursework, and the people I have met. Being able to pursue my PhD is an amazing opportunity and will help me fulfill my goals of being in a position to influence research and policy. I am also a completely different and, I feel, a better person from when I started my graduate education. None of this would have been possible without student loans.

Having said that, there are also significant downsides to student debt. Perhaps the most immediate impact is the entrapment that occurs when one starts borrowing money for school. While education is traditionally seen as something positive, creating opportunities by freeing one from limited employment advancement, allowing for economic improvement, and ultimately raising one's quality of life, with student debt, these positive effects are greatly muted and, in some cases, completely eliminated. At least in my experience, student debt can also impart a significant negative effect on a person's physical and mental health by creating a state of constant stress.

One of the first negative effects of student debt is what I call debt entrapment. Debt entrapment occurs even prior to graduation when someone is forced to continue to take out student loans in order to complete a program because there is no way they will be able to pay off the debt accumulated without the degree they are working toward. I realized this after my first semester in the MSW program, when I looked at how much I owed and what it would take to pay the loan back. Even if I had been able to return to my previous job, I would have difficulty making the loan payments on my old salary. After the first year I was completely trapped, debt-wise, and it was graduate or else. There were no other options. I constantly worried about getting sick or having some other issue come up that would cause me to withdraw or be dismissed from the program. This situation has only progressively worsened as the level of debt has increased. There is now significant pressure to complete my dissertation as quickly as possible so that the debt doesn't increase much more. At this point I have no idea how I'm going to pay it all back. While I feel that it is at the tipping point of being impossible, I also feel that I can't not get my PhD. Without my PhD there won't be any way to get the level of job required to deal with my accumulated debt. While some people might think of this effect as a positive, encouraging people to complete degrees, I think of all those who stick with majors they have decided are wrong for them, don't take a risk on a particular program or opportunity, or otherwise change their life course because of the debt that hangs over their heads. It seems odd, somehow, to call that "financial aid."

When it comes to employment, student debt limits my opportunities in that once I graduate I will be under significant pressure to find employment as soon as possible because student loan payments, including the interest, will start rolling in. Any opportunities that emerge for employment will have to be viewed through the lens of paying off my debt. Finding an area in my field where I can do the most good, or ultimately be best-positioned, will be secondary to getting a paycheck as quickly as possible. In the end, even if I am able to find a well-paying job, the benefits to me will be diminished because of how student debt will impact my paycheck and reduce my ability to pursue real security and economic mobility.

Another area where student loan debt has an impact is the economic improvement, specifically in acquiring assets. There's a reason I keep comparing my student loan debt to my house. When I graduate with my PhD, odds are I will have to move to another state for employment. I'll have to sell my house as part of the process, and given that it is an older house with less than 900 square feet, I hope I can break even on the sale. When I get to wherever it is I end up, it is highly likely that I'm going to have to rent, because even with the help available to me as a veteran, odds are I won't qualify for a mortgage given the extent of my student debt. Also, I compare my student loan debt to a house because, while most mortgages are a 30-year note, the idea of still making student loan payments when I'm 70 sounds horrible.

As ludicrous as it sounds, it could very much become the case where I'm using my Social Security retirement to make my student loan payments. Student loan debt for me means the possibility of retiring and getting old with significant debt but without having any tangible assets on which to rely. This theme continues in other areas of saving, such as for retirement. Instead of contributing to a 401k plan or individual retirement account, I could find myself in the position of paying my student debt instead, leaving me to rely on Social Security when I retire. Rather than allowing me to advance, getting additional degrees by taking out student loans has instead set me on a prolonged course to poverty or, at least, financial insecurity.

Student loan debt also impacts economic improvement in other ways, some of which I also see in my own life. Student loan debt can have a negative effect on one's credit score, which means paying more through higher interest rates for anything that requires credit approval to secure. My current insurance company provides a credit report, and being fiscally conservative, prior to going back to school I had an outstanding credit score and easily qualified for the lowest interest rates. Now my score is much lower and the major negative to my credit rating is, unsurprisingly, my enormous student debt. This will improve slightly when I graduate and obtain employment as I will have a source of income, but then I will also have to start making student loan payments and will begin accruing interest on all of my subsidized loans. So should I need a loan to replace the 20-year-old car I'm currently driving, or anything else that requires a credit check, odds are I will end up paying a higher interest rate, which translates to a higher price, just because my credit score has been lowered due to student debt.

The future I foresee has a significant impact on my quality of life. I frequently wonder if I made the right choice by going into the PhD program and if it will all be worth it when I graduate. I'm fairly certain that getting a PhD will not double my income from what I would have earned as an MSW, at least not anytime soon after graduating, so I question the wisdom in doubling my debt. This, combined with the feeling that I am trapped, economically, in the program contributes significantly to the stress I feel. My student loan debt impacts every facet of my life and adds stress to all of it. I constantly worry about how to afford unexpected problems like car or house repairs or medical issues. I worry about having to delay my graduation or the worst-case scenario of having to leave the program. I worry about and feel ashamed at having to get additional money from my parents. Even when having to consider how to budget what funds I have in order to make the most of my fixed income, student debt adds stress to all of it. This is on top of the stress that is normally felt when completing a PhD program, which is no small amount, particularly on the accelerated timeline I have set for myself because of my financial situation. It is well documented that stress—including financial strain—has negative consequences to both an individual's physical and mental health (see, among others, Kessler, Turner, & House, 1988;

Linn, Sandifer, & Stein, 1985; Roberts, Golding, Towell, & Weinreb, 1999).

Critics will point out that I voluntarily accepted the financial aid. I readily admit that this is true. Putting this "choice" into context, however, requires considering the alternatives. With few available grants or scholarships, today's American financial aid situation has become a Catch-22. In order to advance, one needs financial aid to go to school to obtain a degree. Until one has advanced economically, though, few students have the financial resources at their disposal to pay for the very degree they need in order to climb. I did not see then, and I do not see now, that I had many options other than staying in a job that was financially, intellectually, and emotionally unsatisfying or borrowing a lifeline in order to move up. It is clear to me that the original goal of financial aid, to enable people who could not normally afford to go to college to attend, earn degrees, and then *get ahead*, has been lost. The system needs to be re-examined. Although I have yet to see it in my own life, I believe that the concept that education is beneficial can still be true in our society. We'll have to finance it in a way that keeps that promise from being a lie, though. Otherwise, higher education will return solely to the realm of the privileged and the elite. Those aren't the rules that my parents thought they were playing by. That's not the bargain Americans agreed on. That's not the vision we should accept for our futures.

References

Kessler, R. C., Turner, J. B., & House, J. S. (1988). Effects of unemployment on health in a community survey: Main, modifying, and mediating effects. *Journal of Social Issues, 44,* 69–85. doi: 10.1111/j.1540–4560.1988.tb02092.x.

Linn, M. W., Sandifer, R., & Stein, S. (1985). Effects of unemployment on mental and physical health. *American Journal of Public Health, 75,* 502–506.

Roberts, R., Golding, J., Towell, T., & Weinreb, I. (1999). The effects of economic circumstances on British students' mental and physical health. *Journal of American College Health, 48*(3), 103–109.

Aaron Conrad is a student in the PhD program within the School of Social Welfare at the University of Kansas. His scholarship interests include adult mental health and addiction issues, sexual and gender minority rights, and educational and nutritional justice for marginalized populations.

Introduction

This chapter provides brief profiles of some influential organizations and individuals, active in today's student debt conversation. This is certainly not an exhaustive list; however, these names provide a solid foundation from which to begin a scan of the student loan dialogue and also reference significant research and policy contributions, useful for tracing the arc of the evolving student debt discussion in the country. All information in these profiles is accurate as of summer 2016, although certainly individuals' organizational affiliations and organizations' leadership structures can change rapidly.

Researchers

Beth Akers

Beth Akers is a fellow at the Brookings Institution's Center on Children and Families and the Brown Center on Education Policy. As an expert on the economics of education, with an emphasis on higher education policy, Akers writes on the topics of student loan debt, information in higher education, and extended time-to-degree. Her recent report, titled *How Much Is Too Much? Evidence on Financial Well-Being and Student Loan Debt* (Akers,

Vice President Joe Biden delivers his remarks about the economic challenges facing America's families at the Brookings Institution's Hamilton Project forum, "From Recession to Recovery to Renewal" in Washington, D.C., on April 20, 2010. Student debt figures prominently into American policy discussions about opportunity, equity, and upward mobility. (AP Photo/Manuel Balce Ceneta)

2014), suggested that factors such as degree completion and field of study, as well as a student's initial position, may influence the effect student loan debt has on an individual's financial standing. Another report, coauthored by Matthew Chingos, *Is a Student Loan Crisis on the Horizon?*, tracked the education debt levels and incomes of households between 1989 and 2010. Here, Akers concluded that policies aimed to minimize student debt are unnecessary and may in fact be wasteful, while noting the risk involved with getting a college degree (Akers & Chingos, 2014). Akers published *Game of Loans: The Rhetoric and Reality of Student Debt*, with Matthew Chingos, in 2016.

Akers's status as an expert on student debt has been recognized by media outlets such as MSNBC, the *Wall Street Journal*, and the *Washington Post* and has provided her opportunities to brief policymakers on the topic of student loans. She has been invited to present her work at postsecondary institutions across the United States, independent research institutes, and the Senate Economic Mobility Caucus. She additionally provided testimony in June 2015 about the reauthorization of the Higher Education Act for the U.S. Senate Committee on Health, Education, Labor, and Pensions. Akers previously held a position as staff economist with the President's Council of Economic Advisors, where she engaged in policy work on federal student lending, in addition to other education and labor issues. Her educational background includes a BS in mathematics and economics from SUNY Albany and a PhD in economics from Columbia University.

Sandy Baum

Sandy Baum is a senior fellow in the Income & Benefits Policy Center at the Urban Institute and serves on the board of the National Student Clearinghouse. She is a well-known speaker and writer on topics related to college access and pricing, student aid policy, student debt, and other aspects of higher education finance. With the Urban Institute, she has written and coauthored numerous research reports and briefs on student debt and higher education finance. Baum also has a scholarly presence with the

College Board and the Brookings Institution. Since 2002, Baum has coauthored the annual, widely cited, College Board publications *Trends in Student Aid* and *Trends in College Pricing*. Her work with College Board also includes coauthoring *Education Pays: The Benefits of Higher Education for Individuals and Society* (Baum, Ma, & Payea, 2010; Baum & Payea, 2004) and *How College Shapes Lives: Understanding the Issues* (Baum, Kurose, & Ma, 2013). Baum's work on characteristics of individuals who borrow the most (e.g., Baum & Johnson, 2015; Baum & Steele, 2010) indicates that students in certain fields of study, in certain types of institutions, and of nontraditional status have higher levels of borrowing. These findings have helped to inform nuanced approaches to student borrower relief and highlighted the multiple influences that shape borrowers' outcomes. Baum also chaired study groups with the College Board including the 2008 Rethinking Student Aid study group, which proposed reforms for the federal student aid system, and the Rethinking Pell Grants study group, which included Pell savings accounts among its proposed reforms. At the Brookings Institution, Baum chaired a study group in May 2012 that issued the report *Beyond Need and Merit: Strengthening State Grant Programs* (Baum et al., 2012). Baum additionally has published articles in academic journals such as *Contemporary Economic Policy, Feminist Economics*, and *Journal of Student Financial Aid.*

Baum has been heavily featured in the popular media, including outlets such as the *Washington Post, Time* magazine, the *New York Daily News*, and the *New York Times*. She previously held a research professor position at the George Washington University Graduate School of Education and Human Development and is a professor emerita of economics at Skidmore College. Her educational background includes a BA in sociology from Bryn Mawr College, where she is a current member of the board of trustees, and a PhD in economics from Columbia University.

Meta Brown

Meta Brown is a senior economist in the Microeconomics Studies Function at the Federal Reserve Bank of New York and an affiliate of the Institute for Research on Poverty at the University of Wisconsin-Madison. She is a member of the American Economic Association and the INET Global Human Capital and Economic Opportunity Working Group and Market and Family Inequality Subgroups. Brown currently serves as coeditor for *Economic Policy Review.*

Brown engages in research around many forms of debt including student borrowing. Her work on student debt includes analysis of the relationship between student loan debt and homeownership, other type of debt, and access to credit (Brown & Caldwell, 2013; Brown, Haughwout, Lee, Scally, & van der Klaauw, 2014). Among her findings are those that indicate that student loan debt may negatively affect an individual's ability to own a home, especially following the recent housing recession. The report by Brown et al. (2014) prompted attention from the media and policymakers regarding the potential macroeconomic effects of student debt and has contributed to the growing recognition of the differences between student loans and other types of financial aid, such as grants and scholarships, in terms of their effects on postcollege financial outcomes.

Brown has received several awards from the Federal Reserve Bank of New York for her work. She has presented at numerous seminars and conferences at academic institutions, at independent research institutions, and throughout the Federal Reserve Bank System. Prior to joining the Federal Reserve Bank, Brown was an assistant professor at the University of Wisconsin and received research grants from the National Science Foundation and National Institute on Aging. She holds a BA in economics and English literature from Ohio State University and an MA and PhD in economics from New York University.

Rohit Chopra

Rohit Chopra currently serves as senior advisor with the Office of the Undersecretary, Department of Education. He is a well-known advocate for fair student loan policies that reduce debt burden for young people and has particularly focused on student loan servicing practices. Chopra's work in the area of student loan debt uncovered harmful practices in the student loan industry and highlighted the effect student loans have on homeownership, retirement savings, and small business formation. One of his most notable contributions was his testimony before the U.S. Congress Joint Economic Committee on the limited regulatory oversight of the private student loan sector. Chopra argued for a consumer protection system that provides clearer terms for student loan issuance and financing, better servicing arrangements, assistance for borrowers in financial distress, and more robust antidiscrimination provisions (Chopra, 2015a, b). His work has been highlighted frequently in the popular media, including the *Huffington Post* and C-SPAN, and he has spoken in front of numerous audiences, including the Federal Reserve Bank of St. Louis.

Immediately prior to his current role with the Department of Education, Chopra was a senior fellow at the Center for American Progress. Previously, he was the top student financial services regulator and ombudsman at the Consumer Financial Protection Bureau. He holds a bachelor's degree from Harvard College and a master's degree in business administration from the University of Pennsylvania. Chopra was a recipient of a U.S. Fulbright Fellowship.

Rajeev Darolia

Rajeev Darolia is an assistant professor at the University of Missouri, with appointments to the Truman School of Public Affairs and the Department of Educational Leadership and Policy Analysis in the College of Education. He additionally serves as a policy research scholar at the Institute of Public Policy at the University of Missouri and as a visiting scholar at the Federal Reserve Bank of Philadelphia.

Darolia's research interests include a focus on access to higher education and investigation of student borrowing for education. He recently conducted an experiment to test the effects of student borrowing information on financial aid decision making. The results indicated the intervention had only modest effects on shaping financial aid outcomes, suggesting that education about financial aid likely would have little effect on altering trends in student debt in the United States (Darolia, 2016). Darolia has additionally written on college accountability in student loan repayment (Darolia, 2013a) and the effect of financial aid availability on postsecondary enrollment (Darolia, 2013b). He authored a perspective on bankruptcy law as it relates to student loans for this volume.

Darolia has presented his work at academic conferences and the Federal Reserve Bank of St. Louis. He received the 2014–2015 Early Career Research Award from the W.E. Upjohn Institute for Employment Research. Prior to his current position at the University of Missouri, Darolia worked as an economic consultant to financial institutions and government agencies, as a financial analyst for Sun Microsystems, and as an intern for the U.S. House of Representatives. He received a PhD in public policy and public administration from George Washington University, MA in economics from the University of San Francisco, and bachelor's degrees in finance and Spanish from Washington University in St. Louis.

Jason Delisle

Jason Delisle is a leading expert on federal financing for higher education, including the federal student loan program. He has developed a specific knowledge base around the features and outcomes within the ascendant student loan products known as income-based repayment (IBR) plans. He is affiliated with New America, recently serving as the director of the Federal Education Budget Project, part of the Education Policy program. In addition, he is currently a research fellow at the American Enterprise Institute (AEI). Three of Delisle's notable works include *Shifting Burdens: How Changes in Financial Aid Affected What Students and Families Paid for College from 1996 to 2012* (Delisle, 2016), *A New Look at Tuition Tax Benefits* (Delisle & Dancy, 2015), and *Beware Savvy Borrowers Using*

Income-Based Repayment (Delisle & Holt, 2013). The paper on IBR provides a comprehensive overview of the IBR system, critically analyzing for whom the program provides the most assistance and suggesting reform to better support individuals repaying loans for undergraduate education (Delisle & Holt, 2013). His work provides valuable knowledge in the field of educational debt. His analysis has contributed to the evidence base revealing that students and their parents are borrowing more to pay for college, as increased federal government financial support for postsecondary education—largely in the form of debt packages—has offset much of the decline in state and local subsidies for low-income families and students. Further, Delisle's critical analysis of the tuition tax-benefit policies, including the Lifetime Learning, Hope, and American Opportunity tax credits, indicates that many undergraduate students are unable to utilize the tax credits, which, while beneficial for eligible students attending for-profit institutions, provide little benefit for those attending community college (Delisle & Dancy, 2015). Delisle has testified before the U.S. Congress and in federal court about the federal student loan program. His work has a presence in national popular media outlets, including the *Washington Post*, the *Wall Street Journal*, National Public Radio, and *Fox Business News*. Prior to his work with New America, Delisle served as a senior analyst with the U.S. Senate Budget Committee and as a legislative aide to U.S. Representative Thomas Petri. He holds a bachelor's degree from Lawrence University and a master's degree in public policy from George Washington University.

Rachel E. Dwyer

Rachel Dwyer is an associate professor with the department of sociology at Ohio State University and serves as the director of graduate studies there. She also works as faculty research associate at the Institute for Population Research at Ohio State University. Her work focuses on social inequality and economic sociology, including youth indebtedness. She has served as the principal investigator on a number of research grants from notable funders such as the National Institutes of Health, the National Endowment for Financial Education, and the National Science Foundation. Dwyer's work on student debt and graduation rates has indicated that, while small amounts of educational debt support college completion, debt in excess of about $10,000 reduces the likelihood a person will complete college. Furthermore, different groups of students may not experience even the same amount of student debt identically; for example, low-income individuals are particularly at risk for dropping out when they perceive a debt burden (Dwyer, McCloud, & Hodson, 2012). In addition to a general focus on education debt, Dwyer's work includes the role of gender and debt in dropping out of college. A coauthored piece for *Gender & Society* indicated that while both men and women are more likely to drop out of college when they possess large amounts of debt, men tend to make a decision to drop out at smaller amounts of debt than women (Dwyer, Hodson, & McCloud, 2013). Dwyer has also included explorations of the effect of education debt on parenthood decisions (Nau, Dwyer, & Hodson, 2015), as well as mastery and self-esteem (Dwyer, McCloud, & Hodson, 2011).

The work of Dwyer and her coauthors has been widely cited in the academic literature, as well as by independent research institutions. She has presented at numerous academic conferences and has been invited to speak at universities around the United States as well as the Federal Reserve Bank of Chicago. Dwyer has a BA in history, MS in sociology, and PhD in sociology, all from the University of Wisconsin-Madison.

Susan Dynarski

Susan Dynarski is a professor of public policy, education, and economics at the University of Michigan, where she holds appointments at the Gerald R. Ford School of Public Policy, School of Education, Department of Economics, and Institute for Social Research, and codirects the Education Policy

Initiative. In addition, she holds faculty research associate appointments at the National Bureau of Economic Research and the Center for Analysis of Postsecondary Education and Employment, is a nonresident senior fellow in the Economic Studies program at the Brookings Institution, and currently serves on the board of *Educational Evaluation and Policy Analysis*. Dynarski currently serves as editor of *Educational Evaluation and Policy Analysis*.

Dynarski's research centers on educational economics, including topics such as charter schools, private schools, high school reforms, relationships between postsecondary education and labor market outcomes, and financial aid for postsecondary education. She is an advocate for improving the accessibility of higher education for low-income and first-generation college students through rigorous policy change. She has made specific policy recommendations to move toward greater inclusion, including reducing the length of the Free Application for Federal Student Aid (FAFSA). In the area of student debt, she has recently written on the connection between earnings and student loan default, asserting that it isn't the amount of the loan that matters most for successful repayment, but rather the individual's earning (Dynarski, 2016a). Dynarski (2016a) encourages the creation of better income-based repayment systems that allow for easy access, flexible payments, and longer repayment periods, to ease the burden for low-income borrowers. In a recent study on the connection between student loan and home ownership, Dynarski (2016b) critically examines assertions by the Federal Reserve Bank of New York and others that student debt prevents individuals from owning a home. Dynarski's addition of educational attainment data indicates that while college debt can slow homeownership, much of the disparity in rates in homeownership relates to whether a person has a college degree or not (Dynarski, 2016b).

Dynarski's status as an expert in the field has earned her opportunities to testify before the U.S. Senate Finance Committee, U.S. House Ways and Means Committee, and President's

Commission on Tax Reform (about education and tax policy). She was previously a visiting fellow at the Federal Reserve Bank of Boston and at Princeton University, served as editor of the *Journal of Labor Economics and Education Finance and Policy*, and was on the boards of the Association for Public Policy and Management and the Association for Education Finance and Policy. She has been awarded the Robert P. Huff Golden Quill Award for excellence in research on student aid by the National Association of Student Financial Aid Administrators, as well as the Public Service Matters Spotlight Award by the Network of Schools of Public Policy, Affairs, and Administration. Prior to her appointments at the University of Michigan, Dr. Dynarski served as an associate professor at Harvard University. Her educational background includes an AB in social studies from Harvard, a master of public policy from Harvard, and a PhD in economics from MIT.

William R. Emmons

William Emmons is senior economic advisor at the Center for Household Financial Stability and an assistant vice president and economist at the Federal Reserve Bank of St. Louis. Emmons's area of focus is the relationship between household balance sheets and the broader economy, including the effects—particularly on young households and Americans of color—of student borrowing on broader measures of financial well-being. The work of Dr. Emmons and his colleagues has often revealed surprising relationships between education and wealth and made significant contributions to critical debates about the fortunes of a generation of young American adults. For example, a recent paper on the role of education in protecting wealth found that black and Hispanic Americans experienced less benefit than their white and Asian counterparts (Emmons & Noeth, 2015), particularly in the recent economic recession. This finding could have important implications for considering the role of student debt in predicting these disparities. Also in 2015, Emmons coauthored a paper with a Federal

Reserve Bank of St. Louis colleague that examines the importance of wealth in determining households' outcomes in today's U.S. economy (Emmons & Ricketts, 2015). Underscoring its relevance to policy and public conversations, Emmons's work has been highlighted in the popular media, including the *New York Times* and the *Wall Street Journal*, and he has appeared on national television programs. He has additionally been invited to present at a number of academic and private institutions. His educational background includes a bachelor's and master's degree from the University of Illinois at Urbana-Champaign and a PhD in finance from the J.L. Kellogg Graduate School of Management at Northwestern University.

Richard Fry

Richard Fry is a senior researcher at Pew Research Center, with a focus on empirical research related to college enrollment in the United States, including labor and nonlabor market outcomes, and racial disparities. In the area of student debt, Fry most notably completed an analysis of the effect of student debt on economic well-being among young adults. Fry's analysis indicated college-educated young adults with no student debt experience approximately seven times greater net worth than households headed by a young, college-educated person with student debt (Fry, 2014), a finding that contributed to the growing call to consider the effects of student loans not just on access to and completion of college, but on long-term financial health and well-being as well.

In addition to dissemination of his research through Pew Research Center publications and online distribution channels, Fry's work has been published in journals such as the *American Economic Review* and the *Industrial Relations Review*. His work has also been highlighted in popular media outlets, including the *Wall Street Journal*, the *New York Times*, *C-SPAN*, and *Bloomberg Surveillance*. Prior to joining Pew Research Center, Dr. Fry was a senior economist at the Educational Testing Service. He received a PhD in economics from the University of Michigan.

Sara Goldrick-Rab

Sara Goldrick-Rab joined the faculty at Temple University on July 1, 2016, as professor of Higher Education Policy and Sociology. This move came after Dr. Goldrick-Rab's high-profile criticism of substantial changes in tenure rules in Wisconsin and of significant budget cuts that also affected postsecondary education funding. At the University of Wisconsin-Madison, Goldrick-Rab was professor of educational policy studies and sociology and a senior scholar at the Wisconsin Center for the Advancement of Postsecondary Education. Separately, she is an affiliate of the Center for Financial Security, Institute for Research on Poverty, and the Consortium for Chicago School Research. Notably, Goldrick-Rab was the founding director of the nation's first translational research laboratory, the Wisconsin Harvesting Opportunities for Postsecondary Education (HOPE) Lab, which investigates novel approaches to minimizing barriers to college completion. In 2015, she was identified as one of the top 30 most influential U.S. educational policy scholars by *Education Week.*

Goldrick-Rab's work centers around critical analyses of the "college-for-all" movement in the United States, including financial aid policies, welfare reform, transfer practices, and interventions for improving college attainment for marginalized populations. In addition to her work in the HOPE lab, Goldrick-Rab is currently working on a large experimental, mixed methods, study investigating the impact of need-based financial aid on STEM student behavior (as described in Blumenstyk, 2014). She is also engaged in a longitudinal study, beginning in 2008, on the impact of a private need-based grant program on behavior and academic outcomes and the impact of reductions in student debt on young adult outcomes. She is coeditor of the book *Reinventing Financial Aid: Charting a New Course to College Affordability* (Kelly & Goldrick-Rab, 2014) and has authored the books *Paying the Price: College Costs, Financial Aid, and the Betrayal of the American Dream* (Goldrick-Rab, 2016) and *Putting Poor People to Work: How the Work-First Idea Eroded College Access for the Poor* (Shaw, Goldrick-Rab, Mazzeo, & Jacobs, 2006).

Goldrick-Rab has a strong presence in academic journals, including *Educational Evaluation and Policy Analysis, Sociology of Education, Review of Educational Research*, and *Teachers College Record*. Her work is also available for nonacademic audiences, through regular publication in the *Chronicle of Higher Education* and *Inside Higher Ed*, as well as on her blog, The Education Optimists, and through her active Twitter presence. Goldrick-Rab was previously a National Academy of Education/Spencer Foundation postdoctoral fellow, and she has received awards for her work and mentorship, including the Faculty Scholars Award and Mentoring Award from the William T. Grant Foundation and the Early Career Award from the American Educational Research Association. She has received a large amount of funding from a number of national and regional sources, including the National Science Foundation, the Great Lakes Higher Education Guaranty Corporation, the William T. Grant Foundation, the Lumina Foundation, and the U.S. Department of Treasury.

In addition to her research, Goldrick-Rab is active in the community through collaborations with nonprofit organizations and engages in policy-level work with governors and state legislators to develop policies that make college more affordable. She also provides technical support to congressional staff, think tanks, and membership organizations throughout Washington, DC. Goldrick-Rab has also provided testimony on college affordability to the U.S. Senate Committee on Health, Education, Labor, and Pensions. Her educational background includes a BA in sociology from George Washington University and an MS and PhD in sociology from the University of Pennsylvania.

Darrick Hamilton

Darrick Hamilton is associate professor of economics and urban policy at the Milano School of International Affairs,

Management, and Urban Policy, and the Department of Economics, at the New School in New York. At the New School, he also serves as director of the doctoral program in public and urban policy and is a faculty research fellow at the Bernard Schwartz Center for Economic Policy Analysis at the New School. Hamilton holds research appointments at Duke University as co-associate director of the Diversity Initiative for Tenure in Economics, codirector of the Research Network on Racial and Ethnic Inequality, and senior researcher associated with the Samuel DuBois Cook Center on Social Equity. He is president-elect of the National Education Association and serves on the Board of Overseers for the General Social Survey.

Hamilton's research centers on racial and ethnic inequality in economic and health outcomes, including differences in debt. A recent paper for the Federal Research Bank of St. Louis examined the systematic and inequitable differences in opportunities for wealth, criticizing frameworks that often blame people of color for making poor choices that lead to worse wealth outcomes (Hamilton & Darity, 2016). One primary finding is that people of color have a greater reliance on student and medical debt, resulting in higher total debt than white households, an outcome some are then quick to blame on the different "choices" made by households of color. Hamilton and his coauthor suggest wealth transfers at birth for people of color could reduce disparities and promote access to education.

Hamilton has a strong presence in academic journals and popular media outlets. His work has been featured in the *New York Times*, the *Huffington Post*, and the *Washington Post*. He has provided consultation services to governmental and non-profit organizations, including the Federal Reserve System, Demos, and the Council of Economic Advisors at the White House. Hamilton was previously an affiliated scholar with the Center for American Progress and a Robert Wood Johnson Foundation scholar in health policy research. He holds a BA in economics from Oberlin College and a PhD in economics from the University of North Carolina.

Donald E. Heller

Donald Heller is currently provost and vice president of Academic Affairs, and professor of education, at the University of San Francisco. Heller is a leading expert in the areas of educational economics, public policy, and finance. His primary focus is on college access and choice for low-income and minority students. He has published over 175 articles, book chapters, and other publications, as well as edited/coedited six books, including *The States and Public Higher Education Policy: Affordability, Access, and Accountability* (Heller, 2001; 2011); *Generational Shockwaves and the Implications for Higher Education* (Heller & d'Ambrosio, 2009); *State Postsecondary Education Research: New Methods to Inform Policy and Practice* (Shaw & Heller, 2007); and *Condition of Access: Higher Education for Lower Income Students* (Heller, 2002). One notable work in the area of student aid was in the form of a book chapter, titled "The Impact of Student Loans on College Access" (Heller, 2008), where Heller reviews literature on the effects of student debt and finds little evidence to suggest that student loans improve college access or completion; instead, he finds that student loans may actually worsen educational attainment for some populations. While now dated, this review served as an important first step in examining the unintended consequences of the increasing reliance on student loans and highlighted the distinctions between student loans and other forms of financial aid for postsecondary education.

Heller's research has been published in many academic journals, including the *Journal of Higher Education*, *Educational Policy*, and the *Journal of Student Financial Aid*. In addition, his work has been featured in many popular outlets, including the *New York Times*, the *Wall Street Journal*, the *Washington Post*, the *Los Angeles Times*, *USA Today*, *Newsweek*, *U.S. News & World Report*, *Business Week*, National Public Radio, CNN Headline News, and Marketplace Radio. He has additionally consulted with university systems and policymaking organizations in many U.S. states, testified before congressional committees and state legislatures, and appeared as an expert witness in federal court cases. He received the 2001 Robert P. Huff Golden Quill Award for his work on student financial aid from the National Association of Student Financial Aid Administrators. Prior to his current positions at the University of San Francisco, Heller served as dean of the College of Education and professor in the Department of Educational Administration at Michigan State University, as director of the Center for the Study of Higher Education and professor of education and senior scientist at Pennsylvania State University, and as faculty at the University of Michigan. His educational background includes a BA in economics and political science from Tufts University, EdM in administration, planning, and social policy from Harvard, and an EdD in higher education from the Harvard Graduate School of Education.

Robert Hiltonsmith

Robert Hiltonsmith is a senior policy analyst at Demos, a public policy organization engaged in research and discussion aimed at reducing political and economic inequality. While Hiltonsmith originally joined Demos to examine issues surrounding retirement security for young people in the United States, his research has broadened to include student educational debt, a force shaping young adults' financial position and, in turn, their financial readiness for retirement. He has also written on a wide variety of topics, including tax policy, fiscal policy, health care, and the labor market.

One analysis by Hiltonsmith of the role of student debt in reducing lifetime wealth found the average student debt burden for a dual-headed household with bachelor's degree equates to a loss of approximately $208,000 in lifetime wealth (Hiltonsmith, 2013). In an effort to explain the forces shaping student borrowing today, another recent contribution quantified the amount of overall cost increases in tuition and fees attributed to reduced public investment in higher education. Here, Hiltonsmith found that public contributions from states have only marginally improved since the Great Recession, resulting in significantly lower expenditures, in real dollars, than a decade ago (Hiltonsmith, 2014). Hiltonsmith additionally examined this reduced public funding for education for individual states (e.g., Wisconsin, Connecticut, and Virginia). Public education funding, increased need for student loans, and future outcomes for students are further discussed in Hiltonsmith's (2015) brief *Pulling up the Higher-Ed Ladder: Myth and Reality in the Crisis of College Affordability.* This brief highlights the various causes of rising tuition, zeros in on public institutions, and argues for state and federal governments to reinvest in higher education.

Robert's research has been widely covered in the press, including the *Washington Post, Newsweek,* Marketwatch, Reuters, and Kiplinger. He has appeared on national and regional television and radio, including *Fresh Air, Frontline, The Brian Lehrer Show,* and *Fox Business News.* Robert's writing has appeared in a variety of news outlets including *POLITICO, Newsday,* and *the American Prospect.* He has an MS in economics from the New School for Social Research and a BS in mathematics and philosophy from Guilford College.

Jason N. Houle

Jason Houle is an assistant professor of sociology at Dartmouth College. He is also an affiliate of the Center for Financial Security and Center for Demography and Ecology and an honorary fellow at the Department of Population Health Services, at the University of Wisconsin-Madison. Houle's interests include social disparities in health and mental health, processes of social stratification and mobility, life course sociology, and debt. In addition to his work on student debt, his research includes the intersection between health and loan default (e.g., Houle, Collins, & Schmeiser, 2015; Houle & Keene, 2015) and mental health outcomes associated with home foreclosure (e.g., Houle, 2014b; Houle & Light, 2014).

Houle's most notable article on student debt investigates disparities in young adult student loan debt based on parents' socioeconomic status (Houle, 2014a). Results from the study indicated a nonlinear relationship between parents' income and student loan debt, with low- and high-income families having low risks for debt compared to middle-income families, and that the effect of parents' income varies across the debt distribution. In addition, children of college-educated and high-income parents experienced much lower risk of student debt; private and high-cost institutions are associated with greater risk for student debt. This work was featured in the *Society Pages* and on CNBC, NBC, *Real Money*, and *Al Jazeera America*. Houle additionally coauthored a policy-oriented paper on student loan debt and home buying for Third Way, a moderate think tank, finding student loan debt has had little effect on the housing market or home-buying decisions as a whole but may affect certain populations of people (Houle & Berger, 2015). In addition to the popular media features described earlier, Houle's other work has been featured in the *Huffington Post*, the *Washington Post*, *New York* magazine, the *Wall Street Journal*, and *Reuters*. He has also presented his research at numerous academic conferences and institutions. Prior to joining Dartmouth College, Houle was a Robert Wood Johnson Foundation Health and Society scholar at the University of Wisconsin-Madison. His education background includes a BA in sociology from the University of Maine, and an MA and PhD in sociology and demography from Pennsylvania State University.

Mark Huelsman

Mark Huelsman is a senior policy analyst at Demos. His research focuses primarily on college affordability, student debt, financial aid, and state investment in higher education. Huelsman has provided commentary and written numerous publications on the area of student debt, including coauthoring some of the *Great Cost Shift* series articles with Robert Hiltonsmith, also of Demos. Huelsman's (2015) report on *The Debt Divide* looks at how the trend of college being financed through student loans affects college outcomes. With data from the U.S. Department of Education, The Federal Reserve, and other academic literature, Huelsman finds that black and low-income students tend to borrow more frequently and in larger amounts in order to receive a bachelor's degree, and students of color are more likely to drop out of school with student debt than other students. Further, disadvantaged students are borrowing even to obtain entry-level postsecondary education degrees, such as associate's degrees. In another report, Huelsman investigates the personal and familiar characteristics of students who are able to graduate college debt free (Huelsman, 2016). Data from the 2012 U.S. Department of Education National Postsecondary Student Aid Survey indicated only a privileged minority are able to graduate debt free, most coming from families with high incomes and built-in parental support for college and able to complete college without having to work long hours and/or take on large amounts of credit card debt.

Huelsman's prior experience includes a position as a research analyst at the Institute for Higher Education Policy, where he investigated federal financial aid, student loan debt and repayment, institutional accountability, and the need for better higher education data; as a policy analyst at the New America Foundation, where he focused on asset building and college savings for low-income households; and as a legislative assistant with the Retirement Security Project at the Brookings Institution. Huelsman's educational background includes a BA in government and politics from the University of Maryland, College Park, and an EdM in international education policy from Harvard University.

Bridget T. Long

Dr. Bridget Long is academic dean and the Saris professor of education and economics at the Harvard Graduate School of Education and a research associate with the National Bureau of Economic Research (NBER), research affiliate of the Center for Analysis of Postsecondary Education and Employment (CAPSEE), and member of the board of directors for MDRC. She is also a member and former chair of the National Board for Education Sciences (NBES) and the advisory panel of the Institute of Education Sciences (IES) at the U.S. Department of Education.

Long specializes in the study of education, primarily the transition from high school to higher education and beyond, including college access and choice and the factors that influence postsecondary and labor market outcomes. Long is engaged in research on promoting college savings; completion of financial aid applications; college enrollment; effects of financial aid programs and education tax incentives; the impact of postsecondary remediation; and the role of instructor quality, class size, and support programs on student outcomes. She has been engaged in financial aid research for over a decade. In one early, often-cited, article, Long (2004) examined the effects of the Georgia HOPE scholarship on postsecondary institutions' behavior, finding that four-year colleges in Georgia responded to the availability of the HOPE scholarship by increasing student costs. Another article by Long and Riley (2007) discussed a shift in financial aid policy that benefits middle- and upper-income families, rather than improving college access for low-income families. More recently, in a working paper for the National Center for Postsecondary Research, Castleman and Long (2013) tested the effects of the need-based Florida Student Access Grant on college attendance and completion. Results indicated the receipt of the grant increased college attendance and the likelihood of receiving a bachelor's degree within six years.

As an expert in her field, Long has testified multiple times before congressional committees on education issues and has also been awarded major research awards from the Bill & Melinda Gates Foundation, the U.S. Department of Education, and the National Science Foundation (NSF). She was also awarded the Robert P. Huff Golden Quill Award from the

National Association of Student Financial Aid Administrators (NASFAA) and National Academy of Education/Spencer Post-doctoral Fellowship. She has served as an advisor to many organizations, including the College Board, Bill & Melinda Gates Foundation, American Council on Education, Massachusetts Board of Higher Education, Ohio Board of Regents, and the I Have a Dream Foundation. Her educational background includes an AB from Princeton University and an MA and PhD from the Harvard University Department of Economics.

Ben Miller

Ben Miller is currently senior director of postsecondary education at the Center for American Progress, an independent, nonpartisan educational organization. Miller's work is focused on accountability, affordability, and financial aid in higher education. Miller's work on student debt includes an analysis of average student debt for each college graduate, by state (Miller, 2015). The results indicated different relationships between student debt and college completion, depending on the state, demonstrating a need for contextualized consideration when analyzing student debt and pointing to the significance of state policy as an influence on individual outcomes. For example, Louisiana has relatively low average levels of student debt, but this is primarily related to very low levels of college completion rather than evidence of low levels of student debt burden. In Virginia, however, levels of degree completion are higher, making it at least theoretically easier for student borrowers to pay off their student debt. In addition, a recent report by Miller (2016) provides specific technical, resource, and policy recommendations for improving the postsecondary data infrastructure.

Miller's work has been featured in popular media sources, such as the *New York Times* and *Los Angeles Times*, as well as in education-oriented publications directed at lay audiences, such as *The Chronicle of Higher Education* and *Inside Higher Ed*. Prior to his work at the Center for American Progress, Miller worked as research director for higher education at New America and as a senior policy advisor in the Office of Planning, Evaluation, and Policy Development at the U.S. Department of Education. Miller has a bachelor's degree in history and economics from Brown University.

Laura W. Perna

Laura Perna is a James S. Riepe professor in the Graduate School of Education, founding executive director of the Alliance for Higher Education and Democracy (AHEAD), chair of the Higher Education Division, and chair of the Faculty Senate at the University of Pennsylvania. She additionally serves as a fellow of the American Educational Research Association, faculty fellow of the Institute for Urban Research, faculty affiliate of the Penn Wharton Public Policy Initiative, member of the advisory board for the Netter Center for Community Partnerships, and member of the Social Welfare Graduate Group of the School of Social Policy and Practice.

Perna's research is focused on college access and success, including the ways in which social structures, educational practices, and public policies promote or hinder access and success for low-income and minority individuals. She has authored several books, including *Understanding the Working College Student: New Research and Its Implications for Policy and Practice* (Perna, 2010a) and *The State of College Access and Completion: Improving College Success for Students from Underrepresented Groups* (Perna & Jones, 2013). In one notable article on student debt, Perna explored differences between subgroups of students in student borrowing experiences, specifically the presence of debt aversion among students of color and its relationship to educational outcomes (Perna, 2008). She has often written on the importance of understanding and accounting for context in discussions and research on financial aid and resulting college opportunities and access (e.g., Perna, 2010b; Perna & Steele, 2011), including student perceptions and expectations about aid, and the relationships between perceptions/expectations and school characteristics and the aid available (Perna & Steele, 2011).

Perna has held leadership positions in the principal national higher education administration associations, including 2014–2015 President of the Association for the Study of Higher Education, and vice president of the American Educational Research Association's Division J (Postsecondary Education) from 2010 to 2013. She is also associate editor of *Higher Education: Handbook of Theory and Research* and has served on numerous editorial boards, including *American Education Research Journal, Educational Researcher, Educational Evaluation and Policy Analysis, Academe, Journal of Higher Education, Review of Higher Education, Journal of College Student Development*, and *Research in Higher Education*. She has been the recipient of several awards, including the Promising Scholar/Early Career Achievement Award from the Association for the Study of Higher Education, the Christian R. and Mary F. Lindback Foundation Award for Distinguished Teaching from the University of Pennsylvania, and the Robert P. Huff Golden Quill Award from the National Association of Student Financial Aid Administrators. Perna has received funding for her research from a variety of organizations, including the U.S. Department of Education and Lumina Foundation.

Perna's work has been featured in several popular media sources, including the *New York Times, Wall Street Journal, Washington Post*, and the *Huffington Post*. She has additionally provided invited testimony to the U.S. Senate Health and Education Labor and Pensions Committee and several subcommittees in the U.S. House of Representatives. Her educational background includes bachelor's degrees in economics and psychology from the University of Pennsylvania and a master's degree in public policy and PhD in education from the University of Michigan.

Fabian T. Pfeffer

Fabian Pfeffer is research assistant professor for the Survey Research Center and the University of Michigan Institute for Social Research and a faculty affiliate at the Population Studies Center and the Center on the Demography of Aging, also at University of Michigan, as well as a DIW research fellow at the German Institute for Economic Research. His research is focused on social inequality and mobility, education, wealth, cross-national comparisons, and research methodology.

Pfeffer, Danziger, and Schoeni's (2013) investigation of wealth disparities prior to and following the Great Recession provides a lens for understanding differential outcomes associated with student debt. Specifically, results indicated that while all socioeconomic groups experienced wealth declines after the Great Recession, the declines were greater for people of color, individuals with lower levels of education, and individuals with lower incomes prior to the recession. Pfeffer and Hertel (2015) further explored intergenerational mobility across time and how educational expansion in the 20th century has contributed to mobility changes for men. Their investigation indicated a weaker relationship between social class background and social class destination, as more people are achieving higher levels of education than ever before, a finding that underscores the importance of education as a catalyst for upward mobility and greater economic equity.

Pfeffer has received research funding from well-known institutes and foundations, including the Russell Sage Foundation, National Institutes of Health, and Spencer Foundation, and has completed numerous conference and invited presentations. He has been the recipient of several competitive conference and paper awards and was a Fulbright scholar. Prior to his tenure-track appointment at the University of Michigan, Pfeffer was a faculty research fellow at the Survey Research Center. His educational background includes international degrees in economics, sociology, and social sciences from the University of Cologne, and an MS and PhD in sociology from the University of Wisconsin-Madison.

Tom Shapiro

Tom Shapiro is the Pokross professor of law and social policy at the Heller School for Social Policy and Management and director of the Institute on Assets and Social Policy, at Brandeis

University. Shapiro is a leading expert in the fields of asset development and wealth inequality, with particular interest in racial inequities, an injustice to which research suggests student borrowing may contribute. The author of books and many reports on racial wealth gaps and their causes and implications, Shapiro has an active scholarship inquiry today that pulls from qualitative and quantitative data to understand the structural origins of racial wealth disparities. His research and policy brief titled *The Roots of the Widening Racial Wealth Gap: Explaining the Black-White Economic Divide* used household data over 25 years to investigate the total wealth gap between white and African American families in the United States (Shapiro, Meschede, & Osoro, 2013). Results from the study indicated large racial disparities in wealth, with the wealth gap growing from $85,000 to $236,500. The biggest drivers of the growing gap included years of homeownership, household income, unemployment, college education, inheritance, financial support from family and friends, and prior family wealth (Shapiro et al., 2013). Research has indicated that student debt may be related to a number of these drivers, most notably initiation of homeownership, household income, and access to a college education. In addition, even when income gains were equal, racial differences in wealth were present (Shapiro et al., 2013). Shapiro has additionally contributed to an article on the interface between student debt and the black-white wealth gap (Huelsman et al., 2015). This study found that forgiving student debt for all households would actually increase the wealth gap, but targeting families with incomes of $50,000 or below would reduce the wealth gap by nearly 7 percent, and by nearly 37 percent among low-wealth households.

Shapiro's work has been reviewed and discussed in popular media sources, including the *Washington Post*, the *Boston Globe*, *CommonWealth Magazine*, and *Newsweek*. He presents seminars and lectures to academic and general-community audiences around the United States. He was a 2014 recipient of the Asset Builder Champion Award from the Center for Global Policy Solutions, received the C. Wright Mills Award from the Society for the Study of Social Problems, and was a Fulbright scholar in South Africa. Shapiro holds a PhD from Washington University.

Edward P. St. John

Edward St. John is professor emeritus at the College of Education at the University of Michigan. He is a long-time scholar of postsecondary education and student aid, including three decades of research on educational policy. He previously directed the initiative Promoting Equity in Urban and Higher Education, funded by the Ford Foundation, at the University of Michigan's National Center for Institutional Diversity. This initiative included the development of a database to track and monitor data on education opportunity by state, including information on racial/ethnic representation, high school and college graduation rates, and college costs and financial aid.

St. John's research provides a significant contribution to the academic literature and continues to be heavily cited. Among this work is a well-developed research agenda on relationships between financial aid and college persistence, college choice, and recruitment. In addition to scholarly articles, St. John has written well-reviewed books, including *Public Funding of Higher Education: Changing Contexts and New Rationales* (St. John & Parsons, 2005), *Refinancing the College Dream: Access, Equal Opportunity, and Justice for Tax Payers* (St. John & Asker, 2003), and *Left Behind: Urban High Schools and the Failure of Market Reform* (St. John, Milazzo Bigelow, Lijana, & Massé, 2015). In his most recent book, St. John and his team examine education reforms in four charter schools and four public high schools across the United States, discussing contentions between the needs to develop new courses and to provide social support to encourage college attendance and address barriers (St. John et al., 2015). St. John's next book, *College for Every Student: A Practitioner's Guide to Building College and Career Readiness* (coauthored with Rick Dalton), will be published in 2016. St. John serves as series coeditor for *Readings on Equal Education*, which features policy research on initiatives seeking to reduce inequalities and improving the quality of K-12 and postsecondary educational opportunities. He also coedits *Core Issues in Higher Education*, topical texts for professors and graduate students with an interest in the field. St. John is a fellow of the American Educational Research Association and has received awards from other associations for his scholarship.

Journalists

Anya Kamenetz

Anya Kamenetz is currently the lead education blogger at National Public Radio and author of several books about education. She was named a 2010 Game Changer in Education by the *Huffington Post;* received a National Award for Education, reporting two years in a row from the Education Writers Association; and was nominated for a Pulitzer Prize. In Kamenetz's (2006) book *Generation Debt*, she interviewed student debtors to highlight the consequences of their debt on their educational journeys, career decisions, and future life outcomes. She additionally includes evidence from interviews with experts in economics, the healthcare industry, and education, to comprehensively document the difficulties of surviving and building a secure life for today's young people. Kamenetz discusses the topic of student debt within her book *DIY U: Edupunks, Edupreneurs, and the Coming Transformation of Higher Education* (Kamenetz, 2010). Her book *The Test: Why Our Schools Are Obsessed with Standardized Testing—but You Don't Have to Be* (Kamenetz, 2015) discussed the history, current state, and future of standardized testing.

Prior to joining National Public Radio in 2014, Kamenetz was a staff writer for *Fast Company* magazine and contributor to the *New York Times*, the *Washington Post, New York* magazine, and *O, the Oprah Magazine*. She has appeared in documentaries about educational policy and financing, including *Default: A Student Loan Documentary* and *Ivory Tower*. Kamenetz has a bachelor's degree from Yale University.

Nicholas Lemann

Nicholas Lemann is the Joseph Pulitzer II and Edith Pulitzer Moore professor and dean emeritus (2003–2013) of journalism at the Columbia University Graduate School of Journalism. In addition, Lemann is a staff writer and Washington correspondent at the *New Yorker*, responsible for the columns *Letter from Washington* and *Wayward Press*. Lemann's article "The Real Student-Debt Crisis" has contributed to today's conversation on student debt (Lemann, 2015). In it, he unpacked the myth of college as a place where students live and come of age and revealed the high debt burden incurred by many students and the changing nature of higher education itself, which increasingly happens online and within for-profit schools. Further he discussed the increasing costs at public colleges and universities and the high level of student borrowing that has become commonplace for degree-seeking undergraduates. Lemann has also authored the books *The Promised Land: The Great Black Migration and How It Changed America*, *The Big Test: The Secret History of the American Meritocracy*, and *Redemption: The Last Battle of the Civil War*. Lemann has lectured at many universities, served on several boards of directors, and was named a fellow of the American Academy of Arts and Sciences. Prior to his current position at the *New Yorker*, Lemann was a national correspondent on politics, education, business, and social policy at the *Atlantic Monthly* and was a writer and editor at the *Washington Monthly*, *Texas Monthly*, and the *Washington Post*. Lemann holds degrees in American history and literature from Harvard College.

Research and Policy Organizations

Access Group

Access Group, formed in 1983, is a nonprofit organization that provides research and policy advocacy, as well as financial education resources for schools and students. Their goal is to promote accessible and affordable legal education, as well as other graduate and professional education. Access Group's research on the affordability and value of a legal or professional education has led to reports such as "Life after Law School," "Loan Counseling for Graduate and Professional Students: The Need for Expanded Financial Literacy Education," and "A Framework for Thinking about Law School Affordability." In regard to student loans, Access Group provides a knowledge center where individuals can access information about student loans regarding both borrowing and repayment. It provides other resources to help students learn more about loans such as videos, forms, fact sheets, and links to other resources.

Center for Responsible Lending

The Center for Responsible Lending (CRL) is a nonprofit, nonpartisan organization, established in 2002 by the Self-Help Credit Union. CRL combats predatory consumer lending through research and policy advocacy. CRL's goal is to create fair and affordable borrowing opportunities for responsible individuals, regardless of their income. CRL has offices in Durham, North Carolina; Washington, DC; and Oakland, California. In addition to its direct provision of financial tools, CRL produces research and advocacy on student loans and predatory lending. Among its analyses, CRL notes that student loan debt is a particular concern for students attending for-profit colleges where the quality of the school and education received may not help students to secure a career that sets them up to repay the loan without significant hardship. CRL's policy positions on student loans, then, include requiring for-profit college and career programs to deliver high-quality education so that students have the ability to pay back loans and also support relief for borrowers such as income-based repayment options, tax-free forgiven balances, and student loans discharge during bankruptcy.

Center on Assets, Education, and Inclusion

The Center on Assets, Education, and Inclusion's (AEDI) mission is to create and enhance opportunities for low-income children and families, within the United States and globally, to climb the economic ladder out of poverty. As such, AEDI's work centers on innovative approaches and research surrounding asset development, education, and financial inclusion. AEDI recognizes the important role postsecondary education plays in catalyzing meaningful opportunities for upward economic mobility for low-income individuals. Accordingly, a major area of AEDI's research has been surrounding Children's Savings Accounts (CSAs), interventions that seek to ensure children, particularly children in low-income families, have both identities consistent with educational attainment and valuable assets to help them accomplish that goal. Building on a solid theoretical foundation and secondary evidence base, AEDI has been conducting original research to examine CSA program models across the United States as well as secondary data analysis and policy analysis to inform stakeholders and policymakers. This work has brought and continues to help bring investments in children's educational attainment into the policy realm.

In recent years, AEDI's director, Dr. William Elliott III, and assistant director, Melinda Lewis, have become active in the area of student debt. Dr. Elliott published some of the early analysis examining the effects of student borrowing on borrowers' long-term financial well-being (Elliott & Nam, 2013; Elliott, Lewis, & Johnson, 2014). Elliott, Lewis, Nam, and Grinstein-Weiss (2014) studied the potential of parental savings to reduce the incidence and extent of student borrowing. Elliott and Lewis published a book on student loans' effects on education's equalizing potential, *The Real College Debt Crisis: How Student Borrowing Threatens Financial Well-Being and Erodes the America Dream*, in 2015. AEDI's work suggests that low-income children and families are not on a level-playing field when it comes to paying for college. Instead, incurring even small amounts of debt may deter degree completion, present financial hardship even after completing a degree, and/or compromise the financial returns higher education is supposed to offer equitably. Rooted in this understanding of the inequity inherent within the current, debt-reliant financial aid system, AEDI continues to spark conversations about student debt and asset alternatives for financial aid.

Demos

Demos, whose name means "the people," is a nonpartisan public policy organization committed to ensuring that all people have an equal voice and opportunity to participate in the U.S. economy. As such, Demos's work is dedicated to decreasing the influence of money in American politics, ensuring all citizens have the freedom to vote, increasing conversations about community and racial inequality to promote equity, and creating trajectories that lead to a larger and more diverse middle class within a sustainable economy.

Demos recognizes the importance of higher education as it pertains to economic mobility for Americans. For the past decade, Demos has been producing research on college affordability, financial aid, and student debt, and considering how these issues impact the economy. Demos continues to demonstrate a commitment to research that informs equitable policy and practice in higher education. A recent Demos publication, "A Leg Up: How a Privileged Minority Is Graduating without Debt," uses the National Postsecondary Student Aid Survey (NPSAS) to describe the characteristics of the small minority of students who are able to complete college debt free and compare them to those leaving with debt. As do most of Demos's reports, this analysis also provides policy recommendations to improve equitable access to college, particularly for students of color and those with low incomes (Huelsman, 2016).

Education Trust

The Education Trust, a nonpartisan, nonprofit advocacy organization founded in 1996, pursues educational equity for students from preschool through college, with a particular focus on closing gaps for students of color and low-income students. The organization has offices in Washington, DC; Royal Oak, Michigan; and Oakland, California. The Education Trust receives support from a diverse group of funders such as the Wallace Foundation, State Farm Companies Foundation, the

College Board, Bill & Melinda Gates Foundation, and the Carnegie Corporation of New York. Through community and stakeholder partnerships, data analysis at the national, state, and local levels and policy work in different governmental systems, the Education Trust works to uncover and eliminate gaps in educational opportunities afforded to students. The Education Trust publishes articles and uses earned and social media to promote conversations surrounding these topics. The organization employs several staff dedicated to working on higher education policy and practice in the areas of (1) access to high-quality postsecondary education; (2) affordability and financial aid for low-income students; (3) postsecondary completion and success; and (4) identifying successful models that support access, affordability, completion, and success.

The Education Trust recognizes the detrimental impact that student loan debt has on low- and middle-income students. The Education Trust works on affordability and financial aid, advocating for the preservation of and improvement to the Pell Grant program as well as innovative strategies to provide equitable financial aid for low-income and working-class students. Some of their work in this area includes reports such as "Doing away with Debt: Using Existing Resources to Ensure College Affordability for Low and Middle Income Families" and "Beyond Pell: A Next-Generation Design for Federal Financial Aid."

Federal Reserve Bank of New York

The Federal Reserve Bank of New York (FRBNY), also called the New York Fed, is part of the Federal Reserve System (The Fed), comprised of 12 regional Reserve Banks within the United States and the board of governors. FRBNY has a head office in New York City, New York, and a regional office in East Rutherford, New Jersey, and employs approximately 2,700 people in total.

The FRBNY generates statistics on student loan debt quarterly, using Consumer Credit Panel data to produce a

"Quarterly Report on Household Debt and Credit." As such, it makes trends in student loan debt and total student loan debt available on a regular basis. The data they collect enables its staff to conduct research that provides relevant information on student loan and its impact on the economy. Researchers at the Federal Reserve Bank of New York, including Meta Brown (see Researchers section), have become recognized experts in student borrowing and its macroeconomic consequences.

The Institute for College Access & Success

The Institute for College Access & Success (TICAS) is a nonprofit organization dedicated to producing and supporting research and advocacy to improve the accessibility and affordability of higher education for all individuals. TICAS has offices in Washington, DC, and Oakland, California. Some of its funders include the Lumina Foundation, the Ford Foundation, and the College Futures Foundation. Since 2005, TICAS has operated the Project on Student Debt initiative, an effort that seeks to keep the public informed about the proliferation of student loans as the primary method of financing college, the resulting levels of debt and loan default, and the impacts student loan debt has on students, families, and the U.S. economy. The Project on Student Debt has a national policy agenda related to reducing student debt burden. That agenda includes increasing needs-based aid to students (through Pell Grants, state investments in higher education, and improved tax benefits), ensuring that important information on debt and college outcomes is available to students who need it, providing easier access to equitable federal loans, making federal loan repayment options easier to understand and the repayment process more efficient, improving borrower protections for students and decreasing their reliance on private loans to fund college, and strengthening policies that promote accountability for higher education institutions to deliver high-quality services.

National Association of Student Financial Aid Administrators

The National Association of Student Financial Aid Administrators (NASFAA), created in 1966, is the largest national postsecondary education association and is known for its work on financial aid. NASFAA's work largely surrounds creating improved access to and success in postsecondary educational institutions. NASFAA has a unique focus on research and advocacy surrounding student financial aid, including legislation, regulation, and training for financial aid administrators. NASFAA conducts original research and uses data to inform its mission of improving access to postsecondary education and increasing student success, providing training and professional development for financial aid administrators, and creating a collaborative forum surrounding student financial aid. Some examples of this work include:

Operating the *Journal of Student Financial Aid*;

Making financial aid data publically available, such as its National Aid Student Aid Profiles;

Offering researchers and members of the interested public annotated bibliographies on topic pertaining to borrowing, debt burden, and repayment;

Convening policy task forces to tackle issues such as simplifying the FAFSA and student loans, debt, and repayment;

Providing resources to help financial aid administrators understand and participate in advocacy related to their areas of work, including maintaining a legislation tracker to keep student financial aid administrators informed while Congress is in session.

National Center on Education Statistics

Housed within the U.S. Department of Education Institute of Education Science, the National Center on Education Statistics (NCES) regularly collects, analyzes, and maintains publically available data. NCES also publishes reports and statistics surrounding K-12 and postsecondary education in the United States. NCES analyses inform much of today's understanding of the dynamics of student loan usage and its effects in the U.S. education landscape today, including many of the figures presented in Chapter 5 of this volume.

Related to student aid, NCES has been using data from multiple data sources to publish reports on the financing of postsecondary education since 1995. The NCES conducts the National Postsecondary Student Aid Study (NPSAS), a study that examines characteristics of America's postsecondary students and the manner in which they finance their postsecondary educations. These data enable NCES to provide research on student aid use that can inform policy on federal aid mechanisms such as Pell Grants and Stafford Loans. NCES also provides an annual report to Congress regarding the condition of education in the United States.

New America

New America is a nonpartisan public policy think tank, founded in 1999, that aims to generate big ideas and foster creative solutions to problems facing America in the Digital Age. New America has offices in Washington, DC, and in New York; employs almost 150 people who work on a variety of projects and initiatives; and operates on a budget of almost $20 million. In addition to traditional policy and data analysis, New America utilizes a variety of media through which to communicate its ideas, including podcasts, blogs, articles, policy briefs, press releases, and events.

New America's Education Policy program has staff dedicated to higher education research and policy. Its work serves to generate public discussion about higher education, including the cost of college and the current financing system. For instance, this year, New America released a provocative paper, "Starting from Scratch: A New Federal and State Partnership in Higher Education," where it proposes that the current, broken federal financial aid system be replaced by a new system that puts the onus on states and colleges to make college affordable and assist financially needy students. This paper was accompanied by a press release in the *Washington Post* and an event in April 2016 where experts debated this approach versus the direct aid to college approach being proposed by Democratic presidential candidates.

United for a Fair Economy

United for a Fair Economy (UFE) challenges the concentration of wealth and power that corrupts democracy, deepens the racial divide, and tears communities apart. UFE uses popular economics education, trainings, and creative communications to support social movements working for a resilient, sustainable, and equitable economy. UFE's areas of emphasis transcend student debt to encompass government budget policies and their disparate effects on communities of color, financial exclusion of marginalized households, and the pervasive racial wealth gap. In recent years, student debt has been more prominent within these analyses, as UFE works to help Americans understand the connections among the economic forces buffeting their prospects.

Veterans Education Success

Veterans Education Success (VES) was created to ensure that the GI Bill was implemented correctly and that veterans' rights and opportunities were protected, following an Executive Order signed by President Obama on January 10, 2013. Prior to this order, a Senate Investigation had uncovered predatory practices of for-profit colleges targeting veterans with the goal of securing GI Bill money, while not guaranteeing high-quality educational programming or strong return on degree. VES provides reports and news pertaining to predatory practices of for-profit college and actions being to protect veterans. VES also provides assistance to veterans who have been deceived by for-profit colleges, resulting in student debt and little to show for it. These actions—while currently limited to those eligible for GI Bill benefits—may create a precedent for providing help to those whose educational and wealth prospects have been harmed by predatory institutional practices, a population not confined to veterans.

Woodstock Institute

Woodstock Institute is a leading nonprofit research and policy organization in the areas of fair lending, wealth creation, and financial systems reform. Woodstock Institute works locally and nationally to create a financial system in which lower-wealth persons and communities of color can safely borrow, save, and build wealth so that they can achieve economic security and community prosperity. The Woodstock Institute's key tools with which to accomplish this vision include applied research, policy development, coalition building, and technical assistance. Woodstock Institute has been a recognized economic justice leader and bridge-builder between communities and policymakers in this field since it was founded in 1973. Now based in Chicago, Woodstock works with community and philanthropic groups, financial institutions, and policymakers. Funded by foundation grants, consulting fees, and charitable donations, Woodstock Institute conducts research on financial products and practices, promotes effective state and federal policies, convenes a coalition of community investment stakeholders working to improve access to credit, and helps people use its work to understand the issues and develop and implement solutions. Katie Buitrago, of the Woodstock Institute's staff, has recently focused some of her research energies on student lending, including the predatory practices of for-profit institutions and the private lenders with which they partner. "Starting out Behind: Trends in Student Loan Burdens at For-Profit Colleges" used National Postsecondary Student Aid Study data to draw attention to this perfect storm and the harm rendered to vulnerable potential students.

Young Invincibles

Young Invincibles (YI), now a national organization, is the outgrowth of an effort by a group of law students in 2009 to create a forum for young adults to have a voice in the national healthcare reform debate. YI receives fiscal sponsorship from the Center for Community Change and grants from a variety of foundations such as the Robert Wood Johnson Foundation, the Annie E. Casey Foundation, and the Kauffman Foundation. YI's national office is located in Washington, DC, with others in New York City, New York; Chicago, Illinois; Houston, Texas; and Los Angeles, California. Today, YI continues to mobilize 18- to 34-year-olds to ensure that their interests are represented in policy efforts pertaining to economic opportunity (specifically, health care, education, and jobs).

YI provides easy-to-digest information on higher education financial aid and student debt through the use of blogs, fact sheets, personal stories, infographics, press releases, and social media. In 2015, it released a report titled "College Information Design and Delivery—Insights from the Cognitive Information Processing Literature" to explore how individuals search for information to make financial decisions for college, how they process that information, and how various characteristics influence the processing of this information (Whitsett & Allison, 2015). YI also created an agenda for higher education in the 21st century, calling for reforms to create debt-free college pathways, improve the quality of higher education received, and decrease payments for existing student debt (YI, 2015). YI staff speak frequently on issues relevant to young adults, including higher education financing and, specifically, student debt. Furthermore, YI's Student Impact initiative provides resources and other tools that enable students to organize and advocate for accessible and affordable postsecondary education at the state level. This initiative is currently active in California, Arizona, Texas, Ohio, Virginia, North Carolina, and Florida.

Organizations Providing Resources and Relief for Borrowers

Debt.org

Debt.org provides free, online resources to help people understand and manage their debt and secure financial well-being.

They have resources specifically devoted to helping students understand student loans and student loan debt, providing them with resources to manage that debt and with financial tips such as how to create a budget. This is one of many organizations that provide tools to help consumers manage debt that, then, have increasingly focused on student loans, given the ascendance of this financing mechanism and its consequences on the financial realities of American households.

Hamilton Project

Launched in 2006 as an economic policy initiative at the Brookings Institution, the Hamilton Project is guided by an advisory council of academics, business leaders, and former public policymakers. The project provides a platform for a broad range of leading economic thinkers to inject innovative and pragmatic policy options into the national debate. The project offers proposals rooted in evidence and experience, not in doctrine and ideology, and brings those ideas to bear on policy debates in relevant and effective ways. While the Hamilton Project conducts research related to financial aid and higher education financing, of relevance to those contending with student debt is the Hamilton Project's Undergraduate Student Loan calculator, an interactive feature that shows the share of earnings necessary to service traditional loan repayment for each of 80 academic majors. This tool aims to help students project their own experiences with student loan repayment, even prior to college enrollment.

StudentDebt.org

This site provides education, free counseling, and access to government programs to assist struggling consumers, including those dealing with repayment of student debt. Specifically in regard to student borrowing, the site aims to help borrowers understand the terms of its particular financing, available repayment options, and the implications of various repayment decisions. Underscoring the relative complexity of the system of repayment options, the site also facilitates advisor review of borrowers' current financial situation and student loan debt to help determine if they are eligible for federal programs to assist in paying down student loans.

Student Debt Crisis

As a nonprofit organization operating from the premise that a well-educated workforce is vital to competing in the global economy, Student Debt Crisis pursues reform of the current financial aid system. Student Debt Crisis focuses on education, legislation, and providing resources that support students using student loans. The message education wants to send is that a well-educated workforce benefits society, not just students receiving the education, so education must be available without the crushing burden of debt. Student Debt Crisis provides resources to help students learn about education loans, such as information about different types of loans, repayment options, and default. It also has a blog that provides ongoing information about student loans and higher education and a forum where it shares student debt stories submitted by individuals with personal experience. Student Debt Crisis is an example of organizations pushing for alternatives to debt-dependent financial aid and of the critical role that indebted young people are playing in catalyzing and sustaining this movement.

Student Groups and Movements

Strike Debt/Rolling Jubilee

An offshoot of the Occupy Wall Street movement that advocated for a more democratic economy as a way to reduce inequality, Strike Debt is a nationwide movement of debt resisters fighting for economic justice and democratic freedom. Using direct action, research, education, and creative arts, Strike Debt brings students and other activists together to challenge student debt as an illegitimate system while imagining and creating alternatives. As described in Chapter 1 of this volume, among the actions of this organization are strategic "bailouts" of particular groups of student debtors, a strategy that provides both tangible relief and important publicity to the cause of student debt relief.

Student Labor Action Project, Fighting for a Debt-Free Future

The Student Labor Action Project's (SLAP's) unique model of organizing students as part of a grassroots working-class movement aims to support successful mobilization of student power. Working with Jobs with Justice and the United States Student Association, SLAP supports the growing student movement for economic justice by making links between campus and community organizing. SLAP provides skills trainings to build lasting student organizations and develops campaigns that win concrete victories for working families, all while breaking the poverty cycle by fighting for access to higher education and full and fair employment. This allows students to recognize power relationships in a much larger fight, where students are fundamentally connected to workers and workers to students.

Studentloanjustice.org

Student Loan Justice is a grassroots, citizens organization dedicated to returning standard consumer protections to student loans, including discharge in bankruptcy, stricter limits on servicing tactics, and broader measures for hardship relief. The group was started in March 2005 and has focused primarily on research, media outreach, and grassroots lobbying initiatives.

United States Student Association

The United States Student Association (USSA) is a student-led organization that fights for education justice. USSA is both the largest and oldest national student group in the United States. USSA uses grassroots efforts to empower and mobilize students to work toward a just society. It hosts two conventions each year, during which students elect the board of directors, set the direction of the USSA's work for the year, and participate in policy work. USSA provides resources for students who want to become involved in campaigns, start a USSA chapter, and organize a movement. USSA believes education is a right. As such, its national education justice platform includes multiple items related to public higher education institutions such as tuition-free college, debt forgiveness by the Department of Education, and supporting the Reducing Educational Debt (RED) Act in order to increase Pell Grant awards and allow more equitable refinancing of student loans.

Media Organizations

Hechinger News Service

Hechinger News Service is an independent education news service that produces regular content related to education reform, equity in educational outcomes, higher education financing and stratification, and the perspectives of critical voices within the education sector. Hechinger's mission centers on bringing to light inequities in American education and publicizing promising innovations to close achievement gaps and make education a more equitable force for prosperity and mobility.

Huffington Post

The *Huffington Post*, known as a liberal political media outlet, aggregates news and provides blogs on timely topics. It was founded in 2005 by Arianna Huffington and was acquired by AOL in 2011. In 2012, the *Huffington Post* was awarded the Pulitzer Prize for its national reporting. With strong audiences among young adult readers, the Huffington Post regularly reports on higher education and student debt. The *Huffington Post* features both earned media coverage of new developments in education policy, trends, and outcomes as well as opinion and commentary from prominent analysts, policymakers, and educators and from students contending with different aspects of the educational system.

References

Akers, B. (2014). *How much is too much? Evidence on financial well-being and student loan debt.* Washington, DC: American Enterprise Institute.

Akers, B., & Chingos, M. (2014). *Is a student loan crisis on the horizon?* Washington, DC: Brown Center on Education Policy, Brookings Institution.

Baum, S., Breneman, D. W., Chingos, M. M., Ehrenberg, R. G., Fowler, P., Hayek, J., & Scott-Clayton, J. (2012). *Beyond need and merit: Strengthening state grant programs.* Washington, DC: Brookings Institution, Brown Center on Education Policy.

Baum, S., & Johnson, M. (2015). *Student debt: Who borrows most? And what lies ahead?* Washington, DC: Urban Institute.

Baum, S. R., Kurose, C., & Ma, J. (2013). *How college shapes lives: Understanding the issues.* New York: College Board.

Baum, S., Ma, J., & Payea, K. (2010). *Education pays, 2010: The benefits of higher education for individuals and society. Trends in higher education* series. New York: College Board.

Baum, S., & Payea, K. (2004). *Education pays, 2004: The benefits of higher education for individuals and society. Trends in higher education* series. New York: College Board.

Baum, S., & Steele, P. (2010). *Who borrows most? Bachelor's degree recipients with high levels of student debt. Trends in higher education* Series. New York: College Board. Retrieved from https://trends.collegeboard.org/sites/default/files/trends-2010-who-borrows-most-brief.pdf

Blumenstyk, G. (2014, April 4). More financial aid + less need to work = more STEM graduates. *The Chronicle of Higher Education.* Retrieved from http://chronicle.com/blogs/headcount/more-financial-aid-less-need-to-work-more-stem-grads/38121

Brown, M., & Caldwell, S. (2013). *Young adult student loan borrowers retreat from housing and auto markets* (1–21). New York: Federal Reserve Bank of New York.

Brown, M., Haughwout, A., Lee, D., Scally, J., & van der Klaauw, W. (2014). Measuring student debt and its performance, Federal Reserve Bank of New York Staff Report No. 668. Retrieved from http://www.newyorkfed. org/research/staff_reports/sr668.pdf

Castleman, B.L., and Long, B.T. (2013). Beyond Enrollment: The Causal Effect of Need-Based Grants on College Access, Persistence, and Graduation. Cambridge, MA: National Bureau of Economic Research. Retrieved from: http:// www.nber.org/papers/w19306.

Chopra, R. (2015a, October 8). Consumer protection and higher education financing alternatives: Testimony before the U.S. Congress Joint Economic Committee. Washington, DC: Center for American Progress. Retrieved from https:// www.americanprogress.org/issues/higher-education/ report/2015/10/08/123004/consumer-protectio n-and-higher-education-financing-alternatives/

Chopra, R. (2015b, October 30). Five steps to keep student loans for ruining your life. *Time*. Retrieved on from http:// time.com/money/4092462/student-loans-dont-ruin-life/

Darolia, R. (2013a). *Student loan repayment and college accountability*. Federal Reserve Bank of Philadelphia Payment Cards Center Discussion Paper Series D-2013. Philadelphia, PA: Federal Reserve Bank of Philadelphia.

Darolia, R. (2013b). Integrity versus access? The effect of federal financial aid availability on postsecondary enrollment. *Journal of Public Economics, 106*, 101–114.

Darolia, R. (2016, June). *An experiment on information use in college student loan decisions* (Working Paper No. 16–18). Philadelphia, PA: Federal Reserve Bank of Philadelphia.

Delisle, J. (2016, April 7). *Shifting burdens: How changes in financial aid affected what students and families paid for college from 1996 to 2012.* Washington, DC: New America. Retrieved from https://www.newamerica.org/education-policy/policy-papers/shifting-burdens/

Delisle, J., & Dancy, K. (2015, November 3). *A new look at tuition tax benefits.* Washington, DC: New America. Retrieved from https://www.newamerica.org/education-policy/policy-papers/a-new-look-at-tuition-tax-benefits/

Delisle, J., & Holt, A. (2013). *Beware savvy borrowers using income-based repayment.* Washington, DC: New America. Retrieved from http://www.edcentral.org/beware-savvy-borrowers-using-income-based-repayment/

Dwyer, R. E., Hodson, R., & McCloud, L. (2013). Gender, debt, and dropping out of college. *Gender & Society, 27*(1), 30–55.

Dwyer, R. E., McCloud, L., & Hodson, R. (2011). Youth debt, mastery, and self-esteem: Class-stratified effects of indebtedness on self-concept. *Social Science Research, 40*(3), 727–741.

Dwyer, R. E., McCloud, L., & Hodson, R. (2012). Debt and graduation from American universities. *Social Forces, 90*(4), 1133–1155.

Dynarski, S. (2016a, May 2). How to—and how to not—manage student debt. *Milken Institute Review.* Retrieved from http://www.milkenreview.org/articles/how-to-and-how-not-to-manage-student-debt

Dynarski, S. (2016b, May 3). *The dividing line between haves and have-nots in home ownership: Education, not student debt.* Washington, DC: The Brookings Institution. Retrieved from http://www.brookings.edu/~/media/research/files/reports/2016/05/03-home-ownership-dynarski/home-ownership-final2b.pdf

Elliott, W., & Lewis, M. (2015). *The real college debt crisis: How student borrowing threatens financial well-being and erodes the American dream.* Santa Barbara: Praeger.

Elliott, W., Lewis, M., & Johnson, P. (2014). Unequal outcomes: Student loan effects on young adults' net worth accumulation. Lawrence, KS: Assets and Education Initiative.

Elliott, W., Lewis, M., Nam, I., & Grinstein-Weiss, M. (2014). Student loan debt: Can parental college savings help? *Federal Reserve Bank of St. Louis Review, 96*(4), 331–357.

Elliott, W., & Nam, I. (2013). Is student debt jeopardizing the long-term financial health of U.S. households? *Review, 95*(5), 1–20. Retrieved from https://www.stlouisfed.org/household-financial-stability/events/20130205/papers/Elliott.pdf

Emmons, W. R., & Noeth, B. (2015). *Why didn't higher education protect Hispanic and black wealth?* St. Louis, MO: Federal Reserve Bank of St. Louis. Retrieved from https://www.stlouisfed.org/publications/in-the-balance/issue12–2015/why-didnt-higher-education-protect-hispanic-and-black-wealth

Emmons, W. R., & Ricketts, L. R. (2015). *The importance of wealth is growing.* St. Louis, MO: Federal Reserve Bank of St. Louis. Retrieved from https://www.stlouisfed.org/publications/in-the-balance/issue-13–2015/the-importance-of-wealth-is-growing

Fry, R. (2014). Young adults, student debt, and economic well-being. *Pew Research Center's social and demographic trends project,* Washington, DC. Retrieved on from http://www.pewsocialtrends.org/files/2014/05/ST_2014.05.14_student-debt_complete-report.pdf

Goldrick-Rab, S. (2016). *Paying the price: College costs, financial aid, and the betrayal of the American dream.* Chicago, IL: University of Chicago Press.

Hamilton, D., & Darity, W. (2016). *The political economy of education, financial literacy, and the racial wealth gap.* St. Louis, MO: Federal Research Bank of St. Louise. Retrieved from https://www.stlouisfed.org/~/media/Files/PDFs/HFS/20160525/papers/Hamilton-paper.pdf

Heller, D. E. (2001). *The states and public higher education policy: Affordability, access, and accountability.* Baltimore, MA: Johns Hopkins University Press.

Heller, D. E. (Ed.). (2002). *Condition of access: Higher education for lower income students.* Westport, CT: American Council on Education/Praeger.

Heller, D. E. (2008). The impact of student loans on college access. In S. Baum, M. McPherson, & P. Steele (Eds.), *The effectiveness of student aid policies: What the research tells us* (pp. 39–67). New York, NY: The College Board.

Heller, D. E. (Ed.). (2011). *The states and public higher education policy: Affordability, access, and accountability* (2nd ed.). Baltimore, MA: Johns Hopkins University Press.

Heller, D. E., & d'Ambrosio, M. (Eds.). (2009). *Generational shockwaves and the implications for higher education.* Northampton, MA: Edward Elgar Publishing.

Hiltonsmith, R. (2013). At what cost: How student debt reduces lifetime wealth. Washington, DC: Demos.

Hiltonsmith, R. (2014). The great cost shift continues: State higher education funding after the recession. Washington, DC: Demos.

Hiltonsmith, R. (2015). Pulling up the higher-ed ladder: Myth and reality in the crisis of college affordability. Washington, DC: Demos.

Houle, J. (2014a). Disparities in debt: Parents' socioeconomic resources and young adult student loan debt. *Sociology of Education, 87*(1), 53–69.

Houle, J. (2014b). Mental health in the foreclosure crisis. *Social Science & Medicine, 118,* 1–8.

Houle, J., & Berger, L. (2015). *The end of the American dream? Student loan debt and home buying among young adults.* Washington, DC: Third Way. Retrieved from http://www.thirdway.org/report/the-end-of-the-american-dream-student-loan-debt-and-homeownership-among-young-adults

Houle, J., Collins, J. M., & Schmeiser, M. (2015). Flu and finances: Influenza outbreaks and loan defaults in U.S. cities, 2004–2012. *American Journal of Public Health, 105*(9), e75–e80.

Houle, J., & Light, M. (2014). The home foreclosure crisis and rising suicide rates, 2005–2010. *American Journal of Public Health, 104*, 1073–1079.

Houle, J., & Keene, D. (2015). Getting sick and falling behind: Health and the risk of mortgage default and home foreclosure. *Journal of Epidemiology and Community Health, 69*, 382–387.

Huelsman, M. (2015, May). The debt divide: The racial and class bias behind the "new normal" of student borrowing. Washington, DC: Demos. Retrieved from http://www.demos.org/sites/default/files/publications/The%20Debt%20Divide.pdf

Huelsman, M., Draut, T., Meschede, T., Dietrich, L., Shapiro, T., & Sullivan, L. (2015). Less debt, more equity: Lowering student debt while closing the black-white wealth gap. Washington, DC: Demos. Retrieved from http://www.demos.org/publication/less-debt-more-equity-lowering-student-debt-while-closing-black-white-wealth-gap

Huelsman, M. (2016, July). A leg up: How a privileged minority is graduating without debt. Washington, DC: Demos. Retrieved from http://www.demos.org/publication/a-leg-up-how-privileged-minority-graduating-without-debt

Kamenetz, A. (2006). *Generation debt: Why now is a terrible time to be young.* New York, NY: Riverhead Hardcover.

Kamenetz, A. (2010). *DIY U: Edupunks, edupreneurs, and the coming transformation of higher education.* White River Junction, VT: Chelsea Green Publishing.

Kamenetz, A. (2015). *The test: Why our schools are obsessed with standardized testing-but you don't have to be.* New York: The Perseus Books Group.

Kelly, A., & Goldrick-Rab, S. (Eds.) (2014). *Reinventing financial aid: Charting a new course to college affordability.* Cambridge, MA: Harvard Education Press.

Lemann, N. (2015, July 6). The real student-debt crisis. *The New Yorker.* Retrieved from http://www.newyorker.com/news/news-desk/the-real-student-debt-crisis

Long, B. T. (2004). How do financial aid policies affect colleges? The institutional impact of the Georgia HOPE scholarship. *Journal of Human Resources, 39*(4), 1045–1066.

Long, B. T., & Riley, E. (2007). Financial aid: A broken bridge to college access? *Harvard Economic Review, 77*(1), 39–63.

Miller, B. (2016, May). Building a student-level data system. Washington, DC: Center for American Progress. Retrieved from http://www.ihep.org/sites/default/files/uploads/postsecdata/docs/resources/building_a_student-level_data_system.pdf

Miller, B. (2015, June). The relationship between student debt and college completion. Washington, DC: Center for American Progress. Retrieved from https://www.americanprogress.org/issues/higher-education/news/2015/06/26/116019/the-relationship-between-student-debt-and-college-completion/.

Nau, M., Dwyer, R. E., & Hodson, R. (2015). Can't afford a baby? Debt and young Americans. *Research in Social Stratification and Mobility, 42*, 114–122.

Perna, L. (2008). Understanding high school students' willingness to borrow to pay college prices. *Research in Higher Education, 49*(7), 589–606.

Perna, L. W. (2010a). *Understand the working college student: New research and its implications for policy and practice.* Sterling, VA: Stylus.

Perna, L. W. (2010b). Toward a more complete understanding of the role of financial aid in promoting college enrollment: The importance of context. In J. C. Smart (Ed.), *Higher education: Handbook of theory and research.* New York, NY: Springer Publishing.

Perna, L. W., & Jones, A. (Eds.). (2013). *The state of college access and completion: Improving college success for students from underrepresented groups.* New York, NY: Routledge.

Perna, L. W., & Steele, P. (2011). The role of context in understanding the contributions of financial aid to college opportunity. *Teachers College Record, 113*, 895–933.

Pfeffer, F. T., Danziger, S. H., & Schoeni, F. R. (2013). Wealth disparities before and after the Great Recession. *Annals of the American Academy of Political and Social Science, 650*(1), 98–123.

Pfeffer, F. T., & Hertel, F. R. (2015). How has educational expansion shaped social mobility trends in the United States? *Social Forces, 94*(1), 143–180.

Shapiro, T., Meschede, T., & Osoro, S. (2013). The roots of the widening racial wealth gap: Explaining the black-white economic divide. Waltham, MA: Institute on Assets and Social Policy, Brandeis University. Retrieved from http://iasp.brandeis.edu/pdfs/Author/shapiro-thomas-m/racialwealthgapbrief.pdf

Shaw, K., Goldrick-Rab, S., Mazzeo, C., & Jacobs, J. (2006). *Putting poor people to work: How the work-first idea eroded college access for the poor.* New York, NY: Russell Sage Foundation.

Shaw, K. M., & Heller, D. E. (2007). *State postsecondary education research: New methods to inform policy and practice.* Sterling, VA: Stylus Publishing, LLC.

St. John, E. P., & Asker, E. (2003). *Refinancing the college dream: Access, equal opportunity, and justice for tax payers.* Baltimore, MD: Johns Hopkins University Press.

St. John, E. P., Milazzo Bigelow, V. J., Lijana, K. C., & Masse, J. C. (2015). *Left behind: Urban high schools and the failure of market reform.* Baltimore, MD: Johns Hopkins University Press.

St. John, E. P., & Parsons, M. D. (Eds.). (2005). *Public funding of higher education: changing contexts and new rationales.* Baltimore, MD: Johns Hopkins University Press.

Whitsett, H., & Allison, T. (May 2015). *College information design and delivery—insights from the cognitive information processing literature.* Washington, DC: Young Invincibles. Retrieved from http://younginvincibles.org/collegeinformationdesigndelivery/

YI (June 2015). A higher education promise for the 21st century. Retrieved from http://younginvincibles.org/wp-content/uploads/2015/06/YI-Higher-Ed-Agenda.pdf

AMERICAN EXPRESS
VISA
MasterCard
Calling Benefits:
1 800 308-6537

Data

Figure 5.1 illustrates two critical facts about the distribution of student borrowing in the United States today. First, that some American

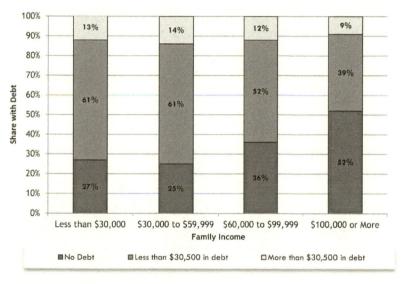

Figure 5.1   Student Debt by Family Income

Source: Figure 1, Student Debt by Family Income, Bachelor's Degree Recipients, 2008. Complete file available at The Debt Divide: The Racial and Class Bias behind the "New Normal" of Student Borrowing. Washington, DC: Demos. Retrieved July 12, 2016, from http://www.demos.org/publication/debt-divide-racial-and-class-bias-behind-new-normal-student-borrowing. Used with permission from Demos.

Student debt has surpassed credit card debt, and even many who practice "responsible" borrowing find themselves contending with unmanageable balances. (AP Photo/Elise Amendola)

*students are still able to complete college—particularly, an under-
graduate degree—without resorting to student loans, although borrowing is widespread, especially for those coming from lower-income
households. Second, while most student borrowers have debts that
most would not consider "high-dollar," low- and moderate-income
borrowers are more likely than the wealthy to owe large student
debts that, of course, they have fewer resources to confront.*

*Figure 5.2 further examines inequity in the student debt distribution,
with African Americans and low-income students (measured by the
receipt of Pell Grants), in particular, more frequently resorting to borrowing to finance their higher educations. The figure also underscores
differences in the usage of student loans among the same groups of
students at different types of institutions, pointing to the significance of
institutional selection as a contributor to student outcomes.*

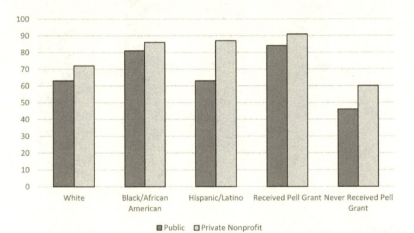

Figure 5.2   Student Loan Debt by Race/Ethnicity and Class

Source: Data from U.S. Department of Education, 2011–2012 National
Postsecondary Student Aid Study, Analysis from The Debt Divide: The Racial
and Class Bias behind the "New Normal" of Student Borrowing. Washington,
DC: Demos. Retrieved July 12, 2016, from http://www.demos.org/publication/
debt-divide-racial-and-class-bias-behind-new-normal-student-borrowing

As Figure 5.3 illustrates, not only do students of color and those disadvantaged by low incomes borrow more frequently than white students and those economically privileged; when they do borrow, they often rely more heavily on student loans to finance their educations, resulting in larger loan balances, as well.

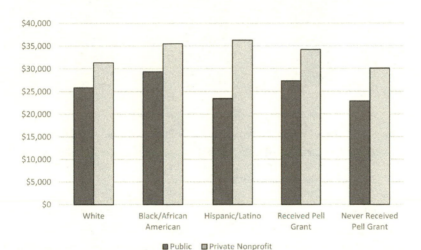

Figure 5.3   Average Debt for Bachelor's Degree Recipients

Source: Data from U.S. Department of Education, 2011–2012 National Postsecondary Student Aid Study, Analysis from The Debt Divide: The Racial and Class Bias behind the "New Normal" of Student Borrowing. Washington, DC: Demos. Retrieved July 12, 2016, from http://www.demos.org/publication/debt-divide-racial-and-class-bias-behind-new-normal-student-borrowing

Figure 5.4 compares the use of student loans and average loan amount for graduates from the class of 2012 receiving their bachelor's degree at different types of institutions: public, private non-profit, and private for-profit. The data underscore that very few students graduate from for-profit institutions without relying on loans and show how different institutional practices and prices can affect overall indebtedness.

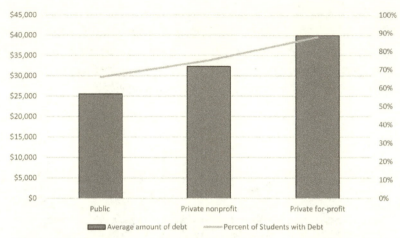

Figure 5.4   Use of Student Loans and Cumulative Debt, by Institution Type

Source: Author's calculations from *Student Debt and the Class of 2012*. Oakland, CA: The Institute for College Access & Success. Retrieved July 12, 2016, from http://ticas.org/content/pub/student-debt-and-class-2012

Bachelor's degree recipients are not the only American students whose student debt burdens have grown in recent years; as Figure 5.5 shows, students striving for associate's degrees have also

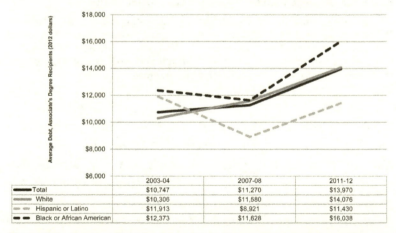

	2003-04	2007-08	2011-12
Total	$10,747	$11,270	$13,970
White	$10,306	$11,580	$14,076
Hispanic or Latino	$11,913	$8,921	$11,430
Black or African American	$12,373	$11,628	$16,038

Figure 5.5   Average Debt for Associate's Degree Recipients, over Time

Source: "During the Great Recession, Average Debt Spiked for Associate's Degree Recipients." Complete document available at The Debt Divide: The Racial and Class Bias behind the "New Normal" of Student Borrowing. Washington, DC: Demos. Retrieved July 12, 2016, from http://www.demos.org/publication/debt-divide-racial-and-class-bias-behind-new-normal-student-borrowing. Used with permission from Demos.

seen increases in their debt accumulation, with African Americans being hit particularly hard by student debt at these early levels of postsecondary educational attainment.

Figure 5.6 shows the change in the composition of higher education finance over the past 20 years, specifically, how net tuition consti- tutes a significantly higher percentage of total education spending, as state support has decreased somewhat, in constant 2015 dollars. Along with analysis that has more precisely attributed increases in student loan burden to eroding public support for higher education, figures such as this illustrate the extent to which today's student debt crisis can be understood as part of the "cost shift" in higher educa- tion, with students and families picking up an ever-greater share of the higher education tab.

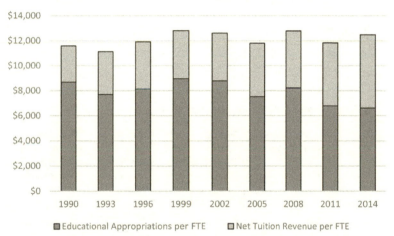

Figure 5.6 Trends in Education Finance: Appropriations for Postsecondary Education and Net Tuition

Source: State Higher Education Executive Officers (2015). *State Higher Education Finance: FY2015.* Retrieved July 12, 2016, from http://sheeo.org/sites/default/ files/project-files/SHEEO_FY15_Report_051816.pdf

Figure 5.7 illustrates how average amount borrowed per under- graduate student tripled between 1993 and 2012, while the per- centage of students incurring student debt rose from fewer than half of students in the early 1990s to almost three-quarters 20 years later.

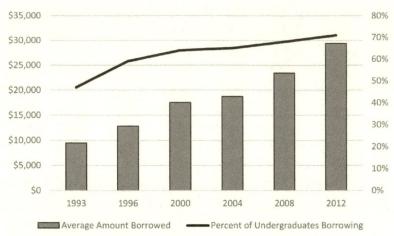

Figure 5.7   Twenty-Year Trend in Student Loan Utilization

Source: Data from U.S. Department of Education, 2011–2012 National Postsecondary Student Aid Study.

Table 5.1 compares student debt holding and average amounts of student debt—in U.S. dollars, converted using a purchasing power parity index—in the United States, Canada, and selected

Table 5.1   Student Debt in Selected Countries

Country	PSE Spending as Percent of GDP	Percentage of Students Who Have a Loan	Average Amount of Loan (in USD, Converted Using Purchasing Power Parity)	Percentage of 25- to 34-Year-Olds with PSE Credential
Australia	1.18	77.1	$3,507	47
Canada	1.88	NA	$4,421	57
Finland	2.08	27.7	$1,200	40
The Netherlands	1.61	33.4	$2,646	43
United Kingdom	1.27	83.9	$10,070	48
United States	1.36	71	$15,510	44

Source: Data from *Student Debt in Selected Countries* (November 2015). European Expert Network on Economics of Education. Retrieved July 12, 2016, from www.eenee.de/dms/EENEE/Analytical_Reports/EENEE_AR25.pdf

European countries. The table also includes spending on postsecondary education, as a percentage of GDP, and the outcome of these higher educational inputs: postsecondary credential holding, among the population aged 25–34.

Figure 5.8 illustrates two important dimensions of the higher education landscape in the United States today. First, there are significant differences in public support for public postsecondary education among states, distinctions that can result in considerably higher tuition prices and student costs in some states—and attendant student debt levels—compared to others. Second, public funding for higher education has declined in most states, in real dollars, since the Great Recession; in many cases, this funding has not been restored, even as states move into economic recovery.

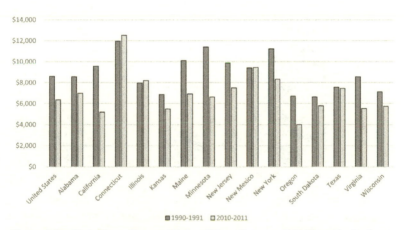

■ 1990-1991   □ 2010-2011

Figure 5.8   State Spending on Higher Education, per Full-Time Equivalent Student, in Constant 2010 Dollars

Source: Data from the Great Cost Shift: How Higher Education Cuts Undermine the Future Middle Class (2012). Washington, DC: Demos. Retrieved July 12, 2016, from   http://www.demos.org/publication/great-cost-shift-how-higher-education-cuts-undermine-future-middle-class

This chart compares estimated undergraduate expenses at three different types of postsecondary educational institutions: public two-year (community college) commuter schools, public four-year institutions (assuming in-state tuition eligibility and on-campus residence), and private nonprofit four-year on-campus living.

Figure 5.9 illustrates the differences in total expected expenditures by institution—more than three times higher at a private non-profit school than a two-year community college—and also the significance of nontuition expenditures—greater than tuition/fees at all but private, nonprofit universities. This latter point is critical for understanding the limitations of "free college" as a solution to the student loan crisis today.

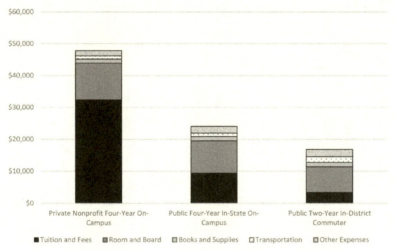

Figure 5.9   Average Estimated Full-Time Undergraduate Budgets, 2015–2016

Source: Data from the College Board Annual Survey, analyzed in *Trends in Student Aid 2015*. Retrieved from https://trends.collegeboard.org/student-aid

Figure 5.10 illustrates that the increase in total student loan debt in the United States, an amount that peaked in 2010, has declined somewhat in recent years, but stands today more than three times greater than 20 years ago. The chart also shows the growth in federal unsubsidized loans, which make up a greater share of total debt held than a generation ago, having grown particularly in relation to federally subsidized student borrowing.

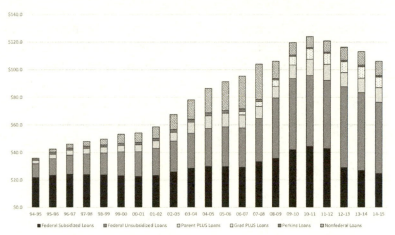

Figure 5.10 Total Student Loan Debt, in Millions of (2014) Dollars

Source: Data from *Trends in Student Aid 2015.* Retrieved from https://trends.collegeboard.org/student-aid

Documents

College Opportunity for a Better America Act (March 18, 2003)

Congress has offered several proposals to expand student loan forgiveness, in an effort to provide politically popular relief to student borrowers while also attempting to mitigate the distorting effects that student debt can have on students' career and life choices. Significantly, this legislation includes language emphasizing the importance of college for upward mobility and expressing concern about the consequences of student borrowing, yet still fails to provide substantial relief to the majority of student borrowers.

To provide student loan forgiveness to Americans employed in service to the public, and for other purposes, Be it enacted by the Senate and House of Representatives of the United States of America in Congress assembled,

Section 1. Short Title; References

(a) Short Title.—This Act may be cited as the "College Opportunity for a Better America Act of 2003".

(b) Reference.—Except as otherwise expressly provided in this Act, whenever in this Act an amendment or repeal is expressed in terms of an amendment to, or repeal of, a section or other provision, the reference shall be considered to be made to a section or other provision of the Higher Education Act of 1965 (20 U.S.C. 1001 et seq.).

Sec. 2. Findings

The Congress finds the following:

(1) Education after high school, including two-year and four-year college degrees, is more important than ever for Americans' future economic security. A four-year college degree is estimated to be worth $1 million in earnings more than a high school diploma over the course of a lifetime.

(2) The cost of attending college has steadily increased faster than the rate of inflation. The average tuition and fees at four-year public and private universities are now $4,081 and $18,273, respectively, an increase of approximately 75 percent over the past decade.

(3) More and more, American students are relying on debt to finance higher education. In 1999–2000, the average student loan debt totaled $16,948, a dramatic increase from the average debt of $9,188 in 1992–93. At the same time, the percentage of students borrowing increased from 42 percent to 64 percent.

(4) Student debt constrains the career options of millions of college graduates. Nearly two-fifths of graduates with debt find it unmanageable, defined as exceeding eight percent of their income. As a result, many college graduates may chose higher-paying jobs rather than enter public service.

(5) Many of our Nation's public service professions, including teaching, nursing, and child care, face shortages of highly qualified personnel that imperil the health and future welfare of our citizens.

(6) Record school enrollments, an aging teaching force, and chronic attrition of new teachers make it difficult to ensure that every child has a qualified, engaged, caring teacher. Excellent teachers are particularly rare in high-poverty schools and in subjects like mathematics, science, and special education.

(7) There is a national shortage of 126,000 nurses, according to the American Hospital Association. At the same time, the number of nursing school graduates decreased by 29 percent between 1995 and 2001.

(8) According to a growing body of research, the single most important determinant of child care quality is the presence of consistent, well-trained child care providers. However, the Nation's child care programs are plagued by high staff turnover fueled by poor compensation.

(9) A well-trained and stable child welfare workforce is needed to protect our country's most vulnerable children and families. The number of unfilled child welfare jobs is large and growing rapidly. Nearly one-tenth of positions in State child welfare agencies are unfilled and staff turnover has doubled since 1991.

(10) The number of infant and toddler specialists are insufficient to meet the health and special education needs of infants and toddlers.

Sec. 3. Loan Forgiveness For Public Service Employees

Section 428K (20 U.S.C. 1078–11) is amended to read as follows:

"SEC. 428K. LOAN FORGIVENESS FOR PUBLIC SER-
VICE EMPLOYEES.

"(a) Purposes.—The purposes of this section are—

"(1) to reduce the burden of student debt, particularly for
Americans who dedicate their careers to meeting certain urgent national needs; and

"(2) to attract more excellent individuals into important
public service careers.

"(b) Loan Forgiveness.—

"(1) In general.—The Secretary shall assume the obligation
to repay, pursuant to subsection (c), a loan made under
section 428 or 428H, a Federal Direct Stafford Loan or
Federal Direct Unsubsidized Stafford Loan, a Federal
Direct Consolidation Loan, or a Federal Perkins Loan
for any new borrower after the date of enactment of the
Higher Education Amendments of 1998, who—

"(A) is employed full time in a qualified public service
position described in paragraph (2); and

"(B) is not in default on a loan for which the borrower
seeks forgiveness.

"(2) Qualified public service positions.—For purposes of
this section, an individual shall be treated as employed
in a qualified public service position if the individual
is any of the following:

[NOTE: Legislation then defines 'highly-qualified teachers in low-income communities and of mathematics,
science, and bilingual and special education', 'early childhood educators', 'nurses', 'child welfare workers', 'nutri-
tion professionals', and 'infant/toddler specialists'. Loan
forgiveness is also outlined for:

"(G) Additional public servants.—An individual who,
as determined by the Secretary of Education by
regulation—

"(i) works in a public service profession that suffers from a critical lack of qualified personnel;

"(ii) serves a low-income or needy community; and

"(iii) is highly qualified.

"(c) Loan Repayment.—

"(1) In general.—The Secretary shall assume the obligation to repay—

"(A) after each of the first or second years of service by an individual in a qualified public service position, 15 percent of the total amount of principal and interest of the loans described in subsection

(b)(1) to such individual that are outstanding immediately preceding such first year of such service;

"(B) after each of the third or fourth years of such service, 20 percent of such total amount; and

"(C) after the fifth year of such service, 30 percent of such total amount.

[NOTE: Legislation also describes treatment of consolidated loans and clarifies that individuals are not eligible for repayment under these provisions and national service awards, simultaneously.]

Source: 108th CONGRESS (1st Session), H.R. 1306: To provide student loan forgiveness to Americans employed in service to the public, and for other purposes (March 18, 2003). Retrieved from https://www.govinfo.gov/content/pkg/BILLS-108hr1306ih/html/BILLS-108hr1306ih.htm

Senate Hearing, "Higher Education, Higher Cost, and Higher Debt" (February 16, 2007)

This excerpt of a hearing of the 110th Congress (1st session) examining college affordability, higher education costs, and student debt considers the expertise shared by leaders from fields of personal

*finance, financial aid, and economic mobility. Coming shortly be-
fore the onset of crises in the housing and labor markets, with the
beginning of the Great Recession, this hearing provides some insights into conditions in student debt and education financing immediately preceding this more widespread financial distress. In the
interest of brevity, only the statements of Senator Edward Kennedy
(chair, D-MA) and Senator Michael Enzi (vice-chair, R-WY) are
included. These statements facilitate comparison and contrast of
the perspectives of both major political parties on student debt,
in regard to the dominant themes of the congressional debate on
student loans.*

The Chairman. We'll come to order. We thank all of our witnesses for coming this morning and it's a pleasure again to be
with my friend and my colleague, Senator Enzi, the Ranking
Member and Senator Isakson and we'll be joined by others as
the morning goes along. We also have a number of students
from George Washington University and the U.S. Students
Association, the American Medical Student Association, even
some young Democrats of America snuck in here this morning.
So we want to welcome all of our students and a very interest-
ing and worthwhile panel. Some 40 years ago, I was here when
the Senate drafted the higher education legislation. It had been
an issue that had been debated and discussed prior to the early
1960s and really, the issue was what is going to be the role of
national policy towards the young people of our country? Are
we going to recognize as a matter of national policy that we
ought to provide some help and assistance to young, talented,
creative, gifted students who are able to gain entrance into our
fine schools and colleges across this country? Because they are
limited in terms of their family's income, their own income,
are they to be denied that opportunity or is the United States
of America going to say to the young people of this Nation,
we're going to find a path so any individual, any student in
this country, young or old alike, that is able to gain entrance
into any school that they choose, will be able to put together

a financial package so that they would be able to go and also be able to come out of school without the heavy indebtedness, which is so often the case today? Assistance so that students during the time of their breaks between the various classes, are talking about their books rather than talking about the size of their student loans?

With the Higher Education Act, after a long debate and discussion, an issue was whether we were going to provide help and assistance to the students or help and assistance to the universities—it was a very hotly contested debate. We made the judgment decision that we were going to provide help and assistance to the students. And at that time, 80 percent of the Federal help and assistance to the students was in the form of grants, 20 percent in terms of loans and that trend has completely reversed in the past several years. We hear political leaders talk about our youth. We hear them talk about the future. We hear how important it is to have an educated youth because we're going to have to deal with the global economy and in order to be a leader in global economy, we're going to have to have an economy of inventiveness—and where will the inventiveness come from if we don't have the young and talented and creative students? We say that we're going to need a national security force that's going to be second to none to deal with the new kinds of threats. Where are we going to be able to get that unless we have the best and the brightest also be interested in protecting the Nation? We say we want our democracy to function and work so that we're the model for the rest of the world in terms of our values and in terms of our respect for human dignity. Obviously, for democracy to be able to work, we need people that know the issues, understand the kinds of questions and are willing to work and pursue their views on these matters. All of this, I think, necessitates that we try and find out how we can move back to that day when we, as a nation, were making education affordable.

What we've seen now in the recent times is that more than 400,000 students who otherwise would not go to college because of financial reasons. It isn't so much even about these students, or about their own obligations but they don't want to bring indebtedness to their families. They respect their parents who have worked hard, played by the rules and now have a very small retirement income. They don't want their parents to go out and have to borrow and indebt themselves even though many do. We have an application for financial aid that is mind-boggling in terms of its complexity and difficulty. Senator Enzi, who is by training and tradition, an accountant and an observer of the flow lines of resources, is helping the young people by making sure that we're going to try and simplify that.

Finally and most of all, a focus for today, we want a student loan program that is going to work for the students. I believe that too often, the student loan program is working for the banks. How can we turn that more towards the student? I think the good, old-fashioned way—by using competition. We found out that the student loan programs needed incentives to begin the program and it seems to me, we ought to be finding out how we can try and use the concepts of incentives and competition to try and move the costs, and the interest rates down, and the Pell Grants up for those young people, and to assist those who want to go into public service, we should put a cap on what they're going to have to pay out of a limited salary as a school teacher, working in child care, working as a legal assistant in public service, a whole range of public service jobs. If they're making $25,000, $28,000 in a career, and are trying to give something back into the community, give something back to their country, we'll ensure they're not going to be overwhelmed by student debt and that they will have their debt forgiven after a period of 10 years. So we have a plan but we are fortunate this morning to have people that have looked at these issues and studied them in depth and we're very grateful for the opportunity to listen to them. I'll put my full statement in the record and I'd ask Senator Enzi for whatever comments he'd like to make.

Prepared Statement of Senator Kennedy

I welcome our colleagues and witnesses for our hearing this morning on the increasingly serious problem of college access and affordability. It's affecting countless young people's basic life choices, from choosing a career to getting married, to buying a house and starting a family. I have a few charts that illustrate the challenges—it's not too much to call it a crisis. It's keeping 400,000 qualified students a year from attending a 4-year college. It's forcing many to rule out careers in public service—such as teaching, social work or law enforcement. They may be lower paying jobs, but many find them deeply rewarding in other ways, and they bring large rewards to our society. It's contributing to the increasing economic inequality in today's America, in which low-income and first-generation students are far less likely than others to earn a college degree, even though higher education is more important than ever to keep the doors of opportunity open in our modern society. In a word, it's a crisis that's tarnishing the American dream for millions, and we in Congress can't ignore it any longer. Today, 60 percent of new jobs require some postsecondary education compared to only 15 percent of new jobs half a century ago.

A major cause of the problem is cost. The cost of college has more than tripled in the past 20 years, and Federal aid hasn't kept up. Twenty years ago, the maximum Pell grant covered 55 percent of the cost of tuition, fees, room and board at a public 4-year college. Today it covers only 32 percent of those costs. As a result of rising costs and declining aid, more and more students are borrowing money to pay for college. In 1993, less than half of all graduates of 4-year colleges used student loans to finance their education. This year, it's two-thirds. The average college student graduates today with $17,500 in Federal student loans on graduation day. At public universities, student loan debt has more than doubled since 1993. Last month, the House of Representatives passed the College Student Relief Act, which cuts interest rates on new subsidized student loans in half. Because the last Congress allowed interest rates to rise, typical student borrowers—already straining under $17,500 in debt—have to pay an additional $5,800 for their college loans. The House bill would prevent this. That's good news for millions of borrowers across the country, and I commend Chairman George Miller and Speaker Pelosi for their leadership in making this legislation such a high priority at the beginning of this new Congress, and I hope the Senate will do the same.

We also need to do more to increase grant aid. Pell grants have been a lifeline to college for many low-income and middle-income students for more than 30 years. But last year, the average Pell Grant fell for the first time in 6 years. In the recent funding resolution, Congress took a significant step forward with a modest increase in the maximum Pell Grant by $260, from $4,050 to $4,310. My hope is that we can raise it to $5,100 in this Congress.

To prevent unreasonable debt burdens on students, we should cap student loan repayments at 15 percent of discretionary income, and offer loan forgiveness after 10 years to students who go into public service.

It's also long past time to reform the Federal student loan programs, so they work for students and families—not the banks. It's a scandal that has allowed these student loan programs to become corporate welfare for big lenders. We pay enormous subsidies to lenders to take part in the Federal student loan programs, and we ignored the enormous growth of the student loan industry.

Forty years ago, subsidies were needed to persuade lenders to take part. But today's, Federal subsidies make student loans the second most profitable business for banks—after credit cards. Something's obviously not right.

Of the two basic programs, the Federal Direct Loan program costs taxpayers much less than the private loan guarantee program funded by the banks and heavily subsidized by the Treasury. We need real competition between the two programs, and we could use the obvious savings from such competition to increase need-based aid.

The difference between the two Federal loan programs is obvious when you look at these charts prepared by the Government Accountability Office. Here is the program funded by the big lenders. It's an incomprehensible maze of rules and responsibilities, involving organizations the Direct Loan program doesn't need, and with money changing hands every which way.

The Direct Loan program, by contrast, is much simpler.

Instead of having lenders and guaranty agencies as middlemen, the government simply lends funds directly to the students—which is one reason why this program is less expensive for taxpayers than the one funded by the banks. Clearly, the Direct Loan program is the better alternative.

In addition, the private student loan market has grown thirteenfold—thirteenfold!—in the last decade. Students deserve protection from such gouging. We also need to be the insight over the sweetheart deals that lenders and schools are increasingly making to offer these loans to students. No students should have to mortgage their future in order to pay for higher education today. All these issues will be addressed in this year's reauthorization of the Higher Education Act. America can't be America without an educated citizenry. It's essential to the Nation's strength. Congress rose to a similar challenge after World War II. For every dollar we invested in the G.I. bill of rights, The Greatest Generation produced $7 in economic growth, and we must do the same today, because the need is so great and the stakes for the future are so profound. So I look forward to the testimony of our witnesses today, and to working with my colleagues in the months ahead to get the job done.

Opening Statement of Senator Enzi

Senator Enzi. Thank you very much, Mr. Chairman. I thank you for holding this hearing and I am particularly pleased that we have college students here and I want to particularly welcome those from the George Washington University—that's my alma mater. I did happen to notice this last week that the Board of Trustees changed the tuition slightly and it is now the most expensive university in the United States. So help is obviously needed. Now, we've built an important record of hearings and roundtables on these issues in the 109th Congress and I hope that when all is said and done, that we have the tools that students need to complete higher education and help them acquire the knowledge and skills to be competitive in the 21st century.

The American system of higher education is renowned. We have more than 6,000 colleges and universities and they enroll over 14-million students and provide access to all types of academic and skill-building programs. In Wyoming, we only have a handful. We have one 4-year university, public or private and seven community colleges. Our grand total of 10 accredited institutions of higher education in the State is the smallest of any State but Alaska. But that doesn't mean that we're any less concerned about a recent report by the Association of American Colleges and Universities that college graduates are less and less prepared to compete in the global economy. The American success story of higher education is at risk of losing those qualities that made it great; that's competition, innovation, access for all. Higher education will continue to be the on-ramp to success in the global economy and it's our responsibility to make sure that our young adults are able to access that opportunity and reach their goals.

The Federal Government does have a role to play in increasing affordability, which is why I support increasing the maximum Pell grant award and why this committee is working on a broader higher education re-authorization bill that will promote innovation and new technologies to keep costs down, to expand the availability of information, and to help students and parents make more informed decisions and to improve the financial literacy across the board, so that students have a better understanding of how they can manage their loans and monthly loan payments. Schools and colleges also have a role to play. They can and must do more to increase accountability and seek efficiencies to bring down the cost of education. Also we need to explore innovative solutions to the complexity of the Federal student aid system. As Senator Kennedy said, we're trying to revise that free application for Federal student aid. I've looked into some of the reasons why it's so complicated and again, it has something to do with action that Congress has taken. Now concern for spiraling costs of college is not new. I plan to submit for the record several articles by Dr. Richard Vedder that provide us insight into the perfect storm that is confronting our institutions of higher education. Declining State support, stagnant productivity and students that are left without the tools they need to make informed choices about their college education. Over the last 20 years, tuition has grown at rates double the increase in family income. At the same time, productivity at our universities is declining, while more students find themselves having to take remedial classes in order to succeed in college-level coursework.

Reauthorization of the Higher Education Act is needed to address these challenges and improve transparencies in ways that will combat these hidden costs of college. Institutions must better communicate the differences between sticker price and net price of a college education and there are many students that transfer from one school to another, only to discover that their hard-earned fully paid credits will not count toward their degrees. Other students enter college without the knowledge and skills they need, requiring them to take remedial courses just to catch up and we'll be doing some things in No Child Left Behind to try and end the wasted senior year of high school. This costs students money and time and adds to the taxpayers' cost. The result is that students graduate with greater debt. It also contributes to higher attrition rates, particularly for low-income students who find themselves no better off economically but likely to be facing monthly student loan payments.

I also want to highlight an issue that I've been championing and see as a critical factor in discussing, which is student financial literacy. We must improve the financial literacy of students so they can weigh the costs and benefits of their college education options. And we can no longer assume that only 18- to 20-year-olds are at issue. We are seeing more working adults, people with college degrees and mid-career Americans pursuing additional education in order to acquire increasing knowledge and skills they need to be successful in the world economy. The choice of whether to pursue a postsecondary education is confronting millions of Americans and they need good tools by which to make those decisions.

I've been a strong advocate for financial literacy because I believe that it gives individuals the tools to understand and shape their future. Senator Sarbanes and I were the authors of legislation enabling the Financial Literacy and Education Commission to develop a national strategy on financial literacy. I should note that next week, the Department of Treasury and Education will be holding the summit on K-postsecondary education—overcoming challenges to help develop the national strategy. In addition, the summit will highlight the challenges to teaching young people about money and saving for college and the rest of their lives. We have members of the panel that have some expertise in that and I look forward to hearing from today's witnesses as we tackle these issues and get ready for that reauthorization of the Higher Education Act. Thank you, Mr. Chairman.

Source: 110th Congress, 1st Session. "Higher Education, Higher Cost, and Higher Debt: Paying for College in the Future." Hearing of the Committee on Health, Education, Labor, and Pensions (February 16, 2007). S. Hrg. 110–151. Washington, DC: Government Printing Office, 2008. The transcript of the entire hearing, including testimony by Suze Orman, Tamara Drout, Jon Oberg, and Sandy Baum, as well as questions and discussion among the conferees and other

members of the committee, is available online at https://
www.govinfo.gov/content/pkg/CHRG-110shrg33516/html/
CHRG-110shrg33516.htm

Senate Hearing, "The Looming Debt Crisis" (March 20, 2012)

*This congressional hearing addressed student loan provisions within
the bankruptcy code, drawing attention to the differential treatment of this type of consumer debt. Conferees included two state
attorneys general and other legal experts. For the sake of brevity,
only the prepared statement of Senator Richard Durbin (D-IL) is
included here.*

Opening Statement of Hon. Richard J. Durbin, a U.S. Senator from the State of Illinois

Senator Durbin. Good morning. This hearing of the Subcommittee on Administrative Oversight and the Courts will come
to order. The title of today's hearing is "The Looming Student Debt Crisis: Providing Fairness for Struggling Students."
I want to thank Chairman Leahy of the Judiciary Committee and Senator Klobuchar, Chair of this Subcommittee, for
allowing me to convene this hearing where we will address the
important issue of student loan debt and a bill which I have
introduced, the Fairness for Struggling Students Act, which
falls within the jurisdiction of this Subcommittee because it
addresses the Bankruptcy Code. I am going to provide a few
opening remarks, recognize the Ranking Member, Senator Ses-
sions, who we hope will be returning from a press conference
shortly, and then turn to our witnesses.

Our Nation faces a serious problem with student loan
debt. Last month, the National Association of Consumer
Bankruptcy Attorneys issued an eye-opening report entitled,
"The Student Loan Debt Bomb." The report pointed out that
American student borrowing exceeded $100 billion in 2010,
and total outstanding student loans exceeded $1 trillion last

year. There is now more student loan debt in this country than credit card debt.

Of course, when used prudently, student loans can be valuable. In many instances, student loans help Americans get a quality education and job skills that they need to repay their loans and have a rewarding life. Unfortunately, it is clear that too many students have been steered into loan arrangements that they will not be able to repay and never be able to escape. According to an analysis by the Federal Reserve Bank of New York, 37 million Americans held outstanding student loan debt as of last year, the average balance $23,300. However, only 39 percent of those student loan borrowers were paying down their balances last year. The New York Fed study found that 14 percent of student loan borrowers—that would be 5.4 million Americans—were delinquent on paying their student loans while the remaining 47 percent of borrowers were either in forbearance or were still in school and adding to their debt.

Last month, Standard & Poor's issued a report saying that "Student loan debt has ballooned and may turn into a bubble." And Moody's Analytics recently said, "The long-run outlook for student lending and borrowers remains worrisome." While the overall growth in student indebtedness is troubling, the most pressing concern are private student loans. According to the Project on Student Debt, the most recent national data shows that one-third of bachelor degree recipients graduated with private loans at an average loan amount of $12,550. These private student loans are a far riskier way to pay for an education than federal loans. Federal student loans have fixed, affordable interest rates. They have a variety of consumer protections built into them, such as forbearance in times of economic hardship. They offer manageable repayment options such as income-based payment plans.

On the other hand, private student loans have high variable interest rates, often two or three times the interest rate that a student pays on the federal loan, hefty origination fees, and a lack of repayment options. And private lenders have targeted low-income borrowers with some of the riskiest, highest-cost loans. Once a student takes out a private loan, the student is at the mercy of the lender. Every week my office hears from students who say private lenders will not work with them to consolidate loans or work out any manageable repayment plan. And if the student falls behind on payments, private lenders are aggressive with collection efforts. In many respects, private student loans are just like credit cards, except unlike credit card debt, private student loan debt cannot be discharged in bankruptcy. In 2005, Congress changed the bankruptcy law and included a provision making private student loan debts non-dischargeable in bankruptcy except under very rare circumstances.

I ask myself: How in the world did that provision get in the law, giving to these private loans the same status as a federal student loan or payments that are owed for taxes, alimony, and child support? It turns out it was a mystery amendment. We cannot find out who offered it. We certainly know who benefited from it. While the volume of private student loans is down from its peak in 2007 when it accounted for 26 percent of all originated student loans, we know that private lending is still being aggressively promoted by the for-profit college industry, and you will hear from the witnesses about that industry, particularly the Attorneys General who are here.

The Project on Student Debt reports that 42 percent of for-profit college students had private loans in 2008, up from 12 percent in 2003. For-profit college students also graduate with more debt than other students who graduate from public and private nonprofit colleges. For-profit colleges have a business model of steering students into private student loans, even when they still have eligibility left under the federal student loan, which has a fraction of the interest payment. And as a result, many students are pushed into taking out private loans when they are still eligible for federal loans, even when the lenders know the students are likely to default.

We need to take steps now to address this looming student problem. It is necessary to help struggling students and help our economy. We are going to have an opportunity come July. The interest rate on federal student loans will double without Congressional action. We cannot allow that to happen, but we need to not only use that as an opportunity to do the right thing for students in terms of interest rates, but also to address this looming crisis of student debt.

I have introduced legislation, the Fairness for Struggling Students Act, to restore the pre-2005 bankruptcy treatment of private student loans. There is no reason why private student loans should get treated any differently than other private debts in bankruptcy. And it is especially egregious that these private loans are non-dischargeable in cases where the student was steered into a loan while they were still eligible for safer, lower-cost federal loans. I believe we should also require full private student loan certification to ensure that students take advantage of their federal student aid options before turning to private loans. We should push for meaningful accreditation for for-profit institutions. Wait until you hear the testimony, which I have read, about some of these for-profit schools, even in my State of Illinois, and what they are doing to these students. And we should encourage the Consumer Financial Protection Bureau, currently collecting data and complaints about private student loans, to use its authority to take corrective steps. Today we have a distinguished panel of witnesses who will discuss the problems that we face and ways to address them, and I look forward to their testimony.

Source: 112th Congress, 2nd Session. "The Looming Student Debt Crisis: Providing Fairness for Struggling Students." Hearing before the Subcommittee on Administrative Oversight and the Courts of the Committee of the Judiciary (March 20, 2012). Serial No. J-112–64; S. Hrg. 112–899. Washington, DC: Government Printing Office. Retrieved from https://www.judiciary.senate.gov/imo/media/doc/CHRG-112shrg89723.pdf

Student Loan Affordability Act (April 11, 2013)

This legislation sought to extend the reduced interest rate on Federal Direct Stafford Loans, set to expire in 2013, to 2015.

It is an example of the dominant theme in the student loan debate at the time, which largely centered on interest rates and other financing terms, modification of which can result in short-term relief for student borrowers while falling short of fundamental reform. This framing is vividly captured by the senators' suggested short title, the Student Loan Affordability Act of 2013, despite the lack of any explicit provisions to guarantee affordability.

Mr. Reed (for himself, Mr. Franken, Ms. Stabenow, Mr. White-house, Mr. Sanders, and Mr. Brown) introduced the following bill; which was read twice and referred to the Committee on Health, Education, Labor, and Pensions
A Bill
To amend the Higher Education Act of 1965 to extend the reduced interest rate for Federal Direct Stafford Loans.
Be it enacted by the Senate and House of Representatives of the United States of America in Congress assembled,

Section 1. Short Title

This Act may be cited as the "Student Loan Affordability Act of 2013".

Sec. 2. Interest Rate Extension

Section 455(b)(7)(D) of the Higher Education Act of 1965 (20 U.S.C.
  1087e(b)(7)(D)) is amended—

(1) in the matter preceding clause (i), by striking
    "2013" and inserting "2015"; and
(2) in clause (v), by striking "2013" and inserting
    "2015".

Source: 113th CONGRESS (1st Session), S. 707. Retrieved from https://www.govinfo.gov/content/pkg/BILLS-113s707is/html/BILLS-113s707is.htm

President Obama's Remarks on Signing the Bipartisan Student Loan Certainty Act of 2013 (August 9, 2013)
Reflecting widespread public concern about the effects of student debt, President Barack Obama used the occasion of the signing of new legislation fixing interest rates for federal student loans to make broader statements regarding college affordability and other needed student loan reforms.

The President. Well, before I sign this, I just want to say thank you to this extraordinary coalition that helped make this signing possible. I want to thank Chairman Kline, all the Members of both House and Senate from both parties that came together to design a sensible, commonsense approach to keeping student interest rates at a reasonable level so that young people have a better opportunity to go to college, get the education that they need, not only to better their own lives, but also to strengthen the country's economy. And I want to thank the advocates, including some of the young people, I suspect, will be benefiting from lower student loans—or lower student loan interest rates, because without their voice, without their participation, we probably would not have gotten this bill done. Last point I'll make, and I suspect the Senators and Congressmen behind me will agree with this, even though we've been able to stabilize the interest rates on student loans, our job's not done, because the cost of college remains extraordinarily high. It's out of reach for a lot of folks, and for those who do end up attending college, the amount of debt that young people are coming out of school with is a huge burden on them. It's a burden on their families. It makes it more difficult for them to buy a home. It makes them more difficult—more difficult for them if they want to start a business. It has a depressive effect on the economy overall. And we've got to do something about it. So I'm going to be looking forward to engaging this same coalition to see if we can continue to take additional steps to reform our higher education system, and I'll have some more things to say about that in the weeks to come. But for now, I want to celebrate what we accomplished here and again thank everybody here for their leadership in getting it done.

Source: Compilation of Presidential Documents. Bill Signings and Vetoes. Retrieved from https://www.govinfo.gov/content/pkg/DCPD-201300561/html/DCPD-201300561.htm

Memorandum on Helping Struggling Federal Student Loan Borrowers Manage Their Debt (June 9, 2014)

This memorandum outlines new federal administrative actions aimed at changing the servicing of federal student loans, announced by President Barack Obama and directed at the secretary of the treasury and the secretary of education.

A college education is the single most important investment that Americans can make in their futures. College remains a good investment, resulting in higher earnings and a lower risk of unemployment. Unfortunately, for many low- and middle-income families, college is slipping out of reach. Over the past three decades, the average tuition at a public four-year college has more than tripled, while a typical family's income has increased only modestly. More students than ever are relying on loans to pay for college. Today, 71 percent of those earning a bachelor's degree graduate with debt, which averages $29,400. While most students are able to repay their loans, many feel burdened by debt, especially as they seek to start a family, buy a home, launch a business, or save for retirement.

Over the past several years, my Administration has worked to ensure that college remains affordable and student debt is manageable, including through raising the maximum Pell Grant award by nearly $1,000, creating the American Opportunity Tax Credit, and expanding access to student loan repayment plans, where monthly obligations are calibrated to a borrower's income and debt. These income-driven repayment plans, like my Pay As You Earn plan, which caps a Federal student loan borrower's payments at 10 percent of income, can be an effective tool to help individuals manage their debt, and pursue their careers while avoiding consequences of defaulting on a Federal student loan, such as a damaged credit rating, a tax refund offset, or garnished wages.

While my Administration has made significant strides in expanding repayment options available to borrowers and building awareness of income-driven repayment plans, more needs to be done. Currently, not all student borrowers of Federal Direct Loans can cap their monthly loan payments at 10 percent of income, and too many struggling borrowers are still unaware of the options available to them to help responsibly manage their debt.

Therefore, by the authority vested in me as President by the Constitution and the laws of the United States of America, I hereby direct the following:

Section 1. Expanding the President's Pay As You Earn Plan to More Federal Direct Loan Borrowers. Within 1 year after the date of this memorandum, the Secretary of Education shall propose regulations that will allow additional students who borrowed Federal Direct Loans to cap their Federal student loan payments at 10 percent of their income. The Secretary shall seek to target this option to those borrowers who would otherwise struggle to repay their loans. The Secretary shall issue final regulations in a timely fashion after considering all public comments, as appropriate, with the goal of making the repayment option available to borrowers by December 31, 2015.

Sec. 2. Improving Communication Strategies to Help Vulnerable Borrowers. By December 31, 2014, the Secretary of Education shall develop, evaluate, and implement new targeted strategies to reach borrowers who may be struggling to repay their Federal student loans to ensure that they have the information they need to select the best repayment option and avoid future default. In addition to focusing on borrowers who have fallen behind on their loan payments, the Secretary's effort shall focus on borrowers who have left college without completing their education, borrowers who have missed their first loan payment, and borrowers (especially those with low balances) who have defaulted on their loans to help them rehabilitate their loans with income-based monthly payments. The Secretary of Education shall incorporate data analytics into the communications efforts and evaluate these new strategies to identify areas for improvement and build on successful practices.

Sec. 3. Encouraging Support and Awareness of Repayment Options for Borrowers During Tax Filing Season. By September 30, 2014, the Secretary of the Treasury and the Secretary of Education shall invite private-sector entities to enter into partnerships to better educate borrowers about income-based repayment plans during the tax filing season in 2015. Building off of prior work, the Secretaries shall further develop effective ways to inform borrowers about their repayment options during the tax filing season in 2015, as well as through personalized financial management tools.

Sec. 4. Promoting Stronger Collaboration to Ensure That Students and Their Families Have the Information They Need to Make Informed Borrowing Decisions. By September 30, 2014, the Secretary of Education, in consultation with the Secretary of the Treasury, shall develop a pilot project to test the effectiveness of loan counseling resources, including the Department of Education's Financial Awareness Counseling Tool. The Secretary of Education shall convene higher education experts and student-debt researchers to identify ways to evaluate and strengthen loan counseling for Federal student loan borrowers. Additionally, the Secretaries shall collaborate with organizations representing students, teachers, nurses, social workers, entrepreneurs, and business owners, among others, to help borrowers represented by these organizations learn more about the repayment options that are available to them in financing their investment in higher education and managing their debt, and to provide more comparative, customized resources to those borrowers when possible.

Sec. 5. General Provisions. (a) Nothing in this memorandum shall be construed to impair or otherwise affect:

(i) the authority granted by law to an agency, or the head thereof; or

(ii) the functions of the Director of the Office of Management and Budget relating to budgetary, administrative, or legislative proposals.

(b) This memorandum shall be implemented consistent with applicable law and subject to the availability of appropriations.

(c) This memorandum is not intended to, and does not, create any right or benefit, substantive or procedural, enforceable at law or in equity by any party against the United States, its departments, agencies, or entities, its officers, employees, or agents, or any other person.

(d) The Secretary of Education is hereby authorized and directed to publish this memorandum in the *Federal Register*.

BARACK OBAMA

Source: *Federal Register* Doc 2014–13961. Retrieved from https://www.whitehouse.gov/the-press-office/2014/06/09/presidential-memorandum-federal-student-loan-repayments

President Obama's Remarks at a Question-and-Answer Session on Student Loan Debt and College Affordability with Tumblr Participants (June 10, 2014)
In this excerpt of a longer transcript of an exchange between President Barack Obama and participants in a question-and-answer session on student debt, President Obama spoke about his recent signing of the executive order fixing interest rates and about his support of other reforms in the student loan system.

Tumblr, Inc.,   This is unusual. Thank you. Thank you,
Chief Executive   everyone, and welcome to the White House.
Officer David Karp.   Thank you for having us, Mr. President.
I'm David Karp, the founder of Tumblr, and it is my tremendous privilege to be here with President Obama today and

joined by the Tumblr community. Thank you for joining us, everyone. Yesterday the President signed an Executive order intended to curb the pain of student debt. Americans now hold more than a trillion dollars in student debt, one of the greatest expenses they'll incur in their lifetime. And the generation that's just reaching college age is beginning to wonder if it's even worth it. One-third of Americans who have applied for an education loan this year also happen to use Tumblr, so last week we asked our audience if they had questions that they'd like to ask the President about the cost value and accessibility of higher education. And turns out, they had quite a few. We're not going to be able to get through all of them today, but the President has been kind enough to give us some time at his house to answer some of those questions. [*Laughter*] So again, huge thank you for making yourself available today. Anything you'd like to add before we start?

The President. Well, first of all, this is a rental house. [*Laughter*] And I just want to be clear: My lease runs out in about 2½ years. Second of all, I want to thank David and the whole Tumblr community for participating in this. We're constantly looking for new ways to reach audiences that are relevant to the things we're talking about. And obviously, young people disproportionately use Tumblr. A lot of Tumblr users are impacted by student debt. So for you to be able to give us this forum to

	speak directly to folks is wonderful, and I'm looking forward to a whole bunch of good questions.
Mr. Karp.	Thank you. Okay, so everybody is clear on how the questions worked, so since we closed for questions 5 p.m. yesterday, we brought together a team of influential Tumblr bloggers who helped us select some of the best questions. There are—a few of them, anyway, are joining us in the audience in the State Dining Room here today. Neither the White House nor the President have seen any of these questions in advance. Should we get started?
The President.	Let's go.
President's Student Loan Debt/Tuition Costs Mr. Karp.	All right. So first came in from Caitlin: "I appreciate your willingness to work with legislators to attempt to retroactively diffuse the cost of some student's loans by creating new repayment plans, but this seems to me like an attempt to put a band aid on a broken leg. What are we doing to actually lower the cost of a college degree"—excuse me—"of college tuition so these loans will no longer be necessary?"
The President.	Well, it's a great question. And let me give people some context for what's happened over the last 20, 30 years. I graduated from college in '83, graduated from law school in 1990. And although I went to a private school, through a combination of grants, loans, and working, I had a fairly low level of debt that I was able to pay in 1 year without getting an incredibly well-paying job. I was able to keep my debt burden pretty low. Folks who were

10 years younger than me, they probably paid even less. And if you went to a State school at the time, typically people would come out with almost no debt whatsoever. Today, the average debt burden, even for young people who are going to a public university, is about $30,000. And that gives you some sense of how much the cost has escalated for the average young person. Now, you mentioned earlier some people are wondering, is this a good investment? It absolutely is. The difference between a college grad and somebody with a high school diploma is about $28,000 a year in income. So it continues to be a very smart investment for you to go to college. But we have to find ways to do two things.

One is, we have to lower the costs on the front end. And then, if you do have to supplement whatever you can pay with borrowing, we've got to make sure that that is a manageable debt. And about 12 months ago, maybe 16 months ago, I convened college and university presidents around the country to start working with them on how we could lower debt—or lower tuition, rather. The main reason that tuition has gone up so much is that State legislatures stopped subsidizing public universities as much as they used to, in part because they started spending money on things like prisons and other activities that I think are less productive. And so schools then made up for the declining State support by jacking up their tuition rates. What's also happened is, is that the costs of things like health care that a university community with a lot of personnel has—have to shoulder, those costs have gone up faster than wages and incomes. The combination of those things has made college tuition skyrocket faster than health care costs have. There are ways we can bring down those costs, and we know that because there are some colleges who have done a very good job in keeping tuition low. We also have to do a better job of informing students about how to keep their debt down, because frankly, universities don't always counsel young people well when they first come in. They say, don't worry about it, you can pay for it, not realizing that you're paying for it through borrowing that you're going to end up having to shoulder once you graduate.

Mr. Karp.   What does—what does that help, what does that support look like? So Chelsea sent in a very similar question from Portland. So she asks: "Colleges help students get into debt. They don't often help offer financial planning services before school, after they graduate." Do you guys have a plan to help students make sound financial decisions? I mean, these are teenagers who are making decisions sometimes amounting to hundreds of thousands of dollars that are going to follow them through their entire lives. Hopefully, they have parents who can help them navigate those decisions. But if they don't, are they on their own?

The President.   Well, we are already doing something we call Know What You Owe. And the idea is to work with every college, university, community college out there so that when you come into school, ideally even before you accept an admission from a school, you are given a sense of what your annual loans might be, what your financial package is going to translate into in terms of debt, assuming you go through a 4-year degree on schedule, and what your monthly payments are likely to be afterwards. And so just that one step alone—making sure that schools are obliged to counsel you on the front end when you come in, as opposed to just on the exit interview once you've already accumulated the debt—that in and of itself can make a big difference.

Mr. Karp.   "It wasn't until after I graduated college that I realized what I wanted to do with my life. Now I have a degree that has very little to do with that goal and a mountain of debt. I can't help but wonder if I wasn't pressured to go to college and was better prepared to make that decision—and if I was better prepared to make that decision, that I might be in a better place to pursue my dreams today. How can we change the public education system to better prepare and support young people making this huge decision?" I mean, again, teenagers deciding what they want to do for the rest of their lives.

The President.   Well, one of the things that Haiku Moon—[*laughter*]—is alluding to is that high school should be a time in which young people have greater exposure to actual careers as opposed to just classroom study. And I went to a wonderful school in New York called P–TECH, went there for a visit. What they've done is they have collapsed high school basically into a 3-year program. You can then extend for another 2 years and get an associate's degree. IBM is working with them so that if in fact they complete the curriculum that IBM helped to design, they know they've got a job at IBM on the back end. And that's just one example of what I'd like to see a lot more high schools do, which is give young people in high school more hands-on experience, more apprenticeships, more training. If you are a graphic—somebody who is interested in graphic design, I'd rather have you work at a company doing graphic design your senior year or junior year to see if you actually like it, to get a sense of the training you need. You may not need a 4-year degree. You might only need a 2-year degree. You might be able to work while getting that degree. All that can save you money. So that can make a really big difference for high school kids. At the same time, one of the things that we initiated several years back is something called income-based repayments. And that's something I really want to focus on, is—IBR for short—income-based repayments. What we did in 2011 was to say, all student loans going forward, if you have a debt and you decide you want to go into a job that—like teaching or social work—that doesn't necessarily pay a lot, you shouldn't be hampered from making that choice just because you've got such a significant debt load. So what we said was that we will cap your repayments of your loans at 10 percent of your income above $18,000. And by doing that, that gives people flexibility. It doesn't eliminate your debt. But what it does is it makes it manageable each month so that the career that you choose may not be constrained. And we then have additional programs so that if you go into one of the helping professions—public service, law enforcement, social work, teaching—then over time, that debt could actually be forgiven. Now, the problem with it was that we passed this law in 2011; it only applied going forward. It didn't apply retroactively. So yesterday what I did was sign an executive action saying that the Department of Education is going to be developing rules so that, going backwards, anybody can avail themselves of this income-based repayments. Because I get a lot of letters from people who took out loans in 2005 or 2000; they are also in a situation where they're making regular payments, but it's very hard for them to make ends meet. And we want to ideally finish what's called the rulemaking process—nothing is easy around here—hopefully, by the time, say, the end of next year, the rules will be in place, that will be the law, and then everybody, and not just folks who borrowed after 2011, can take advantage of that. But there's not a lot of knowledge of this, and I hope that the Tumblr community helps to spread the word that this is something already available for loans that you took out after 2011, and hopefully, by next year, it will be available for people even if you took out your loans before 2011.

Mr. Karp.   Where do we find information about it?

The President.   You should go to whitehouse.gov, the White House website. It will then link you to ED.gov, which is the Education Department website. But whitehouse.gov, I figure, is easier to remember. [*Laughter*]

Student Loan Repayment Options

Mr. Karp.   Can you elaborate real quick on encouraging public service? So Josh from Oak Park sent in a really good question about this: "The U.S. has a long history of encouraging college-age men and women to give back to their larger communities through organizations like the Peace Corps, through organizations like Teach for America.

The President.   Right.

Mr. Karp.   Couldn't we make a larger commitment to that by creating tuition loan forgiveness programs for those students who agree to work in those fields or work in those geographic areas in need of skilled employees?" So you can imagine family practice doctors; you can imagine public defenders.

The President.   I mean, right now we have some programs like this in place, but they're typically relatively small, relatively specialized. So there are some loan-forgiveness programs for primary care physicians who are going out to rural communities or inner cities or underserved communities. There are some programs that are available through the AmeriCorps program for people who are engaged in public service. They are not as broad based and widespread as I would like. And we have tried to work with Congress—so far, unsuccessfully—to be able to get an expansion of these areas. And I'll—let's take health care as an example. We know that the population is aging. We know that we are—have a severe shortage of primary care physicians. A lot of young doctors are going into specialized fields like dermatology or plastic surgery because you can make a relatively large profit, you don't end up having a lot of liability, and that's not really what we need more of. And so my hope is, is that over time, Congress recognizes that young people are our most precious asset. We—there are some areas that we know we need people to get into the field, our best and brightest, and right now the financial burdens are precluding them from doing it. And we could open up those fields to a huge influx of talent if we were a little smarter with it.

[NOTE: Discussion of President's career advice removed for brevity.]

The President.   One of the biggest areas where we see a problem is young people who are going, let's say, to technical schools or community colleges or some of these for-profit universities, they're promised a lot. But they haven't done the research to see, okay, does typically a graduate coming out of one of these schools get a job in the occupation? Are they actually making money? If you're going to have $50,000 worth of debt, you better have factored in what are the employment prospects coming out. And so I think it's good for young people—not only good—it's imperative for young people to be good consumers of education, and don't just assume that there's one way of doing things. We tell our daughters—Malia is now—she'll be 16 next month, and she's going to be in the college process. And we tell her, don't assume that there are 10 schools that you have to go to, and if you didn't go to those 10, that somehow things are going to be terrible. There are a lot of schools out there. There are a lot of options. And you should do your research before you decide to exercise one of those options. Having said that, the overwhelming evidence is that a college education is the surest, clearest path into the middle class for most Americans.

Mr. Karp.   Is the White House right now offering any of those tools to be a good a consumer, to navigate all the choices out there?

The President.   Yes, yes. So if you go—again, go to whitehouse.gov, which will link you to

the Department of Education, one of the
things that we're doing is to—we're starting to develop a scorecard for colleges
and universities so you have just a general sense of what's the typical graduation
rate, what's the typical debt that you carry
once you get out, what is the employment
rate for graduates 5 years afterwards. And
over time, one of the things that we're
trying to do is develop a ranking system
that is not exactly the same as the typical
college-ranking systems that you see in
U.S. News & World Report, for example.
Part of the problem with the traditional
ranking systems of schools is that, for
example, high cost is actually a bonus in
the ranking system. It indicates prestige,
and so there may be some great schools
that are expensive, but what you're missing is a great school that may give you
much better value, particularly in the field
that you're in. Now, there's some controversy, I want to confess, about—that a lot
of colleges and universities say, you know,
if you start ranking just based on cost
and employability, et cetera, you're missing the essence of higher education and
so forth. What we're really trying to do is
just identify here are some good bargains,
here are some really bad deals. Then
there's going to be a bunch of schools in
the middle that there's not going to be a
huge amount of differentiation. But what
we are trying to do is make sure that students have some—enough information
going into it that they don't end up in a

	school that is pretty notorious for piling a lot of debt on their students, but not really delivering a great education.
Mr. Karp.	Back to the debt, which is top of mind for everybody here today. So Megan from Tulsa asked an interesting question: "Of my $220,000 in student loans"—
The President.	Yikes.
Mr. Karp.	"from college and law school"—there you go—" less than half is receiving the benefit of loan forgiveness." Why is there no discussion on the mounting private student loan debt?
The President.	Well, there is a discussion. The problem is we just end up having less leverage over that. I mean, the truth is, is that both legislatively and administratively, we have some impact on Federal loans. Private loans—if you take—if you go to a private company and you're taking out a loan, we have the Consumer Finance Protection Bureau that is trying to regulate this area and make sure that you have full information about what you're getting yourself into. It's another version of Know Before You Owe. But it's harder for us to restructure some of that debt. Now, one thing that I think is really important for everybody to know here—because this is actual action you can take, as opposed to just listening to me blather on—this week, there will be a vote in the United States Senate on a bill sponsored by Elizabeth Warren, the Senator from Massachusetts. And what this bill would do

would allow students to refinance their existing loans at today's rates. The reason that's important is because rates have been low, and typically, there's going to be a pretty big spread between the rates that a lot of students—the interest rates that a lot of students have on their debt right now, versus what they could do if they refinanced, the same way that a lot of people refinance their mortgages to take advantage of historically low rates. And so this vote is coming up. It will come up this week. I think everybody on Tumblr should be contacting their Senators and finding out where they stand on the issue, because—and by the way, this is something that will not add to the deficit, because the way we pay for it is, we say that we're going to eliminate some loopholes right now that allow millionaires and billionaires to pay lower rates of taxes than secretaries and teachers. And so it would pay for itself. It's a good piece of legislation. It directly affects folks in their twenties and thirties, and in some cases, their forties and fifties and sixties. But particularly the young people who use Tumblr, this is something that you should pay a lot of attention to. Make sure that you are pushing your Senators around this issue.

Source: *Compilation of Presidential Documents. Addresses and Remarks. Tuesday, June 10, 2014.* Retrieved from https://www.govinfo.gov/content/pkg/DCPD-201400443/html/DCPD-201400443.htm

Student Loan Servicing Reform Fundamentals (2016)

In the wake of the scandal involving student loan servicer Navient, Senator Elizabeth Warren publicly called on the U.S. Department of Education to ascribe to the following "fundamentals" of student loan servicing reform.

1. Put students and families first.

a.   Require all student loan companies to ensure that each borrower is in the program that makes the most sense for them through personalized information, better customer service, and counseling when appropriate.

b.   Require specialized units for certain groups of borrowers, such as service members, disabled borrowers, and borrowers with complaints about for-profit schools.

c.   Ensure that borrower communication is accurate, clear, and easy to understand and use, and that borrowers have easy access to basic account information and history.

d.   Create a single Department of Education portal for personalized information about one's federal student loans, including repayment options, so borrowers are not confused.

e.   Provide real, immediate debt relief through loan discharge or cancellation to borrowers who deserve relief, including group discharges to certain cohorts.

f.   Consult with state attorneys general, consumer advocates, and other federal agencies to develop clear and enforceable borrower servicing rights, and incorporate these rights into contracts with student loan servicers.

2. Punish bad actors that break the rules.

a.   Punish student loan companies and their executives that violate the law or their contracts, including making use of sanctions, fines, contract terminations and other penalties.

b. Ensure that there is an escalated complaint process for borrowers and a process to appeal servicer decisions, including a private right to enforcement.

c. When appropriate, report violations by student loan companies to the Department of Justice, the Federal Trade Commission, or to other relevant state and federal agencies for further enforcement.

d. Avoid propping up "too big to fail" companies by maintaining a transition plan for the exit of any student loan company from the program at any time and capping the loan volume that goes to any one servicer.

3. Change the financial incentives for servicers.

a. Pay companies based on how well they guide borrowers into the program that makes the most sense for them.

b. Hold servicers accountable for the numbers of complaints and complaint resolutions of the borrowers they serve, and eliminate companies with high unresolved complaint volume.

c. Give more loans to the companies that demonstrate the best performance.

d. Open up competition beyond the same old players.

e. Allow borrowers to petition for the Department to reassign them to a new servicer if their current servicer is failing them.

4. Release more and better data.

a. Collect, monitor, and release to the public better aggregate data regarding servicer performance—including loan performance, repayment rates, and default rates—by cohort of borrowers at the servicer level, while protecting student privacy.

b. Make these detailed data public for researchers, policymakers, and advocates to track servicer performance in a manner that protects student privacy and excludes personally identifiable information.

c. Make complaints publicly searchable with optional consumer narratives modeled after the Consumer Financial Protection Bureau's student loan complaint system reports.

d. Provide public information about the results of audits, investigations, and enforcement actions in a timely manner.

e. Publish annual consumer reports on the state of federal student loan servicing, modeled after the Consumer Financial Protection Bureau's annual reports.

f. Set up pilot projects to test and gather data on consumer-friendly improvements to servicing.

5. Step up aggressive oversight.

a. Expand and reform the oversight of servicers and other financial institutions.

b. Require the Department's Inspector General to regularly audit customer service provided by servicers by regularly reviewing materials provided to borrowers, and by recording and periodically evaluating calls between servicers and borrowers.

c. Standardize, monitor, and audit the training that servicer staff receives.

d. Create and monitor an effective complaint resolution processes and make sure borrowers know how to use them.

e. Review protocols for identifying borrowers who have criteria that may signal eligibility for discharge and ensure that servicers are proactively identifying borrowers.

f. Set up clear protocols for communicating with servicers in the event of a school closing or other event that has a widespread effect on servicing, and gather (and share) data on borrower response.

Source: Official Senate Web site of Senator Elizabeth Warren (http://www.warren.senate.gov/files/documents/Student_Loan_Servicing_Fundamentals.pdf).

Senator Elizabeth Warren's Questions Following Inspector General Report Detailing Faulty and Inaccurate Review of Servicemembers Civil Relief Act Compliance by Student Loan Servicers (March 3, 2016)

The office of Senator Elizabeth Warren (D-MA), who has been an outspoken critic of student loan issuers and regulators and a leading proponent of financial aid reform, published this press release following her issuance of a letter and official questions to the acting secretary of education, Dr. John King. Senator Warren called on the U.S. Department of Education to answer for servicing actions she alleges violate protections that are supposed to assist U.S. servicemembers whose loan repayment is disrupted by their military service.

Washington, DC—United States Senator Elizabeth Warren (D-Mass.) today sent a letter and a series of "Questions for the Record" to Acting Secretary of Education Dr. John King, seeking answers about the Education Department's (ED's) flawed oversight of student loan servicers' compliance with the Servicemembers Civil Relief Act. Dr. King recently was nominated to serve as Education Secretary and his nomination is being considered by the Senate Health, Education, Labor and Pensions (HELP) Committee. Earlier this week, ED's Office of Inspector General (OIG) released a report explaining that the Department's 2015 review of Navient and other student loan servicers was statistically flawed, inaccurate, and invalid. Senators Warren, Murray and Blumenthal requested the ED OIG report and released a Warren staff report in August that raised concerns with the methodology of the Department's review and about whether it adequately identified servicemembers who had been overcharged.

"This week's independent review is a stunning indictment of the Department of Education's oversight of student loan servicers, exposing the extraordinary lengths to which the Department will go to protect these companies when they break the law. The thousands of servicemembers who were cheated deserve far better. These findings also raise serious questions about whether the Department and its Office of Federal Student Aid can be trusted to protect the millions of borrowers under its care," Warren wrote. "If confirmed as the next head of the Department of Education, you will be responsible for ensuring that private companies who contract with the Department to participate in the student loan program follow the law and are held accountable when they cheat borrowers. We need to get to the bottom of how this happened—and who allowed it to happen—to ensure that it does not happen again." Today, Warren also joined Senators Murray and Blumenthal in sending a letter to Dr. King calling for corrective actions for the military borrowers who were overcharged on their student loans. In their letter, the senators called on the Department to rescind its methodologically flawed reviews, conduct a full review of student loan services to determine how many servicemembers were eligible for the six percent cap on interest rates but did not receive that benefit, and issue all military borrowers who were overcharged a refund for their money.

Source: Official Senate Web site of Senator Elizabeth Warren (https://www.warren.senate.gov/?p=press_release&id=1077). Full text of letter sent to Dr. King is available at http://www.warren.senate.gov/files/documents/2016–3–3_Letter_to_ED_re_King_QFRs.pdf

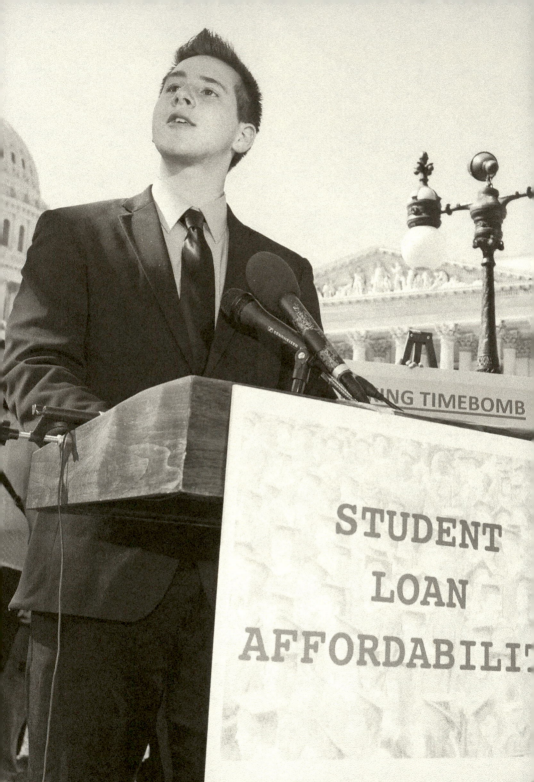

Concern about trends in the increase of student indebtedness, loans'
increasing prominence among financial aid options, and the ways in
which the shift to debt-centric education financing may be reshaping
the educational experience of a generation of American youth has
attracted many voices—often from distinct and even competing vantage
points—to the student debt discussion. While understanding the facts
about student loans is important, including who borrows how much,
what patterns are observed in student indebtedness, and how these
dynamics have changed over time, such data provide only a foundation
for truly grasping the implications of the United States' student debt
model for education finance. To move toward solutions that would
ensure that financial aid complements higher education's role as a
catalyst of equal opportunity and upward mobility for American young
people, research and analysis must also explore divides in student debt
along lines of race and class, as well as the long-term effects of student
borrowing on measures of significance to U.S. policymakers, pundits,
and the general public: homeownership and other asset accumulation,
degree completion and aggregate educational attainment, and overall
well-being. As such, the resources compiled here include both clear-eyed
assessments rooted in hard data and commentary on the state of student
debt today. Of course, this is not an exhaustive list, but the bibliography
provided here should give a scholar of student debt a solid foundation
from which to view the student loan landscape.

Northern Arizona University freshman Tyler Dowden, 18, speaks during a
news conference on Capitol Hill in Washington, D.C. Dowden announced
the collection of over 130,000 letters to Congress to prevent student loan
interest rates from doubling. Student protest movements have gained
momentum, calling for debt relief and affordable paths to educational
attainment. (AP Photo/Manuel Balce Ceneta)

Addo, F.R., Houle, J., & Simon, D. (2016). Young, black, and (still) in the red: Parental wealth, race, and student loan debt. *Journal of Race and Social Problems, 8*(1), 64–76.

Using data from the National Longitudinal Study of Youth 1997 cohort, this study examines racial differences in student loan debt acquisition and parental net wealth as predictors that may contribute to this growing divide. The findings confirm other research showing that black young adults have substantially more debt than their white counterparts, a chasm partially attributed to differences in wealth, family background, postsecondary educational differences, and family contributions to college. Furthermore, the authors show that young adults' net worth explains a portion of the overall racial wealth divide. Finally, the disparity between the debt of white and black young adults is found to be greatest at the highest levels of parents' net worth, where privileged white young adults enjoy the protection of their parents' considerable economic advantages. Policy implications are included in this analysis, which concludes that "student loan debt may be a new mechanism by which racial economic disparities are inherited across generations."

Akers, B. (2014). How much is too much? Evidence on financial well-being and student loan debt. Washington, DC: American Enterprise Institute.

This article examines the incidence of financial hardship among households who have assumed student debt. While the findings that there is not a strong positive relationship between student debt and financial hardship have been taken, by some, to conclude that student lending is not a strong driver of households' financial well-being or lack thereof, a close read of this analysis reveals that this lack of relationship may actually stem from relatively significant effects from small loan balances. Indeed, Akers finds the highest rates of financial hardship among households with relatively little outstanding student loan debt, which suggests that factors other than sheer loan amount—degree completion, for example, as well as field of study and, perhaps, students' initial positions—may help to influence the effects of student debt on Americans' financial standing. In addition, this article may call into question the idea that there is a "safe" threshold of student debt, since factors related to the student and his or her educational trajectory may be just as salient in determining later financial outcomes as the amount or terms of the loan itself.

Baum, S., & Johnson, M. (2015). Student debt: Who borrows most? And what lies ahead? Washington, DC: Urban Institute.
> This analysis, authored by one of the leading voices in federal financial aid policy, looks at recent figures on student borrowing. Among notable findings is a greater increase in the number of borrowers than in the average debt, illustrating growing enrollment and some slowing of the growth in college costs, which may reduce the immediate strain on students. While outstanding aggregate debt now exceeds $1 trillion, 2012, 2013, and 2014 were the years with the slowest growth in college debt over the past decade. Baum and Johnson's analysis points to the importance of considering the differential effects of student loans—or any financial aid policy—on different groups of students, since many borrowers with large balances secured lucrative advanced degrees, while those with small amounts may have even failed to complete their degrees. This Urban Institute report examines differences by fields of study and in relation to different student characteristics.

Baum, S., & Steele, P. (2010). Who borrows most? Bachelor's degree recipients with high levels of student debt. *Trends in Higher Education Series*. Retrieved July 4, 2016, from https://trends.

collegeboard.org/sites/default/files/trends-2010-who-borrows-most-brief.pdf

This brief highlighted the nuances in student indebtedness and the ways in which factors such as institution and major of study can influence students' outcomes and later well-being. Among the findings are statistics that emphasize how unlikely it is for a student to receive a degree from a for-profit institution without incurring student debt, as well as the relatively greater student loan burdens shouldered by independent (e.g., "nontraditional") undergraduate students. Analysis such as this can help policymakers to better understand the particular experiences of subgroups of American students and, then, point to different approaches to student aid reform that would target assistance to those most burdened. The College Board, which published this brief, is an excellent source of data on trends in college pricing, use of financial aid, and educational attainment, including analysis specifically of trends in student borrowing.

Brown, M., & Caldwell, S. (2013). Young adult student loan borrowers retreat from housing and auto markets (pp. 1–21). New York: Federal Reserve Bank of New York.

In this analysis, economists from the Federal Reserve Bank of New York use Consumer Credit Panel data to examine the steep drop in mortgage debt among young households with outstanding student loan debt during the recessionary period, a change that has resulted in a reversal of the historic relationship between student debt and housing debt. Specifically, this study details how homeownership rates between 2003 and 2009 were significantly higher for 30-year-olds with a history of student debt than for those without—unsurprising given that student debt holders have higher levels of education on average and higher incomes, factors that make them more likely to buy homes. This homeownership difference expanded during the housing boom: by 2008, the homeownership gap between the two groups had reached 4 percentage points. However, in the recession, while homeownership rates fell across the board, the decline was twice as steep for those with a history of student debt, such that, by 2012, the homeownership rate for student debtors was almost 2 percentage points lower than that of nonstudent debtors. The study also examines student debtors' interactions in other credit markets and raises the possibility that student debt will reshape financial behavior in different contexts.

Brown, M., Haughwout, A., Lee, D., Scally, J., & van der Klaauw, W. (2014). Measuring student debt and its performance. Federal Reserve Bank of New York Staff Reports, No. 668. Retrieved from http://www.newyorkfed.org/research/staff_reports/sr668.pdf
This analysis by the Federal Reserve Bank of New York examines the effects of student debt on borrowers' home purchases, other debt payments, and access to credit. While stopping short of establishing causality, the study suggests that the higher burden of student loans—balances for which almost tripled between 2004 and 2012—may negatively affect these other economic indicators. The report also urges closer attention to the macroeconomic effects of student loan debt, now the second-largest liability on household balance sheets, after mortgages. This report and the media coverage it galvanized were crucial in changing conversations about the financial implications of student loan debt, prompting additional investigations to explore and refute these associations and attracting the attention of policymakers to the potential for macroeconomic effects from growing student indebtedness.

Buitrago, K. (2015). Starting out behind: Trends in student loan burdens at for-profit colleges. Chicago, IL: Woodstock Institute.

This paper, by the nonprofit Woodstock Institute, looks at the effects of postsecondary institution type and student characteristics on students' decision about whether or not to borrow—and how much—to finance their higher education, with a particular examination of borrowing within the for-profit educational sector. Using data from the National Postsecondary Student Aid Study from the 2011–2012 academic year, this study uses a two-stage regression model in order to estimate the impacts of student and institutional characteristics on the probability that a student would borrow and, for students who borrowed, their student debt burdens. Among other findings, the study found that students at two-year for-profit colleges were nearly 50 percent more likely to borrow than students at public colleges, all other factors being equal. Latino and white students at four-year for-profit colleges were significantly more likely to borrow than Latino and white students at public or nonprofit schools. The paper also includes policy recommendations to address the disparities observed by institution type.

Chopra, R. (2015, October 8). Consumer protection and higher education financing alternatives: Testimony before the U.S. Congress Joint Economic Committee. Washington, DC: Center for American Progress. Retrieved July 2, 2016, from https://www.americanprogress.org/issues/higher-education/report/2015/10/08/123004/consumer-protection-and-higher-education-financing-alternatives/

Rohit Chopra was assistant director of the Consumer Financial Protection Bureau, overseeing the bureau's work on student financial services. In his testimony before Congress, he noted that increases in student borrowing make the limited regulatory oversight of the private student loan sector a salient concern for policymakers, particularly in light of recent, documented abuses and the lingering insecurities that followed the U.S. financial crisis. Among the practices Chopra highlights as particularly warranting response are illegal targeting of military service members, institutions pressuring students to take out high-cost loans, and evidence of discriminatory effects on at-risk students. He then outlines a more robust consumer protection system, to include clearer terms for student loan issuance and financing, better servicing arrangements, provisions to help borrowers manage through financial distress, and stronger antidiscrimination provisions. He further urges that student lenders help borrowers build credit histories and take steps to position them for later financial success.

Collinge, A. (2010). *The student loan scam: The most oppressive debt in U.S. history and how we can fight back.* Boston, MA: Beacon Press.

This book traces the history of the student loan industry, particularly pointing out how legislation and regulatory action created the conditions in which student lenders could profit from protections and a captive market. While it tends to focus on the worst abusers rather than the overall patterns in the financial aid system, the book uncovers the origins of the student loan industry in a way that explains much of what is currently observed. Seen as helpful by both students and families contemplating higher education and by those seeking to better understand student loan policies, the facts and figures in the book are nonetheless somewhat outdated in the intervening years since publication, a realization that underscores the dramatic changes in the student loan landscape.

Cunningham, A. F., & Kienzl, G. S. (2011). Delinquency: The untold story of student loan borrowing. Washington, DC: Institute for Higher Education Policy. Retrieved from http://www.ihep.org/assets/files/publications/a-f/delinquency-the_untold_story_final_march_2011.pdf

This report uses data provided by five of the largest student loan guaranty agencies to examine the repayment experiences of student loan borrowers. This snapshot of borrowers' repayment experiences characterizes borrower behavior as falling into distinct categories, with some following the expected path through payments (about 37 percent of borrowers in the 2005 repayment cohort made timely payments), others using repayment tools and options to manage their obligations (23 percent postponed payments through some tool), and others experiencing delinquency but without default (26 percent) or defaulting (15 percent). The study also considers the effects of student and institutional characteristics on these repayment outcomes. As such, it contributed to the discussion of how different initial positions and educational trajectories may shape students' outcomes from education loans, the development of which continues to inform consideration of different policy approaches in education reform and financial aid offerings.

Darolia, R. (2016, June). An experiment on information use in college student loan decisions. Working Paper No. 16–18. Philadelphia, PA: Federal Reserve Bank of Philadelphia.

This study reports on a randomized field experiment conducted at a flagship Midwestern university. The experiment was constructed to test the effects of information about student borrowing on individual students' financial aid decisions. Such investigations are important in light of policy recommendations that pin many problems associated with student debt on students' poor financial choices and, then, seek to provide greater information as a remedy. However, highlighting the multiple, complex forces that shape financial aid outcomes, this investigation reveals only modest effects from the intervention. As the author concludes, it seems that information alone is insufficient to dramatically change student borrowing patterns. While some subgroups of students—particularly those with low grade point averages—changed their borrowing patterns, there were also some unintended consequences observed, including lower Pell Grant receipt. While information may be useful for students contemplating borrowing, then, it is unlikely to be an answer to the nation's student debt concerns.

Default: The Student Loan Documentary. (2011). Retrieved from http://www.defaultmovie.com/

This film chronicles the experiences of student borrowers to illustrate the strains they experience in repayment, particularly given the lack of consumer protections within this particular financing instrument, including inability to discharge debts in bankruptcy and lack of caps on fees and penalties. While this short film cannot fully explore the origins of the policies implicated, it received wide distribution after its publication on the Public Broadcasting Service and, as such, is credited with contributing to the growing public conversation about the ramifications of student debt for individual borrowers and this generation of American young people.

Delisle, J. (2016, April 7). Shifting burdens: How changes in financial aid affected what students and families paid for college from 1996 to 2012. Washington, DC: New America. Retrieved July 2, 2016, from https://www.newamerica.org/education-policy/policy-papers/shifting-burdens/

This analysis uses data from the National Postsecondary Student Aid Study to examine what students pay for school and what trends have emerged over the past decade and a half. The director of New America's Federal Education Budget Project looks at financial trends by family income, a student's dependency status, and school type, using information about college financing at the student level. Among the findings is evidence that colleges selected affect financing trends; students at community colleges and independent students at public four-year colleges did not see an increase in prices. Also, the share of college costs that the federal government financed rose significantly and consistently from 1996 to 2012 for nearly all income groups and school types. For low-income families and independent students, increases in federal aid nearly or completely offset declines in state and local subsidies. This trend was most pronounced at community colleges and for independent students at public four-year colleges. Notably, however, much of this aid comes in the form of student loans. This means that the net effect of the increases in federal aid may be different than that observed in earlier periods, when more of the financial assistance provided to these students was in the form of state and local grants. Across the board, students and their parents borrowed more to pay for college costs between 1996 and 2012. Even where students have not seen higher prices, such as at two-year colleges, they still increased their use of debt relative to out-of-pocket spending. Finally, across almost all income groups of dependent students, parent borrowing increased more than student borrowing.

Delisle, J., & Holt, A. (2013). Beware savvy borrowers using income-based repayment. Washington, DC: New America. Retrieved from http://www.edcentral.org/beware-savvy-borrowers-using-income-based-repayment/

This report, from New America, explains how income-based repayment (IBR) works in the student debt landscape. While highlighting the underutilization of IBR by today's borrowers, the authors make the contention that it is only this limited awareness that makes IBR fiscally and politically sustainable, since, as currently structured, IBR provides larger subsidies to borrowers who attended graduate school (and accumulate high loan balances) than it does to those who borrowed only to finance an undergraduate education, even though graduate school attendance is even more stratified by race and class than most undergraduate programs. Because borrowers with big loan balances can repay their loans under the same IBR terms as those with low and moderate balances, the bigger the loan balance, the bigger the benefit. While touting the benefits of IBR and urging simplification of the process used to access this repayment structure, this report urges reforms that would target subsidies to students and borrowers who struggle to pay for an undergraduate education.

Dugger, R.A., El-Sayed, A.M., Dogra, A., Messina, C., Bronson, R., & Galea, S. (2013). The color of debt: Racial disparities in anticipated medical student debt in the United States. *Plos One*, *8*(9), e74693–e74693. doi:10.1371/journal.pone.0074693

The cost of American medical education has increased substantially over the past decade. Given racial/ethnic inequalities in the access to financial resources, it is plausible that increases in student debt burden resulting from these increases in cost may not be borne equally. This study evaluates racial/ethnic disparities in medical student debt. Authors collected self-reported data from a nonrepresentative sample of 2,414 medical students enrolled at 111/159 accredited U.S. medical schools between December 1, 2010, and March 27, 2011. After weighting for representativeness by race and class year and calculating crude anticipated debt by racial/ethnic category, authors fit multivariable regression models of debt by race/ethnicity adjusted for potential confounders. The authors found that these medical students' anticipated educational debt upon graduation was greater than $150,000. About 62.1 percent medical students anticipated debt in excess of $150,000 upon graduation. The proportion of blacks, whites, Hispanics, and Asians reporting anticipated educational debt in excess of $150,000 was 77.3 percent, 65.1 percent, 57.2 percent, and 50.2 percent, respectively. Both black and white medical students demonstrated a significantly higher likelihood of anticipated debt in excess of $150,000 when compared to Asians (blacks [OR = 2.7, 1.3–5.6], whites [OR = 1.7, 1.3–2.2]) in adjusted models. The authors report that black medical students had significantly higher anticipated debt than Asian students. This finding has implications for understanding differential enrollment among minority groups in U.S. medical schools.

Dynarski, S. (2016, May 3). The dividing line between haves and have-nots in home ownership: Education, not student debt. Washington, DC: The Brookings Institution. Retrieved June 30, 2016, from http://www.brookings.edu/~/media/research/files/reports/2016/05/03-home-ownership-dynarski/home-ownership-final2b.pdf

In this study, Susan Dynarski examines findings asserted by the Federal Reserve Bank of New York and others, indicating that student debt has a corrosive effect on homeownership. This analysis adds educational attainment data to the credit report data relied upon for those other reports and illustrates that the greatest gap in homeownership is between those with college degrees and those without, not between college graduates with and without student debt. However, as pointed out in some of the media coverage of this study (see Johnson, 2016), Dynarski's analysis does acknowledge that those who have to borrow to finance their college degrees get a "slower start to homeownership than those who went to college debt-free," a delay in homeownership in the critical early adult years that can compromise equity accumulation and contribute to wealth divides.

Elliott, W. (2013). Small-dollar children's savings accounts and children's college outcomes. *Children and Youth Services Review*, 35(3), 572–585.

> One of the critiques of student loans as a financial aid mechanism is their inability to deliver improved educational outcomes during the college preparation period. As a "just-in-time" financial aid mechanism that some research has found may even deter some students from enrolling in (see Perna, 2008; Heller, 2008) or completing college, student loans fare poorly compared to early investments in children's academic preparedness and orientation to higher educational attainment. Here, a leading scholar in the field of asset-based education financing uses data from the Panel Study of Income Dynamics to demonstrate that children who have a small amount of money designated for college—even as little as $1—are more likely to enroll in and graduate from college than children with no education savings account. These findings are widely cited as one of the reasons that it is in the country's best interest to explore alternatives to debt-centric financial aid, to include efforts to help economically disadvantaged families build assets for their children's future educations.

Elliott, W., & Lewis, M. (2015). *The real college debt crisis: How student borrowing threatens financial well-being and erodes the American dream*. Santa Barbara: Praeger.

> This book uses the contrasting stories of the authors—the first, who had to borrow in order to finance the education that lifted him from poverty to the ranks of well-regarded academics, and the second, who enjoys greater financial well-being today largely as a result of having relied on her family's comparatively privileged position to finance her own higher education—to illustrate its core thesis: how one pays for education matters, in determining the return on degree and, then, the

extent to which the American education system can be said to constitute an equitable ladder of opportunities to ascend. The book includes data on the effects of student debt on individuals' net worth, later in life, as well as analysis of policies offered as "solutions" to the student debt crisis. Distinct from many other treatments of the student loan system, however, it also includes an explanation of an approach with the potential to upend financial aid: a shift to asset-based policies, such as Children's Savings Accounts (CSAs). The final chapter of the book explains how CSAs work, outlines some examples of this asset intervention in operation today, and suggests that such an investment could equip more American children with an asset base similar to the one that allowed the second author to realize her family's dream of education as a path to prosperity.

Elliott, W., Lewis, M., & Johnson, P. (2014). Unequal outcomes: Student loan effects on young adults' net worth accumulation. Lawrence, KS: Assets and Education Initiative.

This report is a companion to AEDI's earlier piece on student debt, *It Is Not Enough to Say: Most Students Will Eventually Recover*. Whereas that report examined the effects of student loan debt on individuals' postcollege financial outcomes, this analysis highlights the inequities in student loan reliance—particularly by race, income, and institution type—in order to illustrate the different risks that specific populations face of encountering those adverse outcomes. Among these findings are that individuals who have attended graduate school are the most likely to have negative net worth and that this risk is not mitigated even for those with greater levels of disposable income. In addition to detailing the scope and degree of student loans' effects on young adults' asset positions, this report advances Children's Savings Accounts as a policy alternative to debt-dependent college financing, even identifying ways that existing financial aid programs could be repurposed to capitalize such an asset-based approach.

Elliott, W., Lewis, M., Nam, I., & Grinstein-Weiss, M. (2014). Student loan debt: Can parents' college savings help? *Federal Reserve Bank of St. Louis Review, 96*(4), 331–357.

This article, produced for a symposium hosted by the Federal Reserve Bank of St. Louis, uses data from the Educational Longitudinal Survey to examine factors associated with student loan usage, among students who graduated from a four-year college but did not go to graduate school. Using propensity score matching to control for a variety of variables, the study found that parents' college saving was the only factor that reduced the odds of a student borrowing for college. Regarding that finding, specifically, graduates with parents who had savings for them have about $3,200 less debt. There were several factors associated with a higher likelihood of student borrowing and with greater loan amounts. Among those findings, four-year college graduates who attend a private for-profit college have about $16,436 more student debt than graduates who attend a public college.

Elliott, W., & Nam, I. (2013). Is student debt jeopardizing the long-term financial health of U.S. households? *Review, 95*(5), 1–20. Retrieved from https://www.stlouisfed.org/household-financial-stability/events/20130205/papers/Elliott.pdf

This article was among the first to consider the postcollege effects of student loan debt on an individual's financial well-being. Using Survey of Consumer Finances data, the authors examine whether student loans are associated with household net worth and find that, for households without outstanding student debt, median net worth in 2009 ($117,700) is nearly three times higher than it is for households with outstanding student loans ($42,800). Further, multivariate statistics reveal that living in a household with outstanding student debt and median net worth in 2007 ($128,828) is associated with a loss of about 54 percent in net worth in 2009 compared to living in a household with similar levels of net worth but no outstanding student debt. Living in a household with a four-year college graduate with outstanding student debt is associated with a net worth loss of about 63 percent ($185,995.90 less) compared to living in a household with a four-year college graduate without outstanding debt. While this analytical paper does not explicitly call for policy changes, its findings have underscored the need to consider the long-term financial implications of student borrowing, not just the short-term consequences for college financing.

Emmons, W.R., & Noeth, B. (2015). Why didn't higher education protect Hispanic and black wealth? St. Louis, MO: Federal Reserve Bank of St. Louis. Retrieved July 6, 2016, from https://www.stlouisfed.org/publications/in-the-balance/issue12–2015/why-didnt-higher-education-protect-hispanic-and-black-wealth

This analysis finds that, while educational attainment increases the earning potential and wealth accumulation of all Americans, these effects may not be equitable across all populations. Specifically, based on two decades of detailed wealth data, these authors conclude that education does not protect the wealth of all racial and ethnic groups equally. Compared to their less-educated counterparts, the wealth of white and Asian families with four-year college degrees was less adversely affected by the recent recession than Hispanic or African American families. These households have also accumulated much more wealth than Hispanic and black families headed by someone with a four-year college degree. Indeed, highly educated Hispanic and black families fared worse on wealth protection indicators than Hispanic and black families without college degrees. This was true both during the recent turbulent period (2007–2013) and during a two-decade span ending in 2013. The authors attribute these divides to poorer job market outcomes for Hispanic and black college graduates and to financial decision making. While some authors (see Hamilton & Darity, 2016) have pointed out that financial choices are constrained by inequality in initial conditions, it should also be noted that students of color are significantly more dependent on student loans than are white students, a distinction that may also help to explain the difference in their postcollege financial outcomes.

Fry, R. (2014). Young adults, student debt and economic well-being. Washington, DC: Pew Research Center's Social and Demographic Trends Project. Retrieved from http://www.pew-socialtrends.org/files/2014/05/ST_2014.05.14_student-debt_complete-report.pdf

Using similar data sets as previous analysis, this Pew Research Center report finds that households headed by a young, college-educated adult without any student debt obligations have about seven times the typical net worth ($64,700) of households headed by a young, college-educated adult with student debt ($8,700). And the wealth gap is also large for households headed by young adults without a bachelor's degree: Those with no student debt have accumulated roughly nine times as much wealth as debtor households ($10,900 vs. $1,200). This is true despite the fact that debtors and nondebtors have nearly identical household incomes in each group. The wealth gap is much larger than the actual difference in student loan obligations because student debtor households are accumulating less wealth for a variety of reasons. Significantly, this report finds a continued return on college degrees in terms of household income, reiterating that it is the way in which college is financed that may be changing the bargain of higher education for young people today, more than the inherent value of the human capital accrued.

Hamilton, D., & Darity, W. (2016). The political economy of education, financial literacy, and the racial wealth gap. St. Louis, MO: Federal Reserve Bank of St. Louis. Retrieved July 2, 2016, from https://www.stlouisfed.org/~/media/Files/PDFs/HFS/20160525/papers/Hamilton-paper.pdf

This paper, produced for a Federal Reserve Bank of St. Louis discussion on wealth and race—including the effects of student debt—criticizes dominant framing, which often at least partially attributes the inferior wealth positions of people of color to their presumably poor choices, while the evidence points, instead, to systematic and inequitable differences in the opportunities afforded. Hamilton and Darity take issue with the presumption, for example, that variances in debt assumption between white and Asian households, on the one hand, and black and Latino households, on the other, stem from some measure of financial irresponsibility in the latter. As evidence for their case, they point to the fact that white households are more likely to have some unsecured debt; what drives total debt obligations in this category higher, for people of color, is a greater reliance on student and medical debt, patterns that suggest structural disparities as the principal cause. The authors emphasize that language matters, here since defining the "problem" of the racial wealth gap as rooted in the behaviors of people of color themselves reduces the chance of building an effective collective movement for a structural solution. Toward that end, the article concludes with a call for Baby Bonds—wealth transfers at birth—to equalize the standing of people of color, including as they contemplate their educational futures.

Heller, D.E. (2008). The impact of student loans on college access. In S. Baum, M. McPherson, & P. Steele (Eds.), *The effectiveness of student aid policies: What the research tells us* (pp. 39–67). New York, NY: The College Board.

Here, leading scholar of higher education and financial aid policies, Donald Heller, examines the existing literature on the effects of the shift to debt-centric financial aid on students' educational outcomes. This contribution, coming fairly early in the groundswell of public discontent with student debt, emphasizes that there is relatively little evidence to suggest that student loans are strongly facilitative of college access and completion, and even some evidence that they may have a depressing effect on the educational attainment of some populations. While much of the literature examined for this review is now somewhat dated, given rapid changes in financial aid policies, the continued evolution of the higher educational landscape, and new postrecession economic realities, the significance of this chapter as one of the first well-regarded considerations of the possibility that student loans could serve as other than a benign force in students' lives is unabated.

Hiltonsmith, R. (2013). At what cost: How student debt reduces lifetime wealth. Washington, DC: Demos.

This analysis by Demos adds to the evidence of student debt's negative effects on households' wealth positions. Specifically, the model finds that an average student debt burden for a dual-headed household with bachelor's degrees from four-year universities leads to a lifetime wealth loss of nearly $208,000. Nearly two-thirds of this loss comes from lower retirement savings of the indebted households, with most of the rest coming from lower home equity accumulation. These capital effects are perhaps particularly pronounced because student debt repayment occupies a significant portion of financial resources in households' young adult period, when gaps in asset accumulation can widen. This was among the first papers to examine the effects of student loan usage on individuals' wealth positions and made significant contributions to that emerging body of work.

Hiltonsmith, R. (2014). The great cost shift continues: State higher education funding after the recession. Washington, DC: Demos.

> This analysis seeks to quantify the contribution of reduced public investment in higher education to overall cost increases in tuition and fees. The report describes increases in education costs at public institutions as cost shifts, rather than net cost increases, as revenue from tuition paid for 44 percent of all operating expenses at public colleges and universities in 2012, more than twice the share just 25 years ago and the highest share ever borne by individuals and families. Significantly, while dramatic declines in state investment were particularly pronounced during the Great Recession, Demos's analysis reveals that states have only sporadically reinstated this investment in the better economic times that have followed, suggesting that this may be the arrangement for the foreseeable future.

Huelsman, M. (2015). The debt divide: The racial and class bias behind the "new normal" of student borrowing. Washington, DC: Demos. Retrieved from http://www.demos.org/sites/default/files/publications/The%20Debt%20Divide.pdf

> This report uses data from three U.S. Department of Education surveys, the Federal Reserve's 2013 Survey of Consumer Finances, and other academic literature to paint a picture of the effects of debt-dependent education financing on students of color and those otherwise disadvantaged. Data reveal that black, Latino, and low-income students have higher loan balances, poorer educational outcomes, and worse postcollege positions; further, this report draws a connection between those three conditions. Among Demos's key findings: black and low-income students borrow more—in frequency and amount—to receive a bachelor's degree, even at public institutions. Disadvantaged students—particularly African Americans—need to borrow even to secure entry-level

postsecondary education degrees; associate's degree borrowing has grown dramatically in the past decade. Students of color drop out with student debt at higher rates
than other students, which then leaving them to contend
with student debt obligations without the advantages a
degree confers. The report includes policy recommendations, including Demos's "Contract for College," which
would allow most students to graduate debt free.

The Institute for College Access and Success (TICAS). Cohort
default rates. Retrieved July 6, 2016, from http://ticas.org/
content/posd/cohort-default-rate-resources
   This resource tracks student loan cohort default rates, as a
   measure of financial stress among borrowers, institutional
   performance, and the overall function of student borrowing within the higher educational landscape. TICAS uses
   official Department of Education statistics as the basis of
   their measures. Cohort default rates measure the share
   of an institution's federal student loan borrowers who
   default within a specified period of time after entering
   repayment. Of significance for broader education policy,
   colleges with high cohort default rates may lose future
   eligibility for federal grants and loans. Overall, from
   the most recent data available, 13.8 percent of student
   borrowers defaulted on their loans within three years of
   entering repayment.

Johnson, D. (2016, May 27). Brookings report disputes link
between student debt and home ownership rates. *GoodCall*.
Retrieved July 6, 2016, from https://www.goodcall.com/news/
brookings-report-disputes-link-student-debt-home-ownership-
rates-07179
   This news coverage discusses Susan Dynarski's research,
   described earlier, further probing Federal Reserve Bank
   of New York findings related to the effects of student
   debt on homeownership outcomes. Specifically, experts

quoted here underscore the importance of examining not just comparisons in homeownership rates at a particular point in time, but also differences in age of initial home purchase, as a determinant of later equity, and other measures of asset ownership and overall financial well-being, in order to more comprehensively assess the effects of student loan debt on individuals' total financial positions.

Kamenetz, A. (2006). *Generation debt: Why now is a terrible time to be young.* New York, NY: Riverhead Hardcover.

This book, written by National Public Radio education journalist Anya Kamenetz, features profiles of individual student debtors, interviewed by the author in order to expose some of the consequences of student borrowing on students' educational journeys, career decisions, and later life outcomes. While critiqued by some for offering few detailed solutions to the problems of debt dependence, the book captured early sentiment of concerns with the drift toward debt-centric college financing and provides a readable treatment of student debt issues, from the perspectives of borrowers and those similarly close to the situation.

Kuhl, A., Reiser, C., Eickhoff, J., & Petty, E. M. (2014). Genetic counseling graduate student debt: Impact on program, career and life choices. *Journal of Genetic Counseling, 23*(5), 824–837. doi:10.1007/s10897–014–9700–0

The cost of education is rising, increasing student financial aid and debt for students pursuing higher education. A few studies have assessed the impact of student debt in medicine, physical therapy, and social work, but little is known about the impact of student debt on genetic counseling of students and graduates. To address this gap in knowledge, a Web-based study of 408 recent alumni of genetic counseling programs in North America was conducted to assess the impact of student debt on program, career, and life choices. Over half (63 percent; $n = 256/408$) of the participants reported that loans were extremely important in their ability to attend their training program, with most using subsidized loans no longer available to current graduate students. While participants were generally satisfied with their genetic counseling education, 83 percent (n = 282/342) of participants with student debt reported feeling burdened by their debt, which had a median of $40,000–$50,000. This debt is relatively close to the median starting salary reported by survey participants ($45,000–$50,000), breaching the "20–10 rule" that states student debt should not exceed 20 percent of annual net income. In response to this critical issue, the authors propose recommendations for the genetic counseling field that may help alleviate student debt impact and burden.

Miller, B. (2015, June). The relationship between student debt and college completion. Washington, DC: Center for American Progress. Retrieved July 2, 2016, from https://www.american-progress.org/issues/higher-education/news/2015/06/26/116019/the-relationship-between-student-debt-and-college-completion/

This analysis by the Center for American Progress looks at average student debt per college graduate, by state, to attempt to put into context regional differences in student loan burden. The findings reveal some states (e.g., Louisiana) where relatively low average student debt levels mask concerns about actual experienced student debt burden, given very low levels of college completion. Conversely, in states such as Virginia, residents may be comparatively well-positioned to assume their relatively higher levels of student debt, given high rates of degree holding. While average student debt per graduate is lower than average debt per borrower—since many graduates do not have to borrow at all—slicing the data this way introduces examination of the relationship between financial aid mechanisms and educational attainment, often absent from student debt conversations. Research such as this underscores the need to consider student debt in context, analyzing its effects on educational attainment and, then, overall financial well-being, not just the aggregate amount owed.

Mishory, J., O'Sullivan, R., & Invincibles, Y. (2012). Denied? The impact of student debt on the ability to buy a house. Washington, DC: Young Invincibles. http://younginvincibles.org/wp-content/uploads/2012/08/Denied-The-Impact-of-Student-Debt-on-the-Ability-to-Buy-a-House-8.14.12.pdf

This report, coauthored by a policy and organizing group working on young adult issues—the Young Invincibles— examines the effects of student debt on individuals' homeownership prospects. The analysis concludes that the average single student debtor is likely ineligible for a typical home mortgage due to his or her debt-to-income ratio; including a typical mortgage and other debt, the average single student debtor would pay about half of his or her monthly income toward debt obligations, a ratio beyond the limits allowed for FHA loans or many private mortgages. Even when only one buyer in a couple has student debt, securing favorable mortgage terms could be difficult. This report then raises the potential for student loan debt to ripple throughout the economy, by depressing other economic activity and altering the financial behaviors of a generation.

National Center for Education Statistics. (2016). Graduation rates for selected cohorts, 2006–11; student financial aid in post-secondary institutions, academic year 2013–14; and admissions in postsecondary institutions, fall 2014: First look (provisional data). Retrieved July 6, 2016, from http://nces.ed.gov/pubsearch/pubsinfo.asp?pubid=2015181

The National Center for Education Statistics produces a wealth of data and analysis related to various educational topics, including this series, which examines utilization of financial aid instruments and educational attainment measures, by year. Other publications available at NCES' Web site include those related to cohort default rates, student profiles by level of study, and many reports on outcomes in the kindergarten-secondary school system, the latter of which reveal persistent attainment gaps by race and class and speak, then, to the need to find policy levers with which to address these inequities.

New America, Young Invincibles, and NASFAA. (October 2015). Promise and compromise: a closer look at payroll withholding for federal student loans. Washington, DC: New America. Retrieved July 2, 2016, from https://static.newamerica.org/attachments/10370-promise-and-compromise/Payroll-Withholding.7f8090065bc04a5b9d7543e2fb84211a.pdf

This paper discusses proposals to use payroll withholding to collect payments on federal student loans, considering both the political and operational feasibility of such an approach. Incorporating insights of experts working in the arenas of student loans and financial aid in general, as well as the perspectives of student borrowers, the report makes the case for automatic income-based repayment with employer withholding as an improvement on the current, more fragmented, system. As outlined here, "the process would be simple, payments would be deducted automatically from borrowers' paychecks, and borrowers would never have to pay back more than an affordable percentage of their incomes, thus creating a simple insurance mechanism that is more efficient for the government and ensures borrowers never have to make ruinously high monthly payments." However, the authors acknowledge problems not only technical—what types of income should be included in order to calculate amounts owed, how should married borrowers be treated, how would employers be compensated for costs—but also more substantive, including the

potential additional burdens placed on borrowers, employers, and the government. For their part, borrowers worried
that a withholding system would not be able to effectively
deal with unexpected life events that required forbearance
or deferment, concerns that highlight the difficulties many
borrowers have making student loan payments regularly,
even when the amounts owed are not excessively onerous;
they also worried about privacy and desired to keep student
loans secret from their employers. As part of the student
debt conversation that is confined to discussion of how to
best construct systems that will help borrowers deal with
the daily realities of their indebtedness, this report aims
to help policymakers begin to think through design issues
and "the circumstances under which employer withholding
might make sense as the automatic option for student loan
repayment."

Paul, M., Aja, A., Hamilton, D., & Darity, W. (2016,
March 21). Making college free could add a million new black
and Latino graduates. *Dissent Magazine.* Retrieved July 2,
2016, from https://www.dissentmagazine.org/online_articles/
bernie-sanders-free-college-plan-black-latino-graduates
    In this piece, the authors analyze proposals by Hillary Clin-
ton and Bernie Sanders to provide "free college"—from
very different perspectives, with resulting divergence in
approaches and outcomes—in order to assess their potential implications for young people of color. Of particular
interest is evidence provided about the current state of
college financing for students of color. As described here,
black students are 25 percent more likely to accumulate
student debt, borrowing over 10 percent more than white
students on average. They are, then, one-third less likely to
complete their degrees, often because of the greater financial burden; 29 percent of black students and 35 percent
of Latino students who leave college after their first year
do so for financial reasons. From this baseline, the authors

suggest that reducing interest rates on student loans would save the average black bachelor's degree holder more than $8,000 and the average Latino bachelor's degree holder more than $6,500, although, since more white young people attend college, the benefits of such a policy would flow even more generously to those students. However, to the extent to which reducing financial burdens may increase graduation rates among at-risk students, such an effect may be particularly potent for students of color. The authors estimate that preventing African Americans and Latinos from leaving college due to high costs could produce an additional 250,000 African American and 264,000 Latino bachelor's degree holders, numbers that could climb higher if more students were encouraged by the more favorable financing landscape to enroll.

Perna, L. (2008). Understanding high school students' willingness to borrow to pay college prices. *Research in Higher Education, 49*(7), 589–606.

This research was among the first to explore differences in the student borrowing experiences of different subgroups of students. Here, the author looks at debt aversion among students of color to examine how their orientation to financial aid may mediate the effect that student loans have on their educational outcomes. Specifically, the relatively greater reluctance to borrow evidenced by some disadvantaged students who are forced by rising tuition prices and the erosion of strong need-based financial aid to depend disproportionately on loan financing may constrain aggregate educational attainment among these cohorts. Research such as this has helped scholars and policymakers differentiate among different types of financial aid, revealing the limitations of a lens that sees all financial aid as created equal and views such instruments as valuable only as a tool with which to finance college, at the point of enrollment.

Pfeffer, F.T., Danziger, S.H., & Schoeni, F.R. (2013). Wealth disparities before and after the Great Recession. *Annals of the American Academy of Political and Social Science, 650*(1), 98–123.

Today's student debt debate cannot be understood absent a consideration of the ways in which a relatively unprecedented macroeconomic event—The Great Recession—has shaped a generation's experiences and future prospects. The collapse of labor, housing, and financial markets in 2007–2008 created new challenges for American families and brought existing divides into sharper relief. This study examines disparities in wealth holdings leading up to the Great Recession and in the initial years of the recovery. While all socioeconomic groups experienced declines in wealth following the recession—and higher-wealth households saw larger absolute declines—as percentages of their holdings, however, declines were greater for less-advantaged groups, including people of color, those with less education, and those with poorer prerecession financial positions. These different outcomes, which mirror those found by researchers at the Institute on Assets and Social Policy, increase wealth inequality and serve to widen the gap, then, between those at different "rungs" on the U.S. economic ladder.

Pfeffer, F.T., & Hertel, F.R. (2015). How has educational expansion shaped social mobility trends in the United States? *Social Forces 94*(1), 143–180.

This analysis looks at intergenerational social mobility trends in the United States over the long term and considers how dramatic educational expansion in the 20th century has contributed to the observed changes in mobility opportunities for men across cohorts. The authors attribute the modest but gradual increase in social class mobility noted nearly exclusively to the interaction identified as the compositional effect. Specifically, the direct influence of social class backgrounds on social class destinations is lower among the growing number of Americans attaining higher levels of education. The authors further caution against trusting increased aggregate educational attainment to deliver greater fluidity in social class hierarchy in the United States, as class inequality in education has remained stable. Indeed, the impact of parental education on a child's educational and class attainment has grown or remained stable, respectively. In other words, unless changes in education and related policy delink the relationship between starting position and ultimate educational attainment, education's ability to drive more egalitarian end results will be limited, despite education's potential to serve as such an equalizer.

Phillips, J. P., Petterson, S. M., Bazemore, A. W., & Phillips, R. L. (2014). A retrospective analysis of the relationship between medical student debt and primary care practice in the United States. *Annals of Family Medicine, 12*(6), 542–549. doi:10.1370/afm.1697

This study examines the relationship between educational debt and primary care practice, accounting for the potentially confounding effect of medical student socioeconomic status. The authors performed retrospective multivariate analyses of data from 136,232 physicians who graduated from allopathic U.S. medical schools between 1988 and 2000, obtained from the American Association of Medical Colleges Graduate Questionnaire, the American Medical Association Physician Masterfile, and other sources. Need-based loans were used as markers for socioeconomic status of physicians' families of origin. The study examined two outcomes: primary care practice and family medicine practice in 2010. Physicians who graduated from public schools were most likely to practice primary care and family medicine at graduating educational debt levels of $50,000 to $100,000 (2010 dollars; *P* <.01). This relationship between debt and primary care practice persisted when physicians from different socio-economic status groups, as approximated by loan type, were examined separately. At higher debt, graduates' odds of practicing primary care or family medicine declined. In contrast, private school graduates were not less likely to practice primary care or family medicine as debt levels increased. The study concludes that high educational debt deters graduates of public medical schools from choosing primary care, but does not appear to influence private school graduates in the same way. Students from relatively lower-income families are more strongly influenced by debt. Reducing debt of selected medical students may be effective in promoting a larger primary care physician workforce.

Salmi, J. (2003). Student loans in an international perspective: The World Bank experience. LCSHD Paper Series no. 44. Washington, DC: World Bank. Retrieved from http://documents.worldbank.org/curated/en/2003/01/2813144/student-loans-international-perspective-world-bank-experience
While now somewhat dated, this analysis takes a rare global look at student borrowing, tracing students global origins and examining trends in student debt within different educational contexts around the world. Viewing student loans through a development finance lens, the World Bank paper considers institutions' efforts to make such financing available and support borrowers in complying with repayment terms. The discussion also touches on mechanisms that may increase student loans' utility as drivers of aggregate economic activity and greater well-being. Scholars embarking on a study of student loan policy may find the overview of different approaches pursued in various countries particularly useful, although, again, it should be emphasized that some of those details have changed in the intervening years.

Shapiro, T., Meschede, T., & Osoro, S. (2013). The roots of the widening racial wealth gap: Explaining the black-white economic divide. Waltham, MA: Institute on Assets and Social Policy, Brandeis University.

This study, with lead author Tom Shapiro, whose work has focused on examining and explaining the causes and implications of racial wealth divides, traces the same households over 25 years to illustrate the growth in the total wealth gap between white and African-American families. Between 1984 and 2009, this gap increased from $85,000 to $236,500. While this study does not specifically home in on student debt as a contributor to racial wealth divides, student borrowing is a factor in some of the drivers identified here: years of homeownership (which other research has found to be delayed among student borrowers), household income, unemployment, college completion (which evidence finds student loans only weakly support and may inhibit, within some subgroups), and baseline family wealth or inheritance. Importantly, IASP's analysis finds that equal achievements, such as income gains, yield unequal wealth rewards for whites and African Americans, a finding in line with later research by Emmons and others that reveals that even higher education does not pay equal dividends for all Americans.

Sullivan, L., Meschede, T., Dietrich, L., Shapiro, T., Huelsman, M., & Draut, T. (2015). Less debt, more equity: Lowering student debt while closing the black-white wealth gap. Waltham, MA: Institute for Assets and Social Policy and Demos.

This paper uses IASP's Racial Wealth Audit to assess the impact of public policy—here, specifically, student loan and other financial aid policy—on the wealth gap between white and black households. This analysis finds that young black households are far more likely to have student debt than their white peers; over half (54 percent) of young black households have student debt, compared to 39 percent of all young white households. These gaps in student debt holding likely contribute to the substantial racial wealth gap observed among even young households; among typical households ages 25–40, whites have 10 times the wealth of blacks. Considering policy implications, these researchers find that forgiving student debt only for low- and middle-income households would reduce the racial wealth gap, while eliminating student debt for all households would actually increase the racial wealth gap, largely because white students are more likely to complete college and graduate degree programs and, therefore, would benefit disproportionately, despite their lower risk of indebtedness.

U.S. Department of Education. Student aid data. Retrieved July 6, 2016, from https://studentaid.ed.gov/sa/about/data-center/student

The U.S. Department of Education collects data and publishes reports about federal financial aid applicants, recipients, and disbursements, to paint a picture of trends in the use of different financial aid instruments. Information is available by educational institution, for consumers interested in learning more about their particular school, as well as by cohort, for the past several years. The site also includes definitions of relevant terms related to financial aid and serves as the source of data for some of the studies cited here, such as TICAS' analysis of cohort default rates.

Walsemann, K.M., Gee, G.C., & Gentile, D. (2014). Sick of our loans: Student borrowing and the mental health of young adults in the United States. *Social Science & Medicine, 124*(2015), 85–93.

This study examines the association between student loan assumption and psychological functioning of debtors, both on an annual basis, while students are still in school, and in terms of cumulative debt burden and effects on individuals ages 25 to 31. Using data from the National Longitudinal Survey of Youth 1997 (NLSY97), the authors found that student loans were associated with poorer psychological functioning, adjusting for covariates. This association varied by level of parental wealth in only some models and did not vary by college enrollment history or educational attainment, raising questions about the spillover effects of this particular approach to college financing. As part of a growing body of evidence examining the social and psychological effects of financial states—such as student indebtedness—this study has helped to quantify the anxieties often expressed by the current generation of highly indebted students and recent college-leavers, as well as to legitimate such inquiries as part of the financial aid policy conversation.

Students and parents contemplating higher education today often see student debt as an unavoidable feature of their college experience, an inevitable aspect of the modern financial aid system. From this vantage point, it can be difficult to remember that student loans have not always figured as prominently into the U.S. financial aid system and that, at several points in our history, slight policy shifts set the country on a course of debt-dependent financial aid fairly unimaginable at the time. This brief chronology includes some of the major milestones and policy moments in the chronology of student borrowing in the United States. In total, these dates and their significance underscore the reality that alternatives were, at one point, very viable, a truth that reminds us that we can still choose a different course.

1944   The GI Bill (Serviceman's Readjustment Act) began providing funding for higher education for returning veterans. This policy is significant because it expanded access to higher education and set a precedent for providing educational opportunities as a benefit to a particular group.

1958   The National Defense Education Act creates National Defense Student Loans, now Federal Perkins Loans. These low-interest loans, given directly to higher education institutions, aim to increase access to college for low-income students. This legislation also expanded financial aid to students who were not veterans and encouraged higher educational studies in particular subjects deemed essential for global competitiveness.

Today's graduates, the majority of whom will leave college with considerable debts, often confront uncertain futures. (AP Photo/Mel Evans)

1964   The Economic Opportunity Act, which included the College Work-Study program, passes, providing additional financing assistance to low-income prospective college students.

1965   The Higher Education Act (HEA) of 1965 increases federal funding to universities, provides low-interest student loans, and creates scholarships—the National Teaching Corps and Basic Education Opportunity Grants, now known as Pell Grants—for the nation's financially-neediest students. The Guaranteed Student Loan (GSL) program allows private lenders to make loans guaranteed by the federal government.

1972   The 1972 Education Amendments to the HEA shift provision of loans to individuals instead of higher education institutions and create Sallie Mae, an organization that will become the largest private student loan lender.

1978   In 1978, the Middle-Income Student Assistance Act removes the income limit for GSLs, expanding access to grants and loans for middle- and upper-class students.

1980   The Parent Loans for Undergraduate Students (PLUS) program originates in 1980, allowing lenders to make government-subsidized loans to parents of dependent college students. This year also sees the creation of the U.S. Department of Education, now with oversight over financial aid programs across a variety of initiatives.

1985   The Consolidated Omnibus Reconciliation Act (COBRA) makes changes in student loan operations, including instituting a requirement that PLUS and GSL loans must be disbursed in multiple payments and restricting access to future student loans for students with defaults on other loans.

1986   Amendments to the Higher Education Act change practices for student loan processing and servicing and, most notably, authorize a pilot income-contingent student loan program.

1988   The GSL program becomes the Robert T. Stafford Loan program. In the 1980s, students increasingly rely on student loans and purchasing power for Pell Grants diminishes.

1992   The 1992 HEA reauthorization renames the Stafford Loan program as the Federal Family Education Loan (FFEL) program. FFEL includes four types of federal loans: Subsidized Stafford Loans, Unsubsidized Loans, PLUS loans, and Consolidated Loans. Eligibility criteria and loan limits expand, increasing access to borrowing. This reauthorization also consolidates the application for federal financial aid into one application, now known as the Free Application for Federal Student Aid (FAFSA).

1993   The Student Loan Reform Act of 1993 increases the limits on unsubsidized student loans.

1994   The Direct Student Loan program is introduced and piloted with 100 schools. Today, more than 1,200 institutions participate.

1997   The Hope Scholarship and Lifelong Learning Credit are part of the Taxpayer Relief Act. Other measures relevant to higher education include a tax deduction for interest on student loans and the creation of education IRAs (now known as ESAs, or Education Savings Accounts) for tax-free higher education saving.

1998   Sixty percent of all federal aid to students is in the form of loans, up from 45 percent a decade ago. Pell Grants continue to lose purchasing power as tuitions rise. Amendments to the Higher Education Act change the formulas used to determine eligibility for Pell Grants and increase the authorization of funding for the program. The legislation also includes some changes to student loan regulation.

2004   Outstanding federal student loan debt totals $435 billion (in 2014 dollars).

2005   The Higher Education Reconciliation Act reduces loan fees from 4 percent to 1 percent, increases some annual loan limits, and prohibits consolidation while a student is still in school, among other changes.

2007   The Great Recession intensifies debate about the equalizing power of higher education and the use of student loans as the primary means of financing higher education.

2010   Student loan debt surpasses credit card debt in the United States.

2014   Aggregate student loan debt reaches $1.1 trillion, second only to mortgage debt.

Glossary

Adverse Credit Prior credit conditions that may result in having a credit history that makes an individual ineligible for a federal direct loan. Those conditions include having an account that is more than 90 days past due; the write-off of a federal student loan; foreclosure proceedings currently in process; history of defaulting on a loan, regardless of payment status; any unpaid collection accounts; history of transferring mortgage deed to lender to avoid foreclosure (deed in lieu of foreclosure); and termination of a lease or contract due to default. In addition, experiencing any of the following within the past five years may also constitute as adverse credit history: foreclosure; release from debt due to bankruptcy; repossession of collateral or voluntary surrendering collateral that was subject to repossession; wage garnishment, or federal, state, or local tax lien.

Assets Resources one owns that have economic value.

Children's Development Accounts *See* Children's Savings Accounts.

Children's Savings Accounts (synonymous with Children's Development Accounts) Children's Savings Accounts are savings vehicles, most commonly designed for higher education savings, that often incorporate specific incentives and explicit structures to encourage savings by disadvantaged youths and families who otherwise may not have equitable access to financial institutions (Elliott & Lewis, 2014).

College Affordability   A measure of the perceived ability to pay for a college degree from personal income, amenable to alteration by changes in the cost of college itself and/or changes in the availability and terms of financial aid instruments. Usually refers to the ability to meet the obligation of the "net price," or cost of tuition and room/board/fees, minus financial aid.

College-Bound Identity   An identity rooted in an expectation of attending college. Institutions provide contextual clues that nurture or activate this identity, which may in turn affect an individual's educational attainment.

College Completion   Completion of requirements to earn a postsecondary degree.

College Consumption Expenses   Expenses incurred during the process of attending college but not levied by the educational institution for the purpose of accumulating credits, for example, room and board, but not institutional fees or tuition.

College Student Persistence   Completing one academic semester or academic year and returning for the next, or sequentially completing the requirements for a postsecondary education degree.

Consolidation   The combination of multiple loans into a single loan with one monthly payment, often offered within the context of student loan servicing.

Consumption-Smoothing Device   A financial product or instrument that bridges a gap between a desired standard of living and one's current income capacity. In the context of student financial aid, a loan is a consumption-smoothing device, available to the student during a period of low earnings, to facilitate purchase of educational investments for which current income is inadequate, with the result of an incurred liability that must be paid from future earnings.

Credit Constrained   Limited ability to borrow against future income due to factors such as low income, poor credit, or debt that exceeds acceptable levels.

Debt Aversion   Reluctance to acquire financial debt.

Debt-to-Income Ratio   The percentage of monthly gross income that goes toward paying debts.

Default   Occurs when the borrower does not meet the repayment terms of the promissory note. Missing payments for 270 days, or approximately 9 months, is considering defaulting on most federal student loans.

Deferment   A temporary delay of loan payment obligations that is allowed when certain conditions are met. The government pays the interest during the deferment period for the following three types of federal student loans: Direct Subsidized Loans, Subsidized Federal Stafford Loans, and Federal Perkins Loans. Unsubsidized and Direct PLUS Loans continue to accrue interest during deferment; unpaid interest is then added back to the principal balance when the deferment period ends.

Delinquent   The status of a loan for which payments are not received when due. Loans remain delinquent until payments are made current through payment, deferment, or forbearance.

Direct Loan   Federal loans borrowed directly from the U.S. Department of Education by eligible students or parents at participating institutions. The William D. Ford Federal Direct Loan program makes these loans. Examples include Direct PLUS Loans, Direct Consolidation Loans, and Direct Subsidized Loans.

Direct PLUS Loan   A type of direct loan borrowed from the U.S. Department of Education for which the borrower (students or parents of dependent students) remains responsible for the interest even if the loan's status changes (e.g., during deferment or forbearance).

Earnings Potential   The total amount of money one has the potential to earn in his or her occupation.

Earnings Premium   Typically defined as the difference between median earnings of individuals with bachelor's degrees and those with only high school diplomas; a measure of the marginal value of the educational attainment, then, for individuals' earnings.

Economic Mobility   The ability to move to a different level of economic status. In other words, to improve or worsen one's standard of living.

Educational Attainment   Highest level of education an individual has completed; in the aggregate, the average level of education completed in a particular population.

Entrance Counseling   A session that new borrowers are required to take to learn information about their rights and responsibilities prior to receiving their first federal student loan; an effort to increase consumers' understanding of the terms and conditions of their student loans.

Exit Counseling   A session that half-time or recently graduated student borrowers are required to take to learn information about loan repayment such as when repayment begins, what servicing options are available, and what responsibilities they have.

Extended Repayment Plan   Some loans from the Direct Loan program and the FFEL program allow borrowers to make lower monthly payments (may be fixed or graduated) over a longer period of time than the Standard Repayment Plan.

Federal Family Education Loan (FFEL) Program   The FFEL program utilized private lenders who made loans that were guaranteed by the federal government. The loan types available through the FFEL program included Subsidized Federal Stafford Loans, Unsubsidized Federal Stafford Loans, FFEL PLUS Loans, and FFEL Consolidation Loans. In 2010, the FFEL program was replaced by the Direct Loan Program (see definition) so all federal student loans are now made by the U.S. Department of Education rather than private lenders.

Federal Work-Study   A student aid program where the federal government provides students who have financial need with part-time work to help them pay their educational expenses.

Forbearance   Temporary suspension or reduction of student loan payments for up to one year. Forbearance may be granted by the lender when one cannot make payments due to qualifying circumstances but is not eligible for deferment. Interest accrues for both subsidized and unsubsidized loans during forbearance and is added to the principal balance to be paid following the forbearance period.

For-Profit College or Proprietary Education   Educational institutions operated by private, profit-seeking businesses (in contrast to public institutions or private, nonprofit institutions).

Free Application for Federal Student Aid (FAFSA)   The free application used to apply for all federal student aid, such as federal grants, loans, and work-study.

Graduated Repayment Plan   Repayment plan that starts with lower monthly payments that then increase as an individual's salary increases.

Income-Based Repayment (IBR)   A repayment structure that bases the monthly payment amount on a percentage of the borrower's income, in order to ensure a level of affordability. Also called income-driven repayment, of which IBR is technically a type, the term has become synonymous with any type of student loan that bases repayment obligations on a borrower's income.

Income Contingent Repayment (ICR)   The monthly repayment amount is based on the borrower's income, the total amount owed, and the borrower's family size.

Loan Forgiveness   The federal government excuses the borrower's responsibility to repay some or all of the remaining loan balance. Part of most income-based repayment plans, and a benefit provided to students participating in some targeted recruitment or other incentive programs.

Loan Guarantee   The promise by the guarantor to assume the debt obligation of a borrower if that borrower defaults.

Loan Servicer   A third party that collects and applies payments to loans, handles customer service, and performs administrative tasks associated with the loan on behalf of the lender.

Master Promissory Note   A binding legal contract that lists the terms and conditions for loan repayment as well as the rights and responsibilities of the borrower. It can be used to provide one or more federal loans for up to 10 academic years.

Need-Based Financial Aid   Financial aid determined based on the assets and income of the prospective student and his or her family, rather than measured academic ability or special talent. Need-based financial aid is designed to bridge the gap between a household's own resources and the price of college access.

Net Worth   Total assets minus total liabilities.

Perkins Loan   A program through which students with financial need can obtain low-interest federal student loans.

Postsecondary Education   Education continued after high school.

Predatory Student Lending   Providing loans without regard for the borrower's ability to pay or the risk of default. Often characterized by the issuance with loans with unfavorable servicing terms, high costs, and/or unclear consumer disclosures.

Public Service Loan Forgiveness   A federal program through which certain types of public or nonprofit employees may have their student loans forgiven. A particular type of loan forgiveness.

Relative Debt   The debt-to-asset ratio tells you the percentage of total assets that were financed by creditors, liabilities, or debt.

Risk-Averse   Used to describe students unwilling to borrow money for college even though the expected return of a college degree may outweigh the cost.

Standard of Living   The level of material goods and services associated with living in a specific socioeconomic class.

Standard Payment Plan   Paying a fixed amount toward a student loan for a standard amount of time (generally 10 years but may be up to 30 years for a consolidated loan).

Subsidized Loan   A type of loan that is provided based on financial need, issued with more favorable terms than unsubsidized loans. During times where the borrower is in school, or in a deferment or grace period, the federal government assumes responsibility for paying the accrued interest of subsidized loans. The exception is for Direct Subsidized Loans issued between July 1, 2012, and July 1, 2014, where a borrower is responsible for paying interest that accumulates during a grace period and any unpaid interest amounts are added to the principal balance of that loan.

Subsidy Cost   The money that needs to be set aside at the point of student loan issuance in order to cover the costs to the government over the life of the loan.

Work-Study   *See* "Federal Work-Study."

About the Authors

William Elliott III is an associate professor at the University of Kansas (KU) and founder of the Center on Assets, Education, and Inclusion (AEDI), a research center in KU's School of Social Welfare. He also serves as a faculty director of Asset Building for the Center for Social Development at Washington University in St. Louis, Missouri, and as a nonresident senior research fellow for New America's Asset Building Program. He is a member of the advisory board for the initiative to develop a Human Needs Index at the Center on Philanthropy at Indiana University and was previously a visiting scholar at the Federal Reserve Board of Boston. Elliott has received research funding from such sources as Ford Foundation, Charles Stewart Mott Foundation, W.K. Kellogg Foundation, Lumina Foundation, and Citi Foundation.

Elliott is a leading researcher in the field of children's savings, college matriculation and success, and college debt. He has written extensively on the relationship between assets and children's educational outcomes and is author of many peer-reviewed, well-regarded articles on these topics. In the area of student debt, Elliott has investigated the effect of student debt on long-term financial health ("Unequal Outcomes: Student Loan Effects on Young Adults' Net Worth Accumulation," 2014; "Is Student Debt Jeopardizing the Long-Term Financial Health of U.S. Households," 2013), as well as the effect of parents' college savings on reducing student load debt ("Student Loan Debt:

Can Parental College Savings Help?," 2014). Elliott recently coauthored the book *The Real College Debt Crisis: How Student Borrowing Threatens Financial Well-Being and Erodes the American Dream* (Elliott & Lewis, 2015). The book portrays the contrasting personal experiences of the authors' college journeys: one who borrowed money to finance an education that would lift him out of poverty, and the other who was fortunate to have financial support from family to pay for college and, then, saw a greater and more immediate return on her degree. In addition, the book includes data regarding the effects of educational debt on future net worth, the analysis of policy options that have been offered to reduce the burden of student debt, and the discussion of asset-based solutions, such as Children's Savings Accounts (CSAs). Dr. Elliott has another book under contract (with Oxford Press) regarding CSAs that will feature research he is directing, which examines outcomes from CSA programs around the country.

Dr. Elliott's work has been integral to the initiation of CSA programs such as Kindergarten to College (K2C) in San Francisco and Promise Indiana, which began in Wabash County. His work has been featured by popular news outlets, such as the *Washington Post*, *U.S. News*, and *PBS News Hour*, and highlighted by other respected researchers, including the Federal Reserve Bank of St. Louis. He was the recipient of the 2014 National Award for Distinguished Recent Contribution in Social Work Education and the 2016 University of Kansas Scholarly Achievement Award. Elliott received a bachelor's degree in philosophy from Geneva College and a master's in social work and PhD from the George Warren Brown School of Social Work at Washington University in St. Louis.

Melinda K. Lewis is the assistant director at the Center for Assets, Education, and Inclusion (AEDI), and associate professor of practice at the School of Social Welfare, at the University of Kansas. Her work with AEDI includes conducting research and translating findings into policy changes, specifically around the role of assets in addressing educational inequities and improving upward mobility. Recently, Lewis coauthored the book *The Real College Debt Crisis: How Student Borrowing Threatens Financial Well-Being and Erodes the American Dream.* In addition, Lewis has coauthored articles for academic journals, including an article discussing the research and policy implications of the effect of student debt on financial well-being ("Student Debt Effects on Financial Well-Being: Research and Policy Implications," 2015), as well as numerous research reports for AEDI, particularly regarding CSAs ("Latino Immigrant Families Saving in Children's Savings Account Program against Great Odds: The Case of Prosperity Kids," 2016; "Saving and Educational Asset-Building within a Community-Driven CSA Program: The Case of Promise Indiana," 2016). She frequently presents on student debt, CSAs, and educational inequity. Prior to her current roles at the University of Kansas, Lewis worked as a nonprofit policy advocate, grassroots organizer, and community researcher. Lewis has a Bachelor of Social Work from the University of Kansas and a Master of Social Work from Washington University.